The arrows show in schematic form flight paths for bombers, and for I.C.B.Ms. and I.R.B.Ms. The ends of the arrows bear no relation to the sites of existing bases.

a

DEFENSE OR RETALIATION

DEFENSE

OR

Translated by EDWARD THOMAS

HELMUT SCHMIDT

RETALIATION

A German View

FREDERICK A. PRAEGER, *Publisher*

NEW YORK

BOOKS THAT MATTER

Published in the United States of America in 1962
by Frederick A. Praeger, Inc., Publisher,
64 University Place, New York 3, N.Y.

A translation of *Verteidigung oder Vergeltung: ein
deutscher Beitrag zum strategischen Problem der NATO*,
by Helmut Schmidt, first published by Seewald-
Verlag Dr Heinrich Seewald, Stuttgart-Degerloch
1962. Published in Great Britain by Oliver and
Boyd Ltd 1962

Library of Congress Catalog Card Number: 62—12842

Printed in Great Britain
by T. and A. Constable Ltd., Hopetoun Street,
Printers to the University of Edinburgh

Under no circumstances can the art of war be considered as the tutor of policy. . . . The subordination of the political point of view to the military would be unreasonable. . . . The subordination of the military point of view to the political is, therefore, the only thing which is possible. . . . It is an impermissible and even harmful distinction, according to which a great military event or the plan for such an event should admit a purely military judgment; indeed, it is an unreasonable procedure to consult professional soldiers on the plan of war, that they may give a purely military opinion. . . . It is only when policy promises itself a wrong effect from certain military means and measures, an effect opposed to their nature, that it can exercise a harmful effect by the course it prescribes.

KARL VON CLAUSEWITZ, *On War*, Book 8, Chapter 6(B)
(trans. O. Jolles, New York 1943)

Preface
to the first English Edition

THE original purpose of this book was to give the German public a better picture of the strategic situation of their country than had hitherto been available to them, and to provoke wider public discussion of the elusive and often complex strategic problems confronting Germany. The author attempted, in particular, to make available to German public opinion the findings of writers on strategic problems working in other countries and to evaluate their ideas from the German point of view.

Twelve months after the first German edition went to press many people in Germany can see in sharper relief some of the alternatives which the author had in mind. Naturally enough there are still, on these matters, many different opinions. But thanks to the keen pressure exerted by the Soviet Union—particularly since August 1961—many people are at last beginning to realise that it is imperative to give serious new thought to our common defence.

This pressure has also served to lead peoples of other countries in the alliance to the same realisation and has precipitated quick decisions on the part of some of the governments. We are not yet in sight of a generally agreed solution to the strategic dilemma of how to defend Europe, but important steps are being taken that point emphatically in a new direction. This is true not only of recent military decisions taken by President Kennedy's administration, but also of changes in strategic thinking elsewhere in the West.

Twelve months ago it was, perhaps, not too hard a task to predict the majority of the new strategic policy decisions which the United States Government could be expected to take during 1961. But the fact that these predictions turned out right should not tempt any reader to take it for granted that the book is always sound in its handling of other matters. On the other hand the author feels that world events during the last year have borne out the general tenor of his book and that extensive re-writing of those passages which have been, to some extent, overtaken by events, is not in the circumstances necessary. The Soviet Union's current political aggressiveness—at present focused on Berlin—underscores the correctness of one of the points made in the book's last chapter, viz. that the forthcoming transition period in Western strategy and armaments policy will also be one of danger. This transition must be completed as quickly as possible. To ensure this the necessary action must be taken by the allied powers not later than the spring of 1962. Between now and then the assumptions made and the conditions described in this book will probably not undergo any major change.

Soviet policy during 1961 serves to remind us yet again of the need for both joint and unilateral decisions on the part of the governments of allied nations—and for action also. But joint decisions and common action presuppose the common analysis of problems and mutual understanding on the part of the nations concerned of their separate interests. The author hopes that this English edition will help towards meeting these requirements. He would also like to express his gratitude to the publishers, Messrs Oliver and Boyd, to their editor, Miss Anne Orde, and to the translator, Mr Edward Thomas, who have all made this possible.

Hamburg   HELMUT SCHMIDT
November 1961

Contents

MAPS

Foreword
to the first German Edition

THE author of this book has, over a period of almost eight years, devoted the greater part of his parliamentary activity to defence policy—not always in a fashion that suited his inclinations, and for the most part without deriving any great satisfaction from it. It is his experience that there is little pleasure in being regarded in Parliament as a "defence expert" and in having to do battle on the contentious issues of defence policy-making. It may similarly be no unalloyed pleasure for the reader to immerse himself in the materials which this book offers him.

Nevertheless, I hope to provoke my friends in the German Parliament (Bundestag) and all connected with politics in Germany, the German press and the German armed forces (Bundeswehr) to make bigger efforts to acquaint themselves with the facts and opinions propounded by modern scientific military strategy. This book is intended primarily for them—but I hope equally that it will assist the politically-minded layman to understand contemporary strategic problems.

This book does not reflect the agreed views of a committee or a party: I alone am responsible for all parts of it. It is rooted in the soil of my own political convictions: it is not, however, intended to put forward a Social Democratic defence policy, but rather to present facts and ideas which it is hoped will stimulate the reader to pursue his own studies and make his own judgments.

I have to thank Herr Wolf Loah for the Appendix and Bibliography: the latter is intended to facilitate further individual study.

The libraries of the Bundestag in Bonn, of the Führungs-akademie of the Bundeswehr in Hamburg, and of the Institute of Strategic Studies in London have all kindly given their help which I acknowledge with gratitude. Warmest thanks are also due to Frau Elizabeth Karl and Fräulein Ruth Wilhelm for preparing a manuscript which was dictated in many small fragments.

For their clarifications and corrections I am deeply indebted to a number of specialists working on the same problems, either as colleagues in the Bundestag or as officers in the Bundeswehr. I would like to mention by name, as representative of them all, Herr K. W. Berkhan, Member of the Bundestag (M.B.); Colonel of the General Staff Dr F. Beerman; Fritz Erler, M.B.; Lt.-Col. of the General Staff W. Renner; Brigadier J. Steinhoff; and Karl Wienand, M.B.

In addition I had during 1960 the opportunity of exchanging views personally with a large number of the non-German specialists quoted in this book, and of learning from them. I am particularly grateful to the following for helpful encouragement and stimulus: Professor R. Bowie, Alastair Buchan, Rear Admiral Sir A. Buzzard, Capt. B. H. Liddell Hart, Denis Healey, M.P., Roger Hilsman, General Pierre Gallois, James E. King, Professor H. A. Kissinger, Professor Klaus Knorr, Lt.-Col. F. O. Miksche, Professor R. E. Osgood, Professor T. C. Schelling, Marshal of the R.A.F. Sir J. Slessor, and Professor Arnold Wolfers.

In particular I must mention my respect and gratitude for the encouragement I have received from American authors. None of the individuals named here has, of course, the least responsibility for any of the views put forward in this book; in many matters agreement and dissent go hand in hand. Controversy—and not conformist acceptance of a given doctrine—also marks the strategic discussion in France, Britain, and also the United States. The comprehensive work done by scholars and scientists in Britain and, above all, in the United States is indispensable today to any German wishing to answer the fateful question: what strategy is best calculated to preserve the peace?

Global policy and global strategy are inseparable: the term strategy can justifiably be used to describe the whole complex in which the problems of each interweave and intertwine. This book confines itself to the military aspects of strategy, even though the subject requires frequent reference to foreign policy. I assume that the general direction of German foreign policy is above controversy: I fear, however, that this does not apply to NATO's military strategy and to the role of the Federal Republic within the Alliance.

Hamburg   HELMUT SCHMIDT
November 1960

1

The Dangers of Ignorance

FROM time to time one hears people say how stupid it is for us Germans to be making special preparations on the basis of hypothetical calculations or forecasts of how a future war might run its course: for, firstly, everything would turn out differently from the forecasts; and, secondly, Germany would in any event be physically destroyed in a future war. At the end of this book we will return to these two arguments. In the meantime we will merely note that both contain elements of right and of wrong. At all events they demonstrate the tendency towards the emotional evaluation of military problems that is to be found everywhere in the Federal Republic, and the tendency to brush aside complex and exacting considerations of a rational nature. One hears many such emotional pronouncements: "All future wars will be fought with nuclear weapons"; "There will be no more war, for no statesman would dare destroy the human race"; "No nuclear power will accept defeat without first using its nuclear weapons"; "The next world war will be so appalling that military force is no longer a practicable means of regulating international relations." James E. King writes that there is truth in some, though perhaps not all, such asseverations—but much too little truth. He adds that they also contain lack of realism, fatalism, and wishful thinking. It is indispensable that those who wish to measure up to their responsibilities as citizens or as politicians should rid themselves of every trace of fatalism and wishful thinking.

In recent years all discussion of defence policy and military affairs—or at least all open discussion in the Federal Republic—has been encumbered by a heritage of excessive emotionalism, association of ideas, and prejudice. In consequence the results have often reflected a paucity of sober, sustained reasoning. This is true also of the two major parties during their debates on defence

A

policy in the Bundestag.[1] Nevertheless we must acknowledge that, for the majority of those taking part, the conflict over equipping the Bundeswehr with nuclear weapons is not a conflict between reason and unreason, but a "conflict within reason itself" (von Weizsäcker).

This shortage of sober sustained thought was evident not only in the big debate on nuclear affairs in 1958, but as early as 1950 or 1952. It also emerged in 1955 and subsequently. In many of these debates statements made, or alleged to have been made, by NATO were accepted by the one side as revealed wisdom, as precisely meeting the needs of the situation, and in every way as right and fitting. The other side, by the same token, was inclined to suspect precisely the opposite. The overvaluation of NATO, its elevation to the absolute means and end of foreign policy, led to a corresponding under-valuation on the part of the Opposition. The point was reached where each speaker chose his examples quite arbitrarily. For example, Denmark, Norway and Sweden (irrespective of the fact that only the first two belong to NATO) have all made similar decisions in the field of military policy. None of the three has so far either equipped itself with nuclear weapons or stockpiled nuclear weapons on its territory. On the other hand all three have upheld the principle of national military service and have supplemented this by introducing militia-type territorial systems. The two decisions are, of course, related and derive from the same fundamental concept. In the Federal Republic's domestic discussions, however, the one side has stressed only the first decision and has not wished to acknowledge the second, while the other side has done precisely the opposite. In general the strategic discussions and decisions of the West German parliament have been guided by a sense of high responsibility, but by no means always by an exalted knowledge of the facts.

Strategic Dilettantism

No one will deny that a foreign policy that has been built up on a careful analysis of the situation and carefully checks and works

[1] The writer was one of those who participated in—and must share the responsibility for—the big Bundestag debate of early 1958 on the question of nuclear weapons for the Bundeswehr. Those who recall the frenetic rejoicings of the Bundestag majority on that occasion will nevertheless understand, although it is now a long time ago, that a decisive halt had to be called to the upsurge of emotion in the Bundestag's majority about its resolution on nuclear weapons.

over this analysis, must take into account not only the diplomatic and psychological position, but also economic and technological factors and the changes to which they are subject: it must also consider the military situation. And those responsible for defence policy decisions must reciprocate by taking political, economic, psychological and technological factors into account. Washington and Moscow have not just discovered that the making of decisions in the fields of political and military strategy must be treated as a unified operation, they did so very long ago. Such decisions go hand in hand and mutually influence one another. No highest level political decisions are made in either Washington or Moscow without a clear look beforehand at the military power balance, at the military situation in general, and at its possible future changes. This was the case, for example, when it was decided to fight the Korean War without the use of the atom bomb; it was also the case when the decision was made to intervene militarily in the Lebanon; it was also true of the Soviet decision to use force to suppress the Hungarian uprising, and of Khrushchev's decision to break off the Paris Summit Conference of 1960. No power can take global policy decisions without first sizing up the military power balance, so as to assess the consequences its political decisions might conceivably have. From this it follows that a country wishing to pursue its political aims in concert with, or in opposition to, one of the major powers must constantly remain clear as to the facts of the military balance and in particular as to how the major powers look at it and evaluate it. They must also have a clear idea of the various ways in which the situation might develop. This is as much true for de Gaulle as for Gomulka; it applies to both Cairo and Stockholm. Or—to speak of our domestic scene—it applies to the Government in Bonn as much as it does to the opposition.

It is unfortunate that the Bundestag and public opinion should, in recent years, have been served all too often with superficial, unsound arguments—indeed with entirely bogus arguments—on defence questions. This did not spring so much from a lack of candour as from the inadequacy of the information available to politicians. Both Ministers and deputies, to some extent, lacked their own opinions on strategic questions; therefore, in formulating their views, they were apt to accept the opinions of the military as objective truth and something whose acceptance was obligatory.

On the other hand, the Bundeswehr generals are awaiting political direction—but they receive little enough in their own specific field. The impression has therefore gained ground that the global strategic system of deterrence and counter-deterrence—the whole system of "war without war"—has not for years been fully grasped in Bonn. The reasons for this are not only to be found in the inadequacy of the available information, or in the inadequate co-operation of the politicians and the military: they are also to be found in the perpetuation of old prejudices. Long periods can often elapse before political (and military!) leaders fully grasp the significance of developments in the field of military technology.

It is true that our military officers are accustomed to co-operating with technicians, physicists and economists (although sometimes not nearly closely enough), but—at least in the Federal Republic—there is no co-operation with diplomats, politicians and statesmen. The military man is not yet fully integrated into the general machinery of government. One of the reasons is undoubtedly the exaggerated quest for secrecy which, although it is necessary, must be regarded as dangerous when the high political importance of the classified materials is borne in mind. A further reason is that very many politicians still suspect the military and wish to avoid coming under their political influence.

Military tactics is without question a trade that one has to have learnt professionally as a soldier. It is a field in which the politician has little need to meddle. Strategy must, however, be regarded as the field where joint foreign policy and military decisions are taken and the basic principles underlying them formulated: it is also the political authorities' mandate to the soldier. As a rule soldiers are not educated in taking strategic decisions: the vision of the statesman is much better suited to the task. The strategies of deterrence and counter-deterrence are especially remote from military methods of calculation. They take place in the realm of political psychology—a field for which the soldier's education fits him least of all. Overall political strategy must be reserved for the political direction, whether it is a question of disarmament, of the national arms structure, of day-to-day foreign policy decision-making, or the formulation of medium or long-term national political aims. While carrying out these tasks the political leaders must recognise that incorrect strategic decisions frequently determine not only whether there is to be war or peace, but also the course of a future

war (as did, for example, the decision to build the Maginot Line).
Between tactics and strategy lies the field of operational planning
and direction which as a rule will remain a matter for the military.

In his latest book Liddell Hart writes: "Statesmanship, in the
H-bomb age, must control not only the aims but the operations.
Hence statesmen and their diplomatic advisers must have a
greater knowledge of military technique than they needed in the
past. That is as important as for soldiers to submit to political
direction."[2] Without wishing to enter into an argument over the
operational competence[3] of statesmen, one is tempted to underline
at any rate the statement that "statesmen and their diplomatic
advisers must have a greater knowledge of military technique than
they needed in the past." The term "technique" is certainly used
here in a very general sense. This requirement is met only very
inadequately in the Federal Republic at the present time.[4] Many
non-professionals, and also many educated military officers,
believe that conventional armies with machine guns and tanks
have today been superseded. In fact their significance mounts from
year to year. Public opinion must recognise that we are going to
live less and less under the protection of H-bomb deterrence.
Many military men and politicians believe that this exposure can be
remedied by means of tactical nuclear weapons, but at best this
proposition is not even half true. Many have yet to learn that in
the event of a collision in Europe our peoples would be destroyed
by tactical nuclear weapons every bit as efficiently as by strategic
bombs, and that, furthermore, the fact of their existence scarcely
reduces the risk of the outbreak of war at all. If Liddell Hart, one
of Europe's most respected writers on strategy, can say: "These

[2] B. H. Liddell Hart, *Deterrent or Defence*, London and New York 1960, p. 67.

[3] Liddell Hart clearly means the concept of operational direction to apply to a
wider context than it customarily has in German military language.

[4] Dr Adenauer's statement in the Bundestag debate of 25 February 1955 is
relevant. In this he expressed the view that the Federal Republic's membership
of NATO would make it impossible for Germany to become a battlefield for the
forces of the United States and the Soviet Union in the event of war. Anglo-
American strategic writings deal with this statement, which is often specifically
quoted, with a frown or a shrug of the shoulders. This exaggerated notion, in
Dr Arnold Wolfers's opinion, derives from an inability to understand the military
situation in Europe. Dr Kurt Schumacher, at all events, summed the matter up
five years earlier in terms much closer to the mark: in August 1950 he used the
term "delaying defence" to describe the West's military concept, and pointed
out that Germany "as the glacis between West and East (would be) the worst to
suffer."

governments will be unworthy of their trust unless they tackle the problem of developing a non-suicidal form of defence and providing the minimum military strength required for it"[5] then it is time for those people who wish to have confidence in their government's strategy, to take up the study of these questions. The strategic doctrine of NATO has been in a state of crisis for more than two years. There are many reasons for this; and many different arguments and theories are put forward in consequence. But the Federal Republic, which is the "battlefield country" of NATO, is not adequately informed about the doubtful questions, the controversial arguments or the inferences to be drawn from them. We scarcely participate in the Western world's public debate.

Strategy as a Science

It is a matter for regret that there is as good as no worthwhile literature in Germany on contemporary strategic problems. What little our scholars and soldiers have written on military and strategic problems has been almost exclusively concerned with World Wars I and II. And as far as books by military authors are concerned, these are very often written with the object of self-justification in view—something that is not uncommon in memoirs. Books published in Germany, therefore, can help us but little to gain an insight into the present position. This is not the case in the Soviet Union; and in Britain and above all in the United States public discussion through the medium of serious periodicals and books is even more developed. In the United States there is a wide range of literature with several new publications each year on current military problems and their impact on international affairs. A particularly striking feature of this is the large number of civilian scientists and scholars, both young and old, who have published works of conspicuous insight and impressive authority. Unfortunately Germany has produced almost nothing of the sort. Let us expressly call attention to one of the very few exceptions, namely the slim volume of Professor von Weizsäcker of Hamburg.[6] This book is still today well worth reading by those who seriously wish to study these matters.

It is truly remarkable that such writings are so rare in Germany,

[5] Liddell Hart, *Deterrent or Defence*, p. 91.
[6] C. F. von Weizsäcker, *Mit der Bombe Leben* (Living with the Bomb), Hamburg 1958.

for the subject of military strategy lends itself to illumination by the methods of scholarship—more so, indeed, than the field of contemporary international affairs. Even the latter has had but scant treatment at the hands of German scholars: German universities prefer to occupy themselves with the foreign affairs of past epochs. This, too, is contrary to the practice of American universities. Political and military strategy lend themselves to scientific analysis because the factors underlying them are a good deal more accessible and less in need of interpretation than are those of many other social sciences. As a social science, strategy is in many ways comparable to economics. This is true not only because both disciplines rest on the principle of economy, whereby a given object is to be attained with the least possible means, or the biggest possible effect with given means, but in particular because of their methods of reaching their conclusions. Common to both disciplines is the fact that precise judgments are only possible—other than in historical research—if a whole string of precise assumptions are made. Economists talk, for example, of "a set of data," i.e. the conditions which they regard as fixed so that they may then proceed to vary one factor and ascertain what happens to the others. In economics this is called working with "models," i.e. one imagines a certain situation with given data and factors, and one then alters one factor to see what effect this will have on the remainder. In the actual world of economic reality such models are not to be met with. In that world every conceivable factor changes simultaneously: sometimes they change interdependently, and sometimes autonomously. It is nevertheless useful for the economist to bring together all he has learnt from varying his intellectual models. When he subsequently comes to consider questions of practical economic policy he must try to adapt the relatively uncomplicated model more and more to the much more complex reality. Essential to this process is the bringing to bear of the so-called "extra-economic" factors, e.g. those of a technological, psychological, socio-political, sociological and—above all—political nature. As the theoretical, abstract model is brought nearer and nearer to politico-economic reality the uncertainty of the judgment increases—the judgment which in the abstract model could still be completely unambiguous. Nevertheless, even the complex situations of economic reality lend themselves, in accordance with procedures established by work on models, to analysis by mathematical and electronic techniques, as is shown by the practical conduct of economic policy by many leading countries.

All this applies equally to the discipline of strategy. It is, moreover, no coincidence that a group of mathematician-economists has attempted to develop a "Theory of Strategic Games."[7]

The Uncertainty of Solutions

Without doubt there are politician-economists who rely on their instinct: they seldom pull it off. As a rule the situation requires them, like chess players, to carry their theories and models in their heads. This applies to strategy also. Nevertheless the two disciplines have it in common that, when confronted by the manifold complexities of reality, they must expect considerable risks and a relatively high level of uncertainty as regards the correctness of their recommendations. Even a chess champion will often recognise only retrospectively, from *ex post facto* analysis, which move it was that—positively or negatively—precipitated the final outcome, an insight which was denied him when making the move.

It is said that global policy and global strategy resemble chess. In fact the strategic problems of chess are more precisely determinable than those which will be brought up in this book. A specific reservation is therefore called for as regards the reliability of our judgment. This applies both to the formulation of the problem and, all the more, to the attempts to solve it.

Under no circumstances can we Germans evade the problem. The part we play in the defence of the West and in establishing its strategic concepts is limited, it is true. But because we are, for better or for worse, bound up with the defence system of the West, we are not only entitled but are under an obligation to participate in the process of deciding what its strategy should be. Anyone who made such decisions on the basis of inadequate knowledge of the situation would be shouldering an intolerable responsibility. Faulty decisions could jeopardise our nation's very existence. They are not to be ruled out even if the very best information were available: a large residue of uncertainty will persist. It is our duty to limit this as far as possible.

[7] One of the most interesting new publications in this field is Thomas C. Schelling's *The Strategy of Conflict*, Cambridge, Mass. 1960.

2

From Korea to Cuba

DURING the last fifteen years the strategic situation has changed at breakneck speed. Those wishing to understand the position today must first take a look at the circumstances leading up to it.

After 1945 the West embarked on an extensive demobilisation of its forces and neglected its armaments in order to devote itself to economic reconstruction: a further reason was that it did not consider itself exposed to any military threat. The Soviet Union exploited this credulity on the part of the American leaders by determinedly extending its sphere of influence. A number of circumstances should, indeed, have compelled the West to analyse Soviet strategic aims at this time—for example, General Markos's revolt in Greece, which was assisted by the Communists from outside, the 1948 *coup d'état* in Prague, and the Berlin blockade from March 1948 to May 1949. While it was the two latter events that led to the signature of the North Atlantic Pact, it took the start of the Korean War in mid-1950 to bring the West to recognise that it must direct its strategy and armament against the Soviet Union. Up to this point there was no reason for the Soviet Union to feel that its expansion had brought about a military threat to itself—this despite its lack of a nuclear capability. The United States, which at the beginning of 1945 had 12 million men under arms, by June 1948 had only 1·5 million.

The Nuclear Monopoly

In a strictly literal sense the period of the nuclear monopoly came to an end in 1949, for the Russians succeeded in detonating their first atom bomb in that year. But since, unlike the Soviet Union, the United States alone was in a position to drop its atom bombs on the territory of its principal enemy, the American monopoly of nuclear strategy continued for a number of years.

They alone disposed of the "means of delivery," as it is known in American professional jargon, that is, the means of bringing the weapons themselves to bear on the enemy.

The Soviet Union, indeed, produced atomic bombs in increasing numbers between 1950 and 1953, but she lacked the means of dropping them on Chicago: she lacked bombers of intercontinental range; and missiles able to perform this task did not as yet exist. As against this, the Americans possessed, both by virtue of their tradition and as a result of World War II developments, an enormous fleet of long-range bombers, modernised and supported by tanker aircraft. A most important addition at this period was the establishment of a comprehensive system of bases round the Eurasian land mass from Greenland through Western Europe, Morocco, the Middle East, the Philippines, Okinawa and Korea and then back to North America via Alaska. This was in essence a system of forward airfields and of bases from which tanker aircraft could take off to refuel in the air the bombers already under way. These bases, which the United States obtained after 1950 through a large number of treaties of alliance, were supplemented by additional "bases" in the shape of aircraft carriers, of which the United States then possessed more than thirty (partly in mothballs, however). On the other hand, the Soviet Union had a great numerical predominance in fighting men, tanks and artillery; but she could not use these to march on Chicago. Her superiority in the field of conventional arms was of consequence only in Europe, and in particular in Central Europe. In this theatre the numerical ratio of Soviet infantry and armoured troops to those of the West was at that time of the order 5 : 1 or 6 : 1.

In this situation the Western countries—and in particular America—went about their business fully confident of their nuclear superiority. This was the period when one heard talk of "roll back" and when a German Secretary of State talked of "integration as far back as the Urals." The strategic concept developed by NATO at that time, however, was content practically —if not fully—with the retention of only small conventional forces on the European continent. Later these forces acquired the name of the "Shield," whose object was, in the event of a Soviet attack, to screen Europe for a couple of days during which the Western "Sword" was meant to carry out its retaliatory mission. The

"Sword" was the name given to the American strategic nuclear forces, i.e. the American long-range air force (S.A.C.).

The Russians for their part judged the situation differently. Under Stalin's influence the following doctrine was taught. Nuclear weapons never decide the outcome of a war. They can be only one of various factors to be taken into account in fighting a war, for its ultimate outcome depends on which side can physically occupy the other's territory. And only the massed fighting men of the Soviet army suffice for this. In fact this doctrine only made a virtue of neccessity since the Soviet Union was not in a position to base its plans on a nuclear strategy, lacking the technical means of carrying it out. The Russians clearly regarded their strategic encirclement by the American bases and S.A.C. as a threat to themselves. The Soviet air defence was confronted by most formidable problems. No one in the Soviet Union at that time dared publicly discuss the risks of nuclear war with the United States.

This sketch of the military situation is somewhat oversimplified. From it we may nevertheless draw the general conclusion that, in the event of war, NATO and the West were at that time greatly superior and would have prevailed if—and the "if" is an important one—the West had in fact immediately brought the whole of its nuclear striking power to bear on the Soviet Union.

The Soviet Union was certainly not at this period under the impression that the West specifically intended to launch such an attack at any given point of time. But she had to bear in mind the possibility that, in the event of a serious clash, the United States might make good its threats. The Russians can have been in no doubt that this one-sided situation contained terrible risks for themselves. For this reason the Soviet Union, despite all its rigidity—it was the period characterised by the Molotovian "nyet" —gave at least the appearance of being ready to compromise on a number of international questions, e.g. the German problem. We need only think of the exchange of notes over Germany in the spring of 1952 and of the Berlin Foreign Ministers' Conference in 1954. Soviet tactics were designed to gain time.

In the negotiations of those years the West clearly failed to exploit its advantages in the field of military power by means of a flexible policy. The concessions offered by the Soviet Union during those years struck many people as too small. Particularly note-

worthy in this respect was the appreciation made at this time by
the government in Bonn, who, in 1952, coined the phrase "policy
of strength"—a phrase that has to some extent since been dis-
carded. Behind this phrase lay the idea, since proved wrong, that
if the West continued to build up its armaments, and in particular
were to supplement its strength by building up the as yet unarmed
Federal Republic, it could become much stronger *vis-à-vis* the
Soviet Union: the latter, after a series of shifts in the balance of
power in favour of the West, would soon be prepared to make
greater concessions in negotiation.[1] The West made no serious
effort to probe the at least apparent readiness of the Soviet Union
(from March 1952 to the Malenkov era) to permit the reunification
of Germany by stages on the basis of the debolshevisation of the
Soviet-occupied zone, a concession to be offset by Western concessions regarding the military status of the Federal Republic and
its status in the alliance.[2] Bonn, in particular, believed in the
possibility of bringing the Soviet Union to a greater readiness
to make concessions through building up German military
power over a number of years. Bonn therefore believed it could
afford to make no effort to extract the concessions which it then
seemed possible that the Soviet Union might make.

Other Western capitals were more sceptical on this point. Even
in those days some Western circles had begun to voice doubts as
to whether it would ever be possible to use nuclear weapons in
every kind of war. Everyone knows that the Korean War ran its
course as what is now known as a "limited war." Although the
Americans had a monopoly of nuclear weapons, they made no use
of them: they refrained after making a careful appreciation of both
the strategic consequences and of the political and psychological
reactions throughout the world. The fact that, in Korea, the
leading Western power did not use its mightiest weapon should
even at that time have been a clear hint that the theoretical concept
of massive retaliation was not in practice applicable to every
contingency.

[1] Cf., for example, Bradford's interview with Dr Adenauer (Federal Govt.
Bulletin, 25 March 1952) in which Bradford pointed out to the Chancellor that,
in the opinion of many observers, the Soviet note of 10 March 1952 had left the
distinct impression that the Soviets were now on the defensive. The Chancellor
replied: "Yes. But they must be driven even more on the defensive."
[2] Cf. in particular the article by Flora Lewis in the *Washington Post* of 3 July
1960.

Massive Retaliation

Even in 1954 the United States possessed a considerable nuclear preponderance. The Soviet Union had, indeed, in the meantime developed its first hydrogen bomb (first U.S. thermo-nuclear test —Eniwetok, November 1952: first Soviet test—August 1953); but the American nuclear stockpile continued to be substantially greater; and, in particular, the Americans retained a vast superiority in the means of delivery. Nevertheless, in 1954 the Soviet Union showed clear signs of making progress in the field of production of the larger type of bomber. The numbers were as yet small, and it was doubted whether these bombers were able to fly to the United States, drop their bombs, and then return to the Soviet Union. We in the West had to assume, however, that the Russians would in an emergency have been prepared to accept the non-return of their bombers. Of long-range missiles there was as yet scarcely a whisper. The West was still fully confident of its nuclear superiority. This consciousness led to the use, at that time, of such phrases as "massive retaliation at the time and place of our choosing" (first coined by Dulles in early 1954) —phrases that are still widely heard although they have lost all their meaning. This threat of retaliation—a posthumous tribute to the theories of air warfare of the Italian, Douhet—seemed to the Western world of those days a completely realistic answer to every conceivable form of military aggression from the East. At any rate Western statesmen appeared to believe in the reality of the unrestricted threat of retaliation. Consciousness of this superiority led Dulles to coin that later phrase—we must be prepared to go "to the brink of war."

The fact that the United Kingdom had in the meantime become a nuclear power (first British test—Australia, 1952), and that the original nuclear monopoly had now become a triangular relationship, affected strategic thought neither in the West nor in the East—apart, that is, from Britain itself. The world had the impression that the nuclear capabilities of the United States and the United Kingdom would be handled as a unity in all military and political aspects of warfare—if war were to come.

In the Soviet Union at that time—after the death of Stalin— questions of nuclear strategy began to be discussed more openly. This is shown by a number of contributions to military journals.

It was remarkable that Malenkov, as Head of Government, could publicly declare that, in the event of atomic war, there would be a danger of world civilisation being destroyed. This was a complete *volte-face* from the thinking of Stalin's day which regarded nuclear weapons as just one weapon among others. The Soviet Government was now most keenly sensitive to the fact of its nuclear encirclement, and must have been particularly disquieted by the American bases deployed on its very threshold.

In 1954 NATO had over 15 conventionally armed divisions at its disposal in Western Europe, backed by conventional air and naval forces. There had indeed been a decision in Lisbon two years earlier to raise 96 divisions in Europe so as to be able to build a defence line between Basle and the Zuider Zee, and between the Brenner Pass and Trieste. The West's consciousness of its strategic nuclear ascendency, however, allayed any particular disquiet at the failure to reach these planned levels of conventional strength. Not a single leading politician in Europe had taken the Lisbon decision of the NATO Council as a seriously intended guideline, and only a quarter of the formations decided on at Lisbon were in fact raised. The West felt a sense of security such as has not been felt again since those days. Nobody at the time believed that serious efforts were necessary to raise more divisions. In the United States Eisenhower and Radford introduced the "New Look" which envisaged a considerable reduction in American armed personnel and in overseas commitments in order to facilitate the concentration of America's armaments effort entirely on nuclear warfare. It is true that Soviet propaganda made extraordinarily skilful use of the Western threat of massive retaliation, and that the NATO Council's 1954 decision to redress the lack of divisions by permitting and encouraging the use of tactical nuclear weapons pointed to changes ahead. Nevertheless, these symptoms had no practical effect on strategic decision-making There was no doubt in anyone's mind that the balance of military power was favourable, and it was probably never more favourable to the West at any time during the past decade than in 1954.

The Balance of Terror

In October 1957 Dulles contributed an article to *Foreign Affairs* in which he watered down the doctrine of the universality of the application of massive retaliation. He said that it might be possible in the sixties to enforce on the aggressor the decision to initiate nuclear war. The United States was still preponderant in the field of strategic nuclear power. Nevertheless the Soviet Union was now in a position to inflict unacceptable losses on North America. In the first place the Soviet Union had developed a bomber fleet of the necessary range: and, secondly, she had achieved considerable successes in the field of ballistic missiles— a field neglected by the United States. The launching of Sputnik I in 1957, which gave a profound shock to American public opinion, was of particular military significance since it furnished proof of the enormous thrust of Soviet long-range missiles and the accuracy with which they could be fired. From that time on American thinking became strongly influenced by the Soviet missile threat, even though the Russians were still in the research and development phase and had by no means got as far as series production of I.C.B.Ms. This did not, however, prevent the Russians from making political use of their missile threat: these methods were employed for the first time against London and Paris at the time of the Suez crisis. The nature of the training of Soviet officers, moreover, furnished unambiguous evidence that the Russians were prepared to use these weapons in the event of war.

At this time a new doctrine was worked out in the back rooms of the West. At first it was only tentative and by no means achieved public recognition. Its starting-point was acknowledgment of the fact that to coerce the Soviet Union with massive retaliation was no longer possible. Instead, people talked of "nuclear stalemate" or of "two scorpions in a bottle." The point of this latter expression is that neither scorpion is able to attack the other; for at the precise moment when one scorpion prepares to attack his opposite number, he is forced to expose his soft underbelly to the other. The idea of this equilibrium was comforting to many. Specialists were, however, worried lest a nuclear war should break out unpremeditatedly. There were many theories of "accidental war" such as might be unleashed by technical error (we all know of the case when bombers were alerted and ordered into the air as a result of geese on the radar screen), by enemy miscalculation of one's own actions, or by catalytic action, i.e. where a third party, by acts of violence, manœuvres one of the great powers into a nuclear war against the real intention of the latter.

Although the concept of the nuclear stalemate cast doubt upon the strategy of massive retaliation, the British Government adopted this principle and that of nuclear deterrence as the exclusive basis of its strategy as late as 1957. It announced that, in its weapons policy, it would place the main stress on the H-bomb and on aircraft as the means of its delivery. Conventional equipment and civil defence were to take second place, and national service would in due course be dispensed with. The adoption of this concept led the British to remove a large proportion of its troops from Western Germany (and, let it be noted, without obtaining the prior approval of NATO). They were not the only ones: France did the same to an even greater extent, though for different reasons.

In Germany at this time the first criticisms of the concept of massive retaliation could be heard and doubt was expressed for the first time. For example, at the beginning of 1958, von Weizsäcker argued as follows: if I have for my defence only one weapon, and this weapon kills me at the same time as my attacker, it can—paradoxically enough—protect my life better than it can protect my property. For anyone with designs on my life must be afraid that, since I am to die anyway, I will have recourse to my weapon if only to drag him to death along with me. To this extent my weapon can deter him. But someone with designs on my briefcase will reflect that this article will be less valuable to me than my life. He will assume that I will not make use of a weapon that will destroy both of us, since no one is going to blow himself up for the sake of his briefcase. If the thief is right in this supposition then I shall lose my briefcase: but if he is wrong and I resort to my weapon then I will die along with him. A cynic coined the saying: he who shoots first, dies second.

The Discovery of Limited War

Well before this time doubts had been expressed in Britain and America about the concept of massive retaliation, and these doubts had been supported by arguments both logical and incisive. Liddell Hart had attacked the strategy of massive retaliation soon after its first emergence, and instead had spoken of limited war. In 1954 numerous other British and American authors were concerned to demonstrate both the infeasibility of all-out nuclear war and the implications that followed for national strategic planning.

In 1954 attention was given to the subject of limited war by Kennan, Brodie, Sir John Slessor, Sir Anthony Buzzard, Vannevar Bush, and later by William Kaufmann, Hanson Baldwin and others. When Henry Kissinger's book on nuclear weapons and foreign policy appeared in the United States in 1957—a book which has become widely read, particularly in Germany—it could build on the very comprehensive discussion that had gone before. All these authors agreed that, in the event of a limited Soviet attack, it would be out of the question to base one's defence on strategic annihilation of the enemy, since no one would wish to precipitate the destruction of his own country. A limited attack could only be answered by limited measures. In any event the alternative of limited war had already been clearly developed by Clausewitz. This historical fact was also rediscovered.

For all that, the definitions and theories of limited war took many different forms and did not coincide with one another. Limited war was defined by the aims set for it, by the area of the conflict, or by the effects of the weapons employed. Limited war, it was postulated, could take place between two secondary powers, though it could take place between two major nuclear powers also. A distinction was made between total war, limited war, local war and cold war. "War by proxy," an example of which was furnished by the Korean War, was considered by some to be an aspect of cold war. A heated discussion began—and continues to this day— as to the feasibility of limited war with nuclear weapons.[3]

There is no doubt that one quintessential point of this discussion was fairly generally acknowledged, viz. that one must refrain from driving one's enemy to the point where he is forced, as a last resort, to use his nuclear weapons. One must therefore have alternative weapons so as to be able to fight a limited war. If the threat of strategic annihilation is no longer suitable for deterring an adversary from less than all-out aggressions, then lesser threats also are necessary. The point of having the means for fighting limited war is not just to make war possible, but rather to avoid the fatal dilemma into which the West is in danger of drifting, of

---

[3] Cf. the discussion in Chapter 6 under the heading: Can Nuclear Weapons Replace Men? (pp. 92 ff.).

B

having to choose between yielding in face of attacks or encroach-
ment, and world devastation. If we wish to oppose an attack at the
periphery, we must meet it with limited means, we must limit the
objectives of our defensive action, and we must avoid endangering
the enemy's vital interests if we are not to force him to resort to
nuclear retaliation. Kissinger was particularly impressive on this.

This discussion led to understanding of the fact that even in a
conventional war against a nuclear power the latter must not be
driven into a corner: nor must his retaliatory bases be seriously
threatened since there would otherwise be a danger that he might,
from despair if not from rational calculation, resort to his strategic
nuclear weapons and so unleash world-wide devastation. It thus
became clear that, even in limited war, it is impermissible to aim
at decisive "victory" over a nuclear power. It became equally clear
that limited war could give rise to a special form of misunderstanding or miscalculation: the enemy must not mistake a decision to
fight a limited nuclear war as indicating an intention to fight all-out
war.

The theory of limited war soon found its way into the councils
and decisions of Western governments. It had been applied by
both sides several years earlier in the Korean War, albeit uncon-
sciously: the U.N. forces had not bombed enemy airfields north of
the Yalu, and the Chinese and the North Koreans had not
attacked Pusan, the U.N. forces' only supply port, or the American
fleet. No use was made of atomic weapons in the Suez operation;
and, during the landing in the Lebanon, the American marines
were not allowed to take their Honest John missiles ashore with
them so as to avoid any possibility of a misunderstanding. The
nuclear potential of the Sixth Fleet also was held in the background.

In the winter of 1957 and the spring of 1958 the NATO Council
faced up to the implications of the new theories. It made resolutions in accordance with the recommendations of the celebrated
document MC 70. Since it was assumed that the available weapons
and troops were not enough for limited war, it was decided to
stiffen the "Shield" forces with "tactical" nuclear weapons. The
tactical nuclear weapons were intended to redress the numerical
superiority of the conventional Soviet forces in the event of
limited war. At the same time it was decided to increase NATO
troops in Europe to 30 divisions. It is true that these resolutions

made no mention of the phrase "limited nuclear war": nevertheless, the thought of it was uppermost in the minds of those responsible for making the decisions. In saying this we must not lose sight of the fact that a prime purpose of the NATO resolutions of 1957-8 was to restore the somewhat jaded confidence of European governments in the reliability and efficiency of the West's defences.

Forward Strategy

Since the founding of NATO the conviction had come to prevail in the United States that it was only by means of peripheral defence (i.e. "forward" of the national boundaries) that North America could be effectively defended. This contrasted with the "Fortress America" concept. Acknowledgment of this fact had led to the fighting of the Korean War, to the suppression of the Communists in Greece long before, to the assistance accorded to Persia to help it against the Soviet Union, and to the support of the French in Indo-China and of Chiang Kai-shek in Formosa. The discovery of the principle of limited war inevitably posed the question of whether the available forces were adequate for this type of peripheral defence now that it was becoming ever clearer that nuclear weapons, and S.A.C. in particular, were not suited to meet such contingencies.

The possibility of further such incidents and of regionally limited military clashes at the periphery loomed all too clearly ahead. The United States was under obligation, through its various military agreements, to give military support, in case of need, to a large number of states in Europe, South-East Asia, the Far East, and in the American continent itself. The question arose whether the United States was at all capable of giving such support within a politically meaningful space of time in view of the paucity of her operational troops and her very limited ability to transport these quickly by land or sea to the areas where they might have to be used.

The history of the last fifteen years shows that Soviet strategy has exploited this situation very skilfully. It switched the cold war fronts very rapidly from Greece to Azerbaijan, from Korea to Indo-China, later in the Middle East to Syria, Egypt, Iraq, and then once again back to Formosa: finally new fronts were set up in Berlin, Cuba and the Congo. No one can say how dangerously the situation might develop in the Congo and other parts of Africa, notably Algeria, inflamed as they are by Communist infiltration, by economic and military support, by promises of military protection—all aggravated by Western errors. The strategic potential of the Eastern Bloc comprises many diverse capabilities—ranging from I.C.B.M. threats to giving training in civil war methods, from the despatch of military missions to the absorption of the vital exports of small under-developed countries, from promises of military support to massive military threats. In face of all this the West's strategy has not up till now proved itself outstandingly successful.

3

Deterrence Analysed

NOTWITHSTANDING the obviously revolutionary significance of the atomic bomb, it seemed at the close of World War II as though the four-engined long-range bomber would long remain the decisive weapon carrier of modern air warfare. At all events the United States, and later the Soviet Union, built up their strategic weapons on this concept. Even today S.A.C. consists almost exclusively of long-range bombers. Aircraft have, of course, very greatly improved their performance during the last fifteen years. S.A.C. has at the moment over 1,200 B 47 bombers with a range of about 3,000 miles and a speed of about 600 m.p.h. The 500 strong B 52 fleet is, however, more important: this eight-engined aircraft has a range of 6,000 miles and a speed of about 650 m.p.h. As well as these combat aircraft there is a large fleet of tanker aircraft whose purpose is to refuel the former while in flight: S.A.C. has brought this technique to a fine art.

The Soviet Union disposes of about 100 four-engined bombers with the NATO code name "Bison." These are believed to have a range of 6,000 miles and a speed of 600 m.p.h. There are also smaller numbers of a turbo-prop bomber with poorer performance characteristics which has evidently been converted into a tanker aircraft. The Russians also have at their disposal 1,000 twin-engined medium bombers (NATO code name "Badger") of medium range and a speed of about 600 m.p.h. Whereas the United States has by far the greater numerical strength in heavy bombers the Russians are stronger in medium bombers. The United States Air Force is at present receiving increasing numbers of the supersonic B 58 bomber in place of the B 47: it may be that the Russians are developing a similar aircraft.

Quite apart from its numerical superiority, the American long-range bomber force is far ahead of its Soviet counterpart in both experience and training. Nevertheless the Soviet long-range force has, since 1954, posed an ever-growing threat to North America. For this reason the United States has been making since this date considerable efforts to build up its active air defences: these efforts are comparable to those made earlier by the Soviet Union. The United States has surrounded its territory with a system of radar warning chains: the outermost (with stations in Alaska, Greenland and Scotland) is now under construction. In recent years the United States has brought large numbers of interceptor fighters into service and pressed on with its anti-aircraft missiles. The standard missile used for this purpose is the liquid-fuel Nike-Ajax with a range of about 25 miles and a speed just exceeding that of sound. An improved version, the solid-fuel Nike-Hercules, with a range of 80 miles and supersonic speed, has recently been brought into service: it carries a nuclear warhead. Furthermore, during the last two years a conventional anti-aircraft missile, the Hawk, has been introduced in order to combat low-level bomber attacks: this has a range of up to 20 miles and great launching flexibility. The United States has several other types of guided interceptor weapons (e.g. Bomarc) which are, however, of no great numerical significance.

Soviet air defence is based on similar weapons and, by common consent, is numerically stronger than the American. In the field of radar the Soviet Union appears also to be qualitatively superior. Hanson Baldwin estimated in 1958 that, in face of the strong Soviet air defences, S.A.C. would need about 100 B 47 bombers to guarantee the delivery of at least one nuclear bomb on Moscow. None the less, neither side could count on being able to protect its territory anything like completely against the delivery of nuclear bombs. This fact is the more significant since the detonation of a single nuclear bomb over one heavily populated city can do more damage than thousands of World War II type bombs.

The Missile Revolution

It can be seen from these few indications how far-reaching were the implications of the development of long-range air forces. With the emergence of long-range missiles, however, what was merely rapid development became a revolution. Compared with the effect of a 1945-type four-engined bomber, the destructive power of a single nuclear-armed I.C.B.M. is today 10^5 or 10^6 times greater. The speed of a present-day I.C.B.M. is about fifty times greater than that of bombers of that period, and its range has been trebled. This development is characterised in particular by the high accuracy of missiles. American sources give us to believe that Soviet I.C.B.Ms. can achieve an accuracy of about 2 miles (C.E.P.) at a range of 6,000 miles.

The Soviet lead in the field of development and production of ballistic missiles is uncontested, even though it may recently have been reduced. In pursuing their aims the Russians have built on the German World War II developments and have clearly been able, given this basis, to make rapid progress with their own development. As in the case of the United States, the Russians have at their disposal a multiplicity of ballistic missiles of different types and purposes. As early as 1952 the T 1 ballistic missile (developed from the V 2) was in series production: this can carry a nuclear warhead to a range of 400-plus miles. Three years later series production started of a medium-range ballistic missile (T 2) whose range even at that time registered about 1,100 miles. Alongside these two intermediate-range ballistic missiles there are the Komet and Golem missiles for the use of surfaced submarines: some later versions of these two missiles have characteristics corresponding to the T 1 and T 2. What is noteworthy is that the submarine missiles are to some extent solid-fuelled. As early as 1958 the total Soviet stockpile of intermediate-range ballistic missiles with ranges up to 1,850 miles was estimated to number more than 20,000.

Alongside the intermediate-range ballistic missiles the Soviet Union has various types of I.C.B.M.: these types (T 3 and T 3A) have ranges of from 4,500 to 7,500 miles. The Russians are clearly able to extend these ranges further. All I.C.B.Ms. can carry nuclear or thermo-nuclear warheads.

The Soviet armoury also, of course, has its anti-aircraft (surface-to-air) missiles. Of these available at least two (Types T 6 and T 8) have performances corresponding to the American Nike-Ajax: T 8 has an infra-red homing warhead. Anti-aircraft missiles went, remarkably enough, into series production as early as 1953. A fifth group of missiles (e.g. T 5 and T 7 which exist in various versions—also called BB 1, BB 2 and BB 3 in Germany) are intended for tactical support of the ground forces and have ranges of from 15 to 90 miles. Finally the Soviet Union, of course, has air-to-surface missiles (T 4A) which replace free-falling bombs, and also air-to-air missiles. It has also developed and put into production jet-propelled (air-breathing) missiles for various purposes.

The most important comparable American missiles are known to us mainly from the press. First and foremost there is the Atlas I.C.B.M. with a range of just 6,000 miles, which will be followed by the Titan with rather better performance, and some years later by Minuteman. Intermediate-range missiles are represented by Thor and Jupiter: both have been in service since 1958 with ranges of over 1,250 miles. All the above except Minuteman are liquid-fuelled missiles and their launching requires a lengthy countdown. The air-breathing missile Snark, with a range of about 5,500 miles, is also available in limited number for inter-continental use. The most advanced United States ballistic missile technologically is the Polaris I.R.B.M. which has a range of from 1,280 to 1,500 miles and, as a solid-fuel missile, is designed for launching from submarines: its reliability and accuracy, and also the yield of its warhead, appear to leave room for improvement. Further intermediate-range guided missiles are the air-breathing Regulus (naval), Matador and Mace (Air Force) with ranges of 450 to 600 miles. Missiles for tactical use by the ground forces are Redstone, Corporal, Honest John, Little John and Pershing: all are solid-fuelled with the exception of the first two; the two last-named are not yet available on any considerable scale. They vary in range from 12 to 180 miles.

Submarines are acquiring greater significance as missile launchers on account of the difficulties of detecting them. The Soviet Union has about 450 submarines of which a good half are suitable for long-range missions. It has been confirmed that some of these boats have already been equipped with medium-range missiles, but the number of these conversions cannot be estimated. The United States has so far commissioned only a few boats as missile launchers, but their number will probably increase faster during the next few years than was originally planned. Unlike the hitherto familiar types of missile, Polaris can be launched from submerged submarines. Its launching platform is therefore most extensively safeguarded against surprise attack. The importance of the submarine-launched medium-range missile rises with the introduction of nuclear propulsion for submarines, which makes possible a practically unlimited period of submergence. The submarine's ability to navigate under the ice cap of the Arctic Ocean gives rise to a serious threat to both sides. It would appear that the United States has a slight edge over the Soviet Union in the development of this weapons system: nevertheless it is believed that the Soviet Union has already put nuclear-propelled submarines into service.

Ballistic missiles have had a profound influence on the strategy and tactics of air warfare. To begin with, the value of the two already existing radar warning lines round North America was substantially reduced by the advent of ballistic missiles. And even if the outermost warning line now under construction could detect I.C.B.Ms. at the very moment of launching, the warning period even in the most favourable case for the S.A.C. units based in the United States would at best be only twenty minutes. The extent to which modern radar systems are able to counter interference and deception by enemy electronic warfare can scarcely yet be judged. There seems no prospect whatsoever of enemy I.C.B.Ms. or I.R.B.Ms. being intercepted by manned aircraft. The anti-missile missile Nike-Zeus, for all the publicity it receives, is still only in the early stages of development: a further three to five years must elapse before one can expect it to be introduced as a reliable system. Even then it can only be successful in isolated cases because economic considerations will rule out the protection of more than a few highest priority targets by its means. Furthermore it is doubtful whether this missile will find its target when the target (i.e. the enemy I.C.B.M.) arrives, not singly, but in groups or even in massed salvoes. Altogether, one must proceed on the assumption that in the foreseeable future there will be no practicable means of defence against medium and long-range ballistic missiles. This is the first and fundamental fact of the ballistic missile revolution.

Both sides will therefore strive to strike the enemy's launching sites if possible before his missiles leave the ground. These launching sites are pin-point targets which require great accuracy even when thermo-nuclear warheads are used. This in its turn assumes the highest possible degree of accuracy in the geodetic determination of the target's position. In this respect the Russians have a great advantage over the Americans: the whereabouts of the launching sites on Soviet territory are no more than partially suspected and it has been quite impossible up till now to carry out an accurate survey of the whole system. As against this, the few launching sites so far built by the Americans, in particular the I.R.B.M. sites in Europe, are open to accurate geodetic survey by the Soviets by virtue of the "open" nature of society in the democratic countries.

Target reconnaissance therefore becomes a cardinal factor in air warfare. Only in this light do the U 2 reconnaissance flights carried out year after year by the Americans become understandable. For as long as there is no mutual aerial inspection the West will remain at a disadvantage in the matter of target reconnaissance. It must try to make up for this disadvantage by the widest possible deployment and dispersal of its launching sites, by making them mobile, or by "hardening" them.

An important characteristic of ballistic missile armaments is the enormously increased danger of "war by accident." Whereas bombers sent into the air as a result of inaccurate intelligence or faulty decision can always be recalled (or alternatively—as is the case in the United States today—whereas the prosecution of their mission can be made dependent on the receipt of fresh orders or confirmation of previous ones received in the air), ballistic missiles once launched cannot be recalled. Faulty interpretation of radar echoes—or, to put a fine point on it, a fault or breakdown in the computer system—could precipitate World War III. Responsible leadership must therefore not permit I.C.B.Ms., as opposed to bomber fleets, to be launched on the receipt of uncertain radar information.

The weapons systems of present-day ballistic missile warfare are technologically so complex and require such enormous financial outlay that it is scarcely credible that, apart from the Soviet Union and the United States, third powers will successfully compete in this branch of the arms race. A further consideration is that, for the reasons given above, large land areas will be needed for the deployment of land-based ballistic missiles. It therefore seems, as was the case ten years ago with possession of the atomic bomb, that possession of the I.C.B.M. will once again divide the nations of the earth into great powers and others. This distinction will become clearer when, within a few years, earth satellites are adapted for military purposes. Satellites can help with target survey, observation and reconnaissance, warning of surprise attack, aid to navigation, long-distance communications, and meteorological forecasting. Before long thermo-nuclear warheads will be fired from satellites at fixed points on the earth's surface in just the same way as capsules with dogs and monkeys are today brought back from space to previously determined positions. Defence against such attack seems scarcely conceivable to lay opinion today.

And this is not all: we can today form absolutely no idea of all the many different ways in which the future technological development of warfare will be affected by earth satellites.

The Unstable Balance

In 1957-8 the NATO Council resolved to station American I.R.B.Ms. in Europe. This decision was made under the impact of the Soviet long-range missile potential and was designed to offset it. This was duly implemented by the stationing in Britain of Thor, and in Italy of Jupiter. It was also implemented in Turkey. Other European members of NATO refused to station such missiles on their territory, and others were not considered for either military or geographical reasons. The main political motive behind this undertaking was doubtless to restore the diminished confidence of European governments in the efficacy of the strategy of massive retaliation.

This departure aroused great misgivings in Germany and in Eastern Europe—particularly in Poland; the more so as the reasons for it given by specialists were vague and self-contradictory. It would appear that the Soviet Union, by virtue of the great progress which she had herself made in the field of rocket technology, rapidly overcame the sense of additional threat to herself which this resolution instilled, and later used it both to intimidate her Satellites and to bolster her general propaganda. Nevertheless, everyone capable of objective reasoning must concede that the stationing of enemy I.R.B.Ms., so to speak, on its very threshold (Turkey), must produce the psychological effect of a provocation on any great power. One need only imagine how the Americans would react if the Soviets were to station I.R.B.Ms. in Cuba. From the military viewpoint the stationing of American I.R.B.Ms. on European territory is probably of only transitory significance, viz. until the Americans close the so-called missile gap and eliminate the Soviet lead in I.C.B.M. production.

The theoretical models dating from the time of strategic nuclear monopoly and bipolarity have long since become obsolete: the old-fashioned Western concepts which once rested on them have lost their basis. It was only to be expected that the facts of this matter would scarcely so far have penetrated the consciousness of the general public; but Western European governments and leading politicians seem vague as to whether NATO should still follow the principle of retaliation in the event of war, or whether it should develop fresh concepts in its stead. This present-day conceptual uncertainty is to be explained by three new factors:

1. There are today not two nuclear powers, but three and a half (and no one can tell how long it will be before France—the nuclear half power—achieves full nuclear status, or how long it will be before other powers develop their own long-range nuclear weapons). The monopolistic, bipolar situations, which were relatively easy to calculate, have vanished never to return. And in the meantime the several nuclear powers openly pursue their own interests: their behaviour as nuclear powers within the Western alliance also lacks consistency. The problem of the "Nth power," which formerly existed only in theory, has now become real and concrete.

2. Consideration must be given not only to long-range strategic weapons with nuclear warheads, but also to the great variety of other nuclear weapons which has come into existence—weapons of the most different type, purpose, range, and effect—ranging from heavy artillery capable of firing nuclear shells, to tactical missiles such as Corporal or Honest John, to the Matador and Mace guided weapons, to I.R.B.Ms., and finally to bombers with a range of 3,750 to 6,000 miles and I.C.B.Ms. with a range of 6,000 to 7,500 miles. Each year that passes sees the introduction of new types of nuclear weapon and ballistic missile: the situation is becoming less and less easy to survey on account of its complexity.

3. It has been recognised—at least in the United States and the Soviet Union—that the threat of mutual destruction by strategic nuclear weapons posed by the two global powers, and the state of mutual deterrence which this brings about, does not, contrary to earlier ideas on the subject, represent a stable equilibrium. Formerly the view was held that the "balance of terror" (Churchill) would preserve the world from nuclear war. But, as every student of elementary physics knows, an equilibrium does not need to be

stable. A pendulum always returns to its state of equilibrium: a tight-rope walker, on the other hand, must be on his guard—the slightest touch will put him off his balance and send him tumbling. The attempt to preserve the peace solely on the basis of strategic nuclear parity between the United States and the Soviet Union resembles such a tight-rope act.

When discussing limited war we saw that it is impermissible in a conflict with a global power armed with the full apparatus of strategic nuclear warfare to seek to encompass his decisive military defeat other than at the risk of one's own destruction. Retaliatory strategy has led to still other theoretical innovations. Deterrence is admittedly nothing new in human history, and certainly not in the history of armed states; and many may think that war, irrespective of the technical means by which it is fought, is similarly subject to immutable strategic laws. Too superficial a view of the current Clausewitz renaissance in both the East and the West, might well give rise to this impression. But just as we have learned to distinguish between classical and non-Euclidian geometry, between classical and Keynesian economics, we must recognise that fundamental innovations have been made in the field of strategy. Thermo-nuclear deterrence can function only on the following assumptions:

1. that the enemy has adequate intelligence of one's own strategy and military technical capabilities; and
2. that the enemy will act and react in an absolutely rational fashion.

In so far as A believes that he can surprise B, or that he can forestall or neutralise B's automatic retaliation, or that he need not take B's threats of retaliation seriously because his own reconnaissance has revealed a much smaller capacity for retaliation on B's part than the latter had claimed—in all such cases lies the hideous danger that deterrence might break down and encompass the death of millions. The aggressor must conceal his strength as far as possible: a deterer must proclaim it openly.

The Declining Credibility of Soft Missiles

If A decides to launch a strategic nuclear attack on B, the decision assumes certainty on his part:

1. that he (A) can penetrate B's air defences; and
2. that the attack on B's retaliatory weapons will be successful

enough for their effectiveness to be reduced to the point where they can be combated by A's air defences or where their effects will be acceptable to A.

Translated into practical terms this might be taken to mean that if the Soviet Union were to conclude, during an actual conflict with the United States, that the latter's threats of retaliation were to be taken seriously and realistically, she would have to choose between moderating or breaking off the fighting, or herself going over to the offensive and attacking S.A.C. in order to forestall retaliation. The retaliatory forces of the United States at the end of 1960 consisted of a few Atlas missiles in bases generally known in North America; of about 500 B 52 bombers and about 1,200 B 47 bombers based for the most part in the United States; and about 100 Thor and Jupiter I.R.B.Ms. (to take the highest estimate) in at the most seven European bases. These American retaliatory forces operate from a total of less than 100 bases. To them must be added the nuclear forces of the Sixth and Seventh Fleets, a few Polaris submarines, and several hundred NATO fighter-bombers in Europe: the latter's range enables them to carry a nuclear bomb load at least to the western frontier area of the Soviet Union. It is assumed, on the basis of the reliability, accuracy and presumed payload of present-day Soviet I.C.B.Ms., that it would take the Russians three I.C.B.Ms. to inflict the necessary destruction on a S.A.C. bomber base. These S.A.C. airfields and the few United States missile launching sites so far in commission are open, unprotected sites. It is easy to work out the number of I.C.B.Ms. the Russians would have to fire simultaneously to achieve, with complete statistical probability, the elimination of the retaliatory bases of the United States—or at least of S.A.C. The S.A.C. Commander, General Power, in the spring of 1960 put this figure at 300. He clearly assumed that three enemy missiles per base would be sufficient. We must of course make allowances for the fact that Power had his own reasons for making out S.A.C.'s present-day posture to be one of maximum "softness," i.e. he was anxious to bolster the U.S.A.F.'s claim on the economic resources of the nation. For our purposes, however, it is immaterial whether the right figure is in the order of 300 or 600 I.C.B.Ms. What we must grasp is that, at this very day, if the Soviet Union were to launch a missile attack that achieved both surprise and simultaneity of salvo, only a relatively small residue of S.A.C.'s nuclear retaliatory forces would remain intact. It is true that the carrier-borne air forces and, to some extent, the fighter bombers stationed in Europe would also survive.

For technical reasons it would, of course, not be easy for the Soviet Union to achieve something approaching simultaneity of salvo: its missiles would have to engage their targets at greatly varying ranges—some medium and others inter-continental. S.A.C. might hope to get some warning from this difficulty. Should S.A.C.'s radar cover operate with maximum efficiency, the warning period would be sufficient for a minority of S.A.C. aircraft to get into the air.

On the hypothetical assumption that the Soviet Union could bring all its presently available missiles to bear on their targets, we should have to expect that the relatively small percentage of the American retaliatory forces that would survive undamaged and effective would not be enough to destroy all the operational bases of the Soviet long-range air force. It is true that the surviving United States strategic forces available for a nuclear retaliatory blow, put by some shrewd American experts at between 10 and 20 per cent. of the original force, would probably be sufficient to devastate the majority of Soviet cities: for relatively few weapons with relatively low accuracy would be needed to devastate the large target area presented by a city. If, however, such a retaliatory blow against Soviet cities were to leave unattacked the airfields of the Soviet long-range air force, we could then expect that the Soviet air force, with its strength undiminished, would at once mount a devastating blow against the major American cities. The air defences of the United States, faced with meeting this attack, would be in a state of disarray and greatly reduced efficiency as a result of the previous Soviet first strike. This prospect would confront the Americans with the difficult question of whether they could afford to launch a retaliatory blow against Soviet cities in view of the risk to their own.

In the hypothetical case just quoted, therefore, the possibility arises (and is supported by calculations far more detailed than any we have attempted) that the United States would neither, on the one hand, be able to cripple the Soviet long-range air force by a "counterforce strike" nor perhaps, on the other, exploit the chance she would have of retaliating against Soviet cities ("counter-city strike") for reasons of self-preservation.

This model, of course, works also the other way round. Calculations can, of course, also be made for the case of an American surprise attack on the Soviet Union. These would be handicapped by inadequate knowledge of the number of Soviet I.C.B.Ms. and launchers now actually operational. All calculations of this sort lead to the conclusion that an aggressor who carries out an all-out nuclear surprise attack scores so *tremendous* an advantage over his victim that the latter would probably not be able to restore the position as the war progressed.

A number of preventive counter-measures can, of course, be taken against surprise attack. These have to some extent already been adopted by both sides. It is possible, even though at horrendous expense, to maintain part of S.A.C. permanently in the air where (until now) they would not be vulnerable to surprise attack. The occasions—times of political tension—on which formations of S.A.C. have been ordered into the air are not to be interpreted as aggressive gestures: they were, on the contrary, defensive measures. The popular notion that the Americans keep a third of their strategic air forces in the air is, for all that, completely wrong: both for financial and (particularly) for technical and personnel reasons it is impossible to maintain so high a degree of readiness for more than a few days at the most. We shall not go far wrong if we assume that S.A.C. can as a rule maintain no more than 5 to 10 per cent. of its aircraft in the air at any one time. Over and above this S.A.C. could scramble a proportion of its squadrons if it should obtain clear radar warning of the approach of enemy missiles. I pointed out above the difficulty of obtaining timely warning in such an eventuality.

The dispersal of aircraft among a much greater number of airfields, such as has already begun, and the provision of blast protection on the airfields, are for this reason more important and effective steps. Both measures will, of course, be applied to missile launching sites also.

So long as measures of this sort are only partially carried through, S.A.C. will remain essentially an exceedingly vulnerable instrument—a "soft" system. In its present condition it is scarcely fitted to fulfil its mission of massive retaliation after absorbing a Soviet surprise attack. On the contrary, it is only fitted for carrying out a surprise attack itself.

S.A.C.'s qualified ability to carry out "massive" retaliation after absorbing an enemy surprise blow is not, of course, something recognised only by the U.S. Air Force and American savants: it is also known to the Soviet Air Forces and the Soviet political direction. This knowledge has severely circumscribed the credibility of the American threat of retaliation. The paradoxical fact also emerges, moreover, that in Soviet eyes the weapon developed by the Americans for massive retaliation not only is unsuited for retaliation but, on the contrary, may well seem intended for a surprise attack.

It is, of course, inconceivable that any American administration should decide to carry out a surprise attack on the Soviet Union with H-bombs and missiles: we must nevertheless bear in mind the fact that the Soviet Union, in view of S.A.C.'s present-day posture, may regard this force as an aggressive weapon. A further relevant fact is that relatively little has been done in the United States for the protection of the lives and property of its civilian population—at any rate, clearly less than in the Soviet Union. A country, however, which from its frequently repeated threats of massive retaliation, clearly reckons with the possibility of thermonuclear war and yet does nothing to protect the population from its effects, can by this very token create the impression that it is arming, not for a retaliatory blow or riposte, but, on the contrary, for a surprise attack.

These considerations have given rise, both in the Soviet Union and in the United States, to thoughts of what in America is called "pre-emptive" strike—the theory of the forestalling attack. According to this theory, in a military conflict where the situation between two great powers has become critical, the decisive factor may well be which of the two will be the first to draw his nuclear revolver and surprise the other. If one of them had grounds for assuming that the other intended to carry out a surprise attack, he would be well advised to forestall his adversary and himself deliver a pre-emptive blow.

Should such considerations come to influence the strategy of the Soviet or American leaders (and nobody can rule this out), this would mean that strategic nuclear forces would have lost their power to deter and would possibly have become a source of provocation to the enemy. The pre-emptive blow presupposes, by its very definition, prompt receipt of unambiguous intelligence of the impending enemy surprise attack. In the conditions likely to

C

exist in war unambiguous intelligence of this sort is unlikely to be forthcoming. Nevertheless the West seems to assume that, in the event of nuclear war, it would start with its nuclear forces unimpaired. This is an assumption for which, as we have seen above, there is little justification on practical military grounds.

Theories of pre-emptive attack have been discussed publicly and in detail both in the Soviet Union and in the United States. These discussions and the war games carried out in connexion with them bring home to us in all its hideousness the instability of the alleged balance of terror. This instability has its origin mainly in the high degree of vulnerability of the strategic nuclear forces now in being and their consequent implausibility as retaliatory forces; in the enormous advantage to be gained by the side delivering a surprise attack; in the compulsion felt by both sides to pre-empt an enemy surprise attack suspected to be imminent; in the frightening speed of the missile launching process (which is automated to the greatest degree possible, and is irreversible); and finally in a factor that will later be discussed in greater detail—in the expectation that all new members of the nuclear club, all new fourth, fifth, and sixth powers, will enter the field with an excessively vulnerable nuclear striking force which, for this reason, will be suitable only for attack, and not for retaliation.

Hard Systems

The total number of powers with a nuclear capability could conceivably matter less for the future preservation of peace than whether they dispose of a relatively invulnerable striking force such as would enable them to survive an enemy attack and not feel compelled by vulnerability to attack first. British and American writers therefore distinguish between a "first strike" and a "second strike" capability. The latter expression could perhaps also be rendered as "counterattack system."

The following requirements must be satisfied in a counterattack system: its economic cost must not represent an impossible financial burden; it must have a high relative security in face of enemy air or missile attack; it must be secure against going off accidentally; it must be backed by reliable command and intelligence machinery; its range must be adequate to strike the strategic targets in the enemy's own country; it must be able to penetrate the enemy's air defences in sufficient numbers; adequate intelligence and survey information must be available regarding the targets on enemy territory; it must have sufficient accuracy and—particularly against blast-protected targets—power of destruction. Only if a strategic nuclear weapons system meets these technico-military requirements will the threat of massive retaliation be constant and credible. Only if these requirements are met will the danger of a pre-emptive blow by an enemy threatened with retaliation, become improbable.

A strategic nuclear power must, in its own interest, hope that its adversary will also adopt a similar system. Even the West must wish that the Soviet Union had an invulnerable and secure counterattack system and so be removed from any temptation to seek refuge in a pre-emptive blow that would devastate our cities. The West's security against a surprise nuclear attack by the Soviet Union grows therefore, paradoxically enough, as the Soviet Union progresses from a "soft" to a "hard" system. The question is therefore pertinent—astounding as it may seem—whether it would really serve Western security if the West, by means of reconnaissance satellites, were to carry out a geodetic survey of all the Soviet I.C.B.M. bases and thereby help to down-grade the Soviet "hardened" counterattack system into a soft system. The transformation of former soft systems into counter-attack systems makes the world balance more stable; but it cannot be denied that they will at the same time probably make the problems of inspection and control more difficult.

Some ways of progressing from a soft to a hard system have been pointed out above. At present the most significant method is to try to avoid basing one's own nuclear striking forces at fixed points and localities which the enemy can fix, survey and, as a result, strike easily. Missiles can, for example, be mounted on freight wagons constantly on the move, or on shipboard on inland water-ways or on the high seas. Without doubt the most modern and, for some time to come, perhaps the most secure method is to mount medium-range missiles in submarines capable of firing them submerged. The missile developed by the Americans for this purpose—the Polaris—has much the same range as the earlier I.R.B.Ms. Thor and Jupiter. Unlike these, however, Polaris is solid-fuelled and has a somewhat smaller warhead. A fleet of as few as ten submarines, each with sixteen Polaris missiles, could threaten 85 per cent of the total population of the Soviet Union's major cities. In order to maintain ten submarines on patrol at any one time the United States would need a fleet of double that number as well as depot ships or bases. Given even the maximum possible effort, it will scarcely be possible to build a fleet of this size before 1963. It takes something of the order of two years to build one boat, and in the meantime the prototypes will be wrestling with teething troubles.

Rationality and Credibility

Our discussion so far has shown that we must distinguish between at least three different types of nuclear strategy:

1. surprise attack (first strike);
2. pre-emptive strike;
3. retaliatory or counter-blow (second strike).

All three strategies presuppose separate and distinct military technological capabilities, and vary also according to the targets to be attacked.

A strategy of surprise attack needs no "hardened" weapons system: all that is necessary is the capability to penetrate an intact enemy air defence system and to cause an adequate degree of destruction to the enemy's retaliatory potential. This strategy must be directed primarily against the enemy's nuclear striking forces (counter-force strike): any effort against mass industrial or population targets counts only as a bonus.

The requirements are the same for a pre-emptive strategy as for surprise attack. A power putting its trust in pre-emption, however, must in addition ensure that its intelligence and espionage services provide it at all times, but particularly at times of extreme tension, with a reliable picture of enemy intentions and capabilities, so that the pre-emptive blow may get off to a timely start. Apart from this significant difference, the requirements are much the same in both cases.

The requirements for carrying out a retaliatory blow are of a quite different order. They include, of course, the means of penetrating the enemy's air defences on an adequate scale, but current and exhaustive cover of enemy preparations and intentions is not, on the other hand, so important. What is essential is that one's own striking forces should be able to survive an enemy surprise attack without substantial loss of capability. Retaliatory strategy, therefore, requires a "hardened" nuclear weapons system.

Since the essence of retaliation is attack on enemy population centres (counter-city strike) rather than on the enemy's now empty missile launchers, there is not the same requirement for geodetic survey of the enemy's bases: his population and industrial centres provide targets so extensive that they are relatively easy to hit.

As regards their actual preparations for war, neither of the major nuclear powers has made the clear-cut choice of any one of the three strategies just mentioned: on the contrary, both strive to be adequately prepared for all three. It is difficult to tell how far their material preparations have gone along the road to a "hardened" system. At the moment it is unlikely that "hardened" means of delivery are yet available in numbers sufficient to be able to retaliate on an adequate scale after absorbing a first strike. A retaliatory capability can only be called "adequate" when it can inflict unacceptable losses on the enemy and when the prospect of such losses restrains him from resorting to an aggressive blow. A power, therefore, that wishes to use its retaliatory capacity to deter an enemy from attacking must ensure that the enemy is in no doubt about the effectiveness of its retaliatory capacity and will to use it. In such a case what matters is not so much the possession of as many ballistic missiles as possible; what is essential is that these missiles should not be sensitive to an enemy aggressive blow and that they should be qualitatively and quantitatively adequate to cause the enemy unacceptable losses.

A state of nuclear stalemate will, in practice, be achieved when both nuclear powers are in a position to inflict an unacceptable retaliatory blow on the enemy, and when both make their calculations with this enemy capability in the forefront of their minds. In such a case it must be in the interest of both powers for the enemy to be able to assess the extent of the other's retaliatory capability: to conceal one's retaliatory capability would be to jeopardise one's own strategy. It will take a long time before politicians and public opinion in the countries concerned are able to grasp this fact. They must, furthermore, understand that the stability of the nuclear stalemate will only be guaranteed for as long as neither power tries, by means of its intelligence, reconnaissance or survey devices, to change its adversary's "hard" retaliatory system into a "soft" system again. There is a similar paradox in the proposition that a state having "clean"[1] bombs should, rationally, share the

---

[1] i.e. nuclear bombs with little nuclear fall-out.

secret with its enemy: for it would be absurd for him to carry out his attack with clean bombs if the enemy's pre-emptive or retaliatory blow were made with "dirty" ones.

All these considerations show that the political strategy of deterrence not only assumes an enemy who behaves rationally, but also an enemy who calculates that one will oneself behave rationally in the event of war. As we have seen above, however, it seems at least doubtful whether a nation that has suffered unprecedented devastation in a surprise attack will take the decision to launch a retaliatory blow. The contemporary interplay of strategic nuclear threats, of nuclear deterrence and counter-deterrence, is indeed a delicately balanced, intellectual system of rational calculations. But at the same time we must bear in mind the possibility that, at periods of tension, neither the political leaders nor the large proportion of the decision-making elements of the great powers do by any means react strictly rationally or expediently—they may react emotionally, instinctively even. The United Kingdom's guarantee to distant Poland offers an historical example of a reaction of this kind. This guarantee was made at the height of the Danzig crisis of 1939 at a time when the United Kingdom—completely unprepared for the coming war—was in no sort of position to honour its guarantee. The subsequent course of the Polish campaign showed that the British guarantee of Poland's integrity had no meaning at this stage. The same example also shows that the opposing power, under Hitler's leadership, was not able to make a rational appraisal of this British decision, courteous and motivated by moral considerations as it was, and to calculate its consequences in advance. Hitler, emotional for his part, underestimated Britain's determination to initiate war if need be, however unfavourable the prospects. The "deterrence" implicit in the British guarantee failed in its object.

It is exceedingly doubtful whether the government of a great power is entitled to expect exclusively rational behaviour on the part of its enemy in times of crisis. This leads to the undermining of the credibility of the enemy's strategic system and the soundness of the judgment behind it. One's own strategy must, correspondingly, allow for the possibility of irrational action on the part of the enemy. The greater the element of theoretical calculation in the nuclear strategy of the one side, the greater will be the uncertainty on the other as to whether the adversary will, in an emergency, act rationally in the sense of his own strategy. The same uncertainty is becoming more and more widespread, however, as regards the rationality of one's own future behaviour in the event of war. Nuclear strategy is becoming today, to an ever greater degree, impossible to calculate. Even a deterrence capability that is satisfactory from the practical military point of view, and the determination to use it in case of need, will be of no avail if the enemy believes that the power threatening him is deluding itself as to its powers of decision in an emergency.

The Problem of the Nth Power

It would be quite misleading to picture every future war as though it could be precipitated only by deliberate action on the part of the Soviet Union. The Suez crisis, for example, did not arise as a result of a deliberate Soviet decision, but it could for all that have led to global war. The same is true of Hungary, of the Congo and Lebanon crises, of Jordan and Algeria. There is an inconceivably wide range of possibilities for the outbreak of war, not necessarily desired by the two major powers themselves but into which they might be drawn as though inevitably and ineluctably. This is particularly true in cases of revolts in countries where the populations are suppressed. The greater the number of countries having their own nuclear capabilities, the greater will be the chances of world peace being jeopardised as a result of such incidents and explosions. But even powers without their own nuclear weapons could, in unfavourable circumstances, and wittingly or unwittingly, unleash a nuclear conflict. Ulbricht's psychotic "Blitzkrieg" propaganda is certainly directed not only against the Federal Republic: there is an indirect addressee sitting in Moscow. The instability of the nuclear moratorium will, however, increase by geometrical progression with each new and relatively uncontrolled (and uncontrollable) government in the Middle East, Latin America or the Far East that acquires its own nuclear capability.

Even if we assumed that the present-day nuclear powers would soon have their own "hard" systems (i.e. invulnerable means of retaliation), this relatively stable situation would probably be made unstable again each time a new power came to dispose of its own nuclear weapons. For we must assume that each new nuclear power—developing on the same lines as did the big nuclear powers before them—will first arrive on the scene with a small "soft" striking force which could at best only be transformed into a "hard" system after a considerable lapse of time and large financial outlay. The emergence of new nuclear powers would destabilise the present world situation in two ways. For one thing, the danger of irrational decisions to initiate war would mount in accordance with statistical probability and the total number of possible combinations; and, for another, the existence of the newly introduced "soft" systems would yet further increase the danger of the launching of aggressive or pre-emptive blows.

Theoretical discussion first mentioned the danger of the "third atomic power" as long ago as 1950. Later, out of respect to the United Kingdom, this expression was replaced by the expression "Nth Power." The danger has many aspects: it can arise because an Nth power asserts itself too self-confidently against another —or, indeed, against a major power. It can arise because an Nth power manœuvres itself into a war into which the major nuclear powers will be drawn the moment it crosses the nuclear threshold and is therefore difficult to call off. It can arise because, as nuclear weapons spread into the hands of more and more governments, irresponsible elements might mislead a major power into launching a pre-emptive or retaliatory blow by exploding "sabotage bombs" in its territory. The total number of possibilities defies thought. This is not the least of the reasons why, for ten years, many people in both the United States and the Soviet Union have been working on proposals designed to prevent nuclear weapons spreading into the hands of Nth powers.

The maintenance of the global nuclear standstill clearly depends to no small degree on whether the spread of nuclear weapons and the means of their delivery into the hands of further powers can be prevented. Three dozen states are conducting nuclear energy programmes. The present state of their technological progress suggests that at least the following countries will be able to produce nuclear weapons with their own resources by 1965: Canada, Belgium, Italy, the German Federal Republic, Poland, China, the so-called "German Democratic Republic" ("D.D.R."), Czechoslovakia and Switzerland. We must assume that, some time later, India, Australia, Denmark, Finland, Jugoslavia, Holland, Austria and Hungary may achieve a similar capability. The nuclear arming of these countries would without doubt in every single case increase, to a varyingly great extent, the risks to the world-wide nuclear standstill. Acquisition of nuclear arms by Switzerland, for example, would appear less hazardous than by the "D.D.R." It is not difficult to see that, in the event of the torpedoing of the Nuclear Club, such states as those of Fidel Castro, Hector Trujillo or Colonel Nasser would before long be in a position to threaten nuclear action. Should the Nuclear Club be once and for all dissolved there is scarcely a state that, in the decade following, would dare to run the risk of not arming itself with thermo-nuclear weapons.

Even if the development and production of nuclear weapons by third powers could be successfully stopped, considerable destabilisation would result from the loan or sale of nuclear weapons to third powers by the two major powers. Even if the major powers should confine themselves to providing their allies with so-called tactical nuclear weapons only, this would, in the event of war, increase the danger that the process of action and counter-action would increase and accelerate in intensity from the use of atomic shells to that of thermo-nuclear bombs.

The mathematical probability of nuclear war grows inexorably with the number of countries able to equip themselves with nuclear weapons—whether war comes through accident, technical failure, faulty interpretation of enemy actions and intentions, the arbitrary and provocative action of a third power, or through the desperate "going-it-alone" of a single fanatical aircrew.

It is clear that in such an age, with nuclear weapons so freely disseminated, even the threat of nuclear retaliation by a major against a minor nuclear power could conceivably—and for no other reason than the utterance of the threat—provoke the unleashing of a nuclear war.

Deterrence as a General Strategic Principle

To think of deterrence only in terms of deterrence by the biggest megaton weapons is the result of a widespread abuse of language. The principle of deterring an enemy from aggression by one's own armed posture and by threatening to use one's own weapons is, on the contrary, as old as the history of warfare itself—or the history of the punishment of offenders.

Looking at the world scene through American eyes, Hermann Kahn distinguishes three categories of deterrence:

1. Deterrence of a direct nuclear assault on the United States by means of the threat of all-out nuclear retaliation (second strike).

2. Deterrence of extreme provocations (including large-scale attack on United States forces, or on the territory of a NATO or SEATO ally or other area of the free world) by the threat of first strike.

3. Deterrence of limited attacks (e.g. cutting off access to Berlin, shelling of Quemoy, etc.) by the threat of limited military and non-military measures.

Donald G. Brennan takes up a different position from Kahn and proposes instead a fourfold list of tasks for deterrence:

1. Deterrence of a direct nuclear attack.

2. Deterrence of extreme nuclear provocation.

3. Deterrence of extreme conventional provocation.

4. Deterrence of limited conventional provocation.

Since we cannot go in detail into every conceivable sort of attack the Soviet Union might make on free Europe, the above two lists of actual tasks to be fulfilled by deterrent strategy will at any rate make it clear that such a strategy need by no means be confined to the sole task of preventing nuclear aggression.

Instead of the above lists the following definitions are also employed, notably in Britain:

1. "Active deterrence," or the threat of first strike in the event of enemy aggression (corresponds to Kahn's Type 2 deterrence).

2. "Passive deterrence," or the threat of a retaliatory blow (second strike) in the event of enemy all-out aggression against one's own territory: this concept is to some extent linked with the idea of "minimum deterrence."

3. "Negative deterrence." This has the object of convincing the enemy, by the form of one's strategy and armament, that one will on no account resort to a first strike, and that he (the enemy) need not therefore resort to a pre-emptive strike. ("Negative deterrence" is a misleading expression that has little to do with deterrence in the strict sense.)

These British ideas about deterrence all refer exclusively to one's own nuclear strategy. Nuclear threats are only one way of playing the hand of deterrent strategy; as, indeed, nuclear strategy is only one variant of general strategy.

In past centuries, the strategic principle of deterrence was—and will remain in the future—a universally applicable principle designed to prevent a potential aggressor from launching an attack. The strategic principle of deterrence embraces a much wider field than that of nuclear retaliation. Its general purpose is, rather, to threaten a potential aggressor with an unacceptable risk. If a deterrent strategy is to be successful, two conditions must be satisfied:

1. Neither the deterer nor the potential aggressor must deceive themselves as to the "unacceptability" of the effects of the weapons constituting the threat. "Unacceptability" may lie in the creation of a risk, the running of which will be judged not to outweigh the possible gain from an attack.

2. Deterrent strategy can only prevent war as long as both sides act rationally.

We will look more closely in Chapters 5 and 6 at the extent to which these general principles of deterrent strategy in fact form the basis of the West's present strategic concept.

4

Soviet Strategy

"WHOEVER thinks seriously about our relations with Russia cannot avoid doing his best to understand its military aspect, and making certain assumptions with regard to it."[1] No one will dispute this dictum of Kennan. It is not only necessary for us in the West to know the facts about the general war potential of the Soviet Union and to weigh them carefully against our own: we must also get to know and to understand a much more important aspect of the problem, namely the Soviet estimate of the situation and Soviet strategic doctrine. It is a fact, however, that our knowledge of these subjects is completely inadequate. The chief reason for the unsatisfactory state of our information is clearly the existence of a "closed society" in the Soviet Union. An additional factor, however, is that the West has not done nearly enough to acquaint itself with the strategic calculations and objectives of the Soviet leadership. The number of political and military specialists in America and Britain who make a routine study of the original Soviet texts is very small, and in the Federal Republic it is almost non-existent. In so far as information on Soviet strategy is available in the Federal Republic, it remains locked up in the safes of the Federal intelligence service and the Defence Ministry. Scarcely any work is done on these materials in other departments, apart from their exploitation for propaganda purposes.

From Clausewitz to Mao

Karl von Clausewitz's famous dictum—"War is no more than a continuation of political intercourse with the admixture of other means"—was popularised by Lenin in a colloquial and simplified version that distorted the sense. This was widely disseminated and used for indoctrination purposes in Communist

[1] G. F. Kennan, *Russia, the Atom, and the West*, London 1958, p. 51.

circles (and not only there). "Marxists have always taken this sentence as the basis for their theoretical interpretation of the significance of any given war, and have been completely justified in so doing. Marx and Engels invariably studied the various wars of history from this standpoint."[2] In this connexion we must remember that, as seen through the eyes of a Communist state, every war against a "capitalist state" is of necessity and by definition a "just" war; it is no more than the continuation of the policy of overthrow. World Communism as directed by the Soviet Union is (and will probably long remain) a force dedicated to the world-wide transformation of all political, social and economic relationships. It is aggressive not only by objective standards, but also by its own lights.

In this context Soviet doctrine lays down for its army the task, not of direct attack or conquest, but of exploiting civil war and revolutionary situations, and of consolidating the ground thus gained. Despite World Communism's aggressive character, therefore, Khrushchev may be speaking with utter frankness (by his subjective standards), and in accordance with his own convictions, when he stresses—as he does repeatedly—that war against what he calls the "capitalist states" is by no means inevitable. Mao Tse-tung and the Chinese Communists are right in seeing here a substantial contradiction of Lenin's theories.[3] The Chinese undoubtedly find much to justify their ideas in the speeches and writings of Lenin; was it not he who, after all, described "the myth of the so-called war to end war as a damaging myth, a product of petit bourgeois mythology"?

Challenging the Chinese Communists, the Soviet Communists round Khrushchev put forward repeatedly and insistently their thesis of the avoidability of war. The compromise formulae agreed in Moscow in the late autumn of 1960 by the top leaders of all Communist parties after lengthy, conciliar deliberations, leave plenty of scope for both the Soviet and the Chinese viewpoints, although the Soviet view seems formally to have prevailed in the matter we are now discussing. Despite its express endorsement of the thesis of co-existence, the Moscow declaration is

[2] Quoted from Lenin's Zimmerwald pamphlet *Sozialismus und Krieg* (Socialism and War). See also Wilhelm Ritter von Schramm's *Staatskunst und bewaffnete Macht* (Statecraft and Armed Force), Munich 1957.

[3] Cf. Gustav Wetter, S.J., *Die sowjetische Konzeption der Koexistenz* (The Soviet Conception of Co-existence), Bonn 1959.

(apart from its misrepresentations) downright aggressive. "Peaceful co-existence" is not, of course, an end in itself to the U.S.S.R. It is also doubtful whether the policy of *détente*, so vocally upheld by Khrushchev, is really motivated by his much-quoted wish to gain a breathing space while the Soviet economy is built up. Many things suggest that we should regard Soviet advocacy of *détente* as an attempt to secure specific and limited gains while incurring equally limited risks. In the final analysis the Communist propaganda campaign for peaceful co-existence and relaxation of tension is just as much part of an overall political strategy as is Khrushchev's embracing of Fidel Castro, the threat of disrupting the United Nations, or the threat to Berlin. For many reasons we should assume that the Soviet leaders believe that it will be possible to extend their influence step by step and in this way gradually to destroy the inner cohesion of the Western alliance, without at the same time being compelled to run the risk of nuclear war. These tactics aimed at making piecemeal gains can at any time lead to war without the Soviet Government's wishing it. Theirs is much more a policy of "at the brink of war" in the sense of American foreign policy at the time when the late Secretary of State, John Foster Dulles, coined this unhappy phrase.

According to the ideas of the Chinese Communists, on the other hand, war is the inevitable result of the exploitation of one class by another, and imperialism is the cause of all modern wars. Until imperialism and the exploiting classes are eliminated there will always be wars. It is immaterial whether these wars are imperialist wars over redividing up the world, wars of aggression and counter-aggression between the imperialists and the nations they suppress, or internal wars of revolution and counter-revolution between the exploiters and the exploited in capitalist countries: all these wars, according to the Chinese, represent a continuation of the policy of certain particular classes. And, distorting the historical sense which Clausewitz originally gave to his sentence,[4] they quote Lenin's maxim "it would be a major theoretical error to forget that all wars are the continuation of policy by other means," and thus ascribe to the Clausewitz quotation the meaning that wars are the inevitable consequence of political differences.

---

[4] i.e. the emphasis on the primacy of policy.

The lack of first-hand experience of nuclear weapons certainly makes it difficult for the Chinese Communists to form a realistic picture of the consequences of nuclear war. But we must also bear in mind the fact that the Chinese, who today number 650 million and by 1970 will probably have passed the 800 million mark, are so conscious of the vast mass represented by their population that they evidently find it impossible to conceive of nuclear devastation of their population on a scale sufficient to seal the fate of China. An article written on the occasion of the ninetieth anniversary of Lenin's birth by the editorial staff of *Red Flag* (the official theoretical organ of the Chinese Communist Party) contains the statement: "Should the Americans or other imperialists refuse to agree to a ban on nuclear and atomic weapons and dare to unleash nuclear war, this would lead to the quick and certain extermination of this monster hemmed in by the world, but not to the extinction of the whole human race. The victorious peoples would, within a short space of time, raise up on the ruins of imperialism a civilisation a thousand times finer, and would shape for themselves a truly resplendent future."

Mao Tse-tung is a prolific writer on the subject of civil and guerrilla warfare. He has great personal experience in this field, and has in addition a great faculty for logical reasoning. His military writings have been translated into many languages and are read by many non-European peoples.[5] Their relevance to the strategic problems of the two major powers of the contemporary world is relatively slight. We should nevertheless take note of one interesting correspondence between Soviet and Chinese ideas: both believe that war will be "long drawn out"; both believe that the final decision in war will be made by massed fighting men—by their training and military morale.

The Strategy of Limited Risk

Those who wish to make a detailed study of Soviet military strategic doctrine are recommended particularly to consult the two latest books of Garthoff;[6] Dinerstein's book[7] reaches conclu-

---

[5] A detailed survey of Mao's writings on military doctrine by Herbert Golz was published in *Wehrkunde* of Feb.-March 1960.

[6] R. Garthoff, *Soviet Strategy in the Nuclear Age*, New York and London 1958, and *The Soviet Image of a Future War*, Washington, D.C. 1959.

[7] H. S. Dinerstein, *War and the Soviet Union*, New York and London 1959.

sions in some respects different. Soviet doctrine is on classical lines: the chief task of the armed forces is to destroy the forces of the enemy. This determines the missions of the various branches of the armed forces. The Soviet leadership does not believe that a war can be won by particular weapons with special performance characteristics: they regard the fighting of a future war as the task of balanced forces. They undoubtedly recognise the great significance of surprise nuclear attack. It is for this reason that the Russians have developed the doctrine of the pre-emptive blow which would become necessary should unambiguous intelligence be received of an intended enemy surprise attack. This theory dates from about 1955. Although, therefore, the Soviet leadership, in accordance with Soviet doctrine, must always be prepared to carry out a pre-emptive blow (since this cannot take place at a time of their own choosing or in accordance with their specific preparations, but must be determined as to timing by the action of the enemy), they nevertheless do not place exclusive emphasis on their capability to carry out a pre-emptive blow or nuclear surprise attack.

It would appear that certain writers in the United States perhaps overrate the danger of a pre-emptive blow by the Soviet Union. For over and over again we find expressed in Soviet strategic articles the conviction that war cannot be decided by the nuclear exchange: its outcome, on the contrary, is still likely to be decided, in the present as in the past, by the "permanent operating factors"—by the military, economic and moral strength of the belligerent countries. This concept is associated with the assumption of a war of long duration, and with the conviction of the importance of well-trained, well-armed reserves. We are justified in asking whether this concept will persist in the future. For the present, however, Garthoff's conclusion still appears valid. He writes: "Soviet leaders are not poised to unleash their—and our—military power as soon as the theoretical probability of military victory crosses some calibrated balance of 50 or 70 per cent., or perhaps indeed 90 per cent. In the Communist view, history cannot be made hostage to the mathematical probability calculations of some communivac."[8]

Despite this well-substantiated judgment of Garthoff, we must

[8] R. Garthoff, *The Soviet Image of a Future War*, p. 7.

not, of course, assume that, if the Russians were to achieve absolute military superiority, they would under no circumstances make direct and aggressive use of their armed power. We must, when considering the various strategic possibilities, bear in mind (amongst others) the hypothetical case that the Soviet Union might use its great superiority in conventional forces to attack a Europe which had failed to look to its defences. In so doing she could regard her conventional forces as her "sword," and her thermo-nuclear striking forces as insurance against the possibility of the West's resorting to all-out nuclear retaliation. This would be a complete reversal of the "Sword-Shield" concept as developed by NATO. We must also bear in mind the fact that the Russians have, in their public statements, over and over again rejected the theory of limited or tactical nuclear warfare. They declare that such limitations are impracticable, since, they say, war with tactical nuclear weapons would without further ado develop into total nuclear war. Although the Soviet ground forces are certainly trained to meet situations they might have to face in tactical nuclear war, the Soviet Union seems to be making no great efforts in the technological field to develop small and very small tactical nuclear weapons, as have the Americans. In formulating their weapons policy the Russians appear not to have put preponderant weight on any one feature of their military establishment. Instead, their armoury has been methodically built up and modernised with a view to meeting any possible contingency in a future conflict. The Soviet Union not only disposes today of a quite appreciable long-range air force, but is also—and will probably remain for some years—the strongest military power in the field of the I.C.B.M. She has by far the greatest fleet of submarines in the world, and is now in the process of converting them to missile launching. She disposes of the largest military air transport fleet, and the largest number of trained parachute troops. Her air defences and tactical air arm are, furthermore, of high quality and numerically strong. And, finally, she has an enormous number of combat-ready infantry and armoured divisions.

If one wished to find a centre of gravity within the Soviet armed forces, one would still have to seek it—despite reductions in its numbers—in the army. That this is so is underlined by the fact that two-thirds of all Soviet aircraft are earmarked for the support of the combat army. This distribution of emphasis is consistent

D

with the concept of a total war of long duration, the outcome of which is sought in the last analysis through the physical occupation of the enemy's territory. The top military leaders of the Soviet Union come almost entirely from the Army.

We must not, however, lose sight of the fact that the Soviet Union's armoury, taken as a whole, allows its leaders a good measure of flexibility. The Soviet Union can fight effectively and for long periods in any form of war. Its ground forces are so armed and equipped that they are under no compulsion to resort to the use of nuclear weapons at an early stage in a conflict. The way in which their armed forces are equipped allows the Soviet leaders much greater latitude in the choice of means than have the Western leaders. This is a decided advantage. The Soviet Union is armed both for total nuclear war and for general war fought with conventional weapons, for geographically limited conventional war and for limited nuclear war (although the feasibility of this latter form of war is rejected by Soviet strategists).

During the last few years there have been a number of signs supporting the judgment that the Soviet leaders now possess a supreme measure of military self-confidence—such as Russia has not experienced in generations. At all events the old Russian inferiority complex, in military matters has been completely overcome. The missile threats uttered against Norway and Pakistan by Khrushchev and Malinovsky belong to the same pattern as that which influenced Dulles's thinking in 1954 when he talked of massive retaliation—except that the Soviet threats have hitherto been directed, not at the chief power ranged against them, but mainly at smaller powers. And this is done with the very object of undermining the trust placed by the smaller powers in American retaliation. The West was first seriously exposed to Khrushchev's missile threats as long ago as the time of Suez. At the same period the leaders of the West were prevented, by the very size of the Soviet armed establishment, from contemplating any sort of intervention in Hungary. The Soviets' military self-confidence and consciousness of their power finds expression in the fact that since the beginning of 1960, 1·2 million men are being released from the forces[9] without the Soviet Union having come to any previous agreement with the United States on disarmament.

[9] N. S. Khrushchev announced in July 1961 that this reduction in the armed forces had been halted.

This labour force can, for one thing, be put to good use in civil production; and, for another, these men are now considered redundant in the light of the Soviet Union's overall military position. The breaking off by the Soviets of the disarmament negotiations in the summer of 1960, and their behaviour at the later sitting of the U.N. General Assembly, reinforce one's suspicions that the Soviet Union now feels not only so secure, but also so superior in her military strength, that there is, in her eyes, no particular urgency about nuclear disarmament at present. Like China, the Soviet Union no longer regards nuclear war as something that will encompass the downfall of world civilisation as it did in Malenkov's day. On the contrary, the Soviet leaders now say that nuclear war is something terrible indeed, for it will destroy millions of lives, but it will in the end bring victory to the Soviet Union.

The Soviet Union is now a power of unprecedented and commanding military potential, whereas ten years ago, though still a great military power, she was this only in the traditional sense by virtue of her strength in infantry and armour. The Soviet leaders show every sign of being aware of this advantageous change in the situation. But it is by no means certain that they will be able to preserve this confidence in their military power indefinitely: it is conceivable that, within a few years, a more sober mood will set in, and that the missile euphoria of the Soviet leaders will, after a while, go through a stage of psychological development similar to that of many Americans, whose one-time euphoria evaporated with the loss of the American nuclear monopoly.

It may be that Khrushchev overestimates the strength of his military position. Without doubt his policy comprises an amalgam of messianic and imperialistic motives. Liddell Hart has good reason to say that the Soviet leaders have hitherto done nothing that might lead us to conclude that they deliberately desire war. Similarly, it not only might be misleading, but might eventually become dangerous to regard Khrushchev's aggressive policy since he precipitated the Berlin crisis in 1958, as the result of Chinese or internal Soviet pressures. Such an interpretation might suggest that Khrushchev was not serious in his policy of "peaceful co-existence"—as, according to their own declaration at all events, the Chinese Communists are not—and that it might therefore be wrong to attempt to meet him on his policy of *détente* and co-existence. Certainly, by co-existence, Khrushchev does not mean the peaceful life of a zoo, in which carnivores and herbivores live at peace with one another, segregated into their own separate iron cages. His form of co-existence certainly embraces dissolution, subversion and revolution—all directed from Moscow—and is intended to lead in the end to the triumph of Communism throughout the world. It is therefore theoretically always conceivable that the Soviet Union might, with whatever means seemed suitable within the wide variety of strategic alternatives open to her at a given time, decide to attack the West at some point where it had neglected its defences. Conversely, should some action of the West or of NATO create the impression in the mind of the Soviet leaders that the West was preparing to initiate hostilities at some moment convenient to itself, then we would have to reckon with the possibility that the Russians might act to forestall a Western attack which they suspected to be imminent.

The successful progress of its foreign policy and the expansion of its sphere of influence since World War II make it extremely unlikely that the U.S.S.R. will deliberately resort to all-out nuclear war as a matter of rational strategy. The Russians have no reason for abandoning their strategy of prosecuting the war by political means—a strategy whose success until now they owe to their policy of limited risk-taking. The potential danger of war resulting from actions of the Soviet leaders lies not so much in their rational decisions as in the possibility that they might miscalculate or misinterpret Western policy, or in the possible extension of local or limited conflicts, or finally in the possibility of irrational decision by the Soviet leadership.

Pattern of Operations in the Event of a War in Europe

Irrespective of whether a major military conflict in Western Europe begins with blitzkrieg-type surprise nuclear blows, or develops from local or limited conventional fighting, the Soviet High Command will attempt, with the support of its superior armoured and infantry masses, to reach the Channel and the Atlantic coast in the shortest possible time. It would be equally logical for the Russians to have this as their operational goal if they were to assume that it was not they that had started the war, but that it had been forced upon them. For only a quick breakthrough to the Channel coast offers the prospect of eliminating effectively the European arm of NATO: only thus will the military conditions be created for the subjugation of the British Isles, and a satisfactory basis be established for the prosecution of global war. Simultaneous thrusts against Norway, Rome, the Dardanelles and the Middle East (Kuwait, Cairo) are also to be expected. The present order of battle of Soviet forces in East and Central Europe seems adequate for such operations. This would also apply if NATO's European forces were to use tactical nuclear weapons in their defence.

We must bear in mind the fact that Soviet military leaders have repeatedly rejected the theory of tactical nuclear war; they have declared such limitations to be militarily impracticable, for, according to their ideas, a war with tactical nuclear weapons would lead to total nuclear war. The Soviet army would, however—and naturally enough—hope to reduce the effective scope for Western employment of such weapons by directing their forces to advance in small detachments and columns, and concentrating them only for the attack: meanwhile they would generally reduce the effectiveness of tactical nuclear weapons by maintaining their forces in close and constant contact with the enemy. At the same time, however, the Russians, too, dispose of a considerable capacity for the employment of tactical nuclear weapons: these can be brought to bear either by the ground forces themselves, or by the tactical air forces supporting them. But the manner in which the Soviet forces are equipped and organised does not compel them to resort to these weapons at the outset. This is because all ground-support nuclear weapons and all the larger missiles are, in peacetime, not subordinated to the ground force formations, but are operated by an independently organised branch of the armed forces. This does not rule out individual components of this special organisation being subordinated to units of the ground forces in appropriate circumstances.

Despite the aggressiveness with which the Soviet leaders have handled the Berlin question, the caution which has informed their various practical steps suggests that the Kremlin does not at the moment regard the limitation or localisation of a conflict over Berlin or its approaches as conceivable: in this their thinking appears to resemble that of the West. Should, however, their strategic nuclear superiority in the I.C.B.M. field continue so to expand over the next few years that the Soviet leaders came to regard themselves as no longer exposed to American all-out nuclear retaliation in the event of limited war in Europe, then the West would have to reckon with the possibility of limited attacks on European territory. But this is not to make any prediction about the probability of such attacks.

5

The Dilemma of the United States

AS little as five years ago American politicians and generals thought of their country with justification as the world's strongest military power. By contrast—and with equal justification—they today stress that the United States must not become too weak in relation to the Soviet Union. The United States has almost entirely lost two advantages which it would formerly have enjoyed in the event of war: its geographical inaccessibility, and the vast preponderance of its war potential. Confronted by the question as to whether they should arm for both all-out nuclear war and conventional war—or even for geographically limited war as well—the American leaders decided during the last decade to arm for all-out nuclear war. Their ability to defend Western territory by conventional means in concert with their allies is therefore exceedingly limited.

The United States, has, furthermore, fallen behind in the very field that was once peculiarly its own—that of nuclear strategy. It is, moreover, encumbered with difficult political and psychological problems *vis-à-vis* its European partners. Should the United States make a determined and powerful response to Soviet threats of aggression, Europe at once becomes fearful lest it be drawn into an "unnecessary" war. Should, on the other hand, the United States appear ready to negotiate, then Europe grows fearful lest the American leaders might possibly be ready to sacrifice European interests on account of the United States' own vulnerability to strategic nuclear attack.

The Missile Gap

For the next two to three years at least we must accept the fact that the Soviet Union will have a considerable numerical, and perhaps even qualitative, lead over the United States in the I.C.B.M. field. Air defence against missiles is, of course, infinitely more difficult than that against attacking bomber squadrons—the vehicle on which the United States must continue to rely to a decisive extent for some years to come. It is generally assumed that by 1961-2 the ratio of operational Soviet I.C.B.Ms. to those of the United States will be of the order 3 : 1. Figures published by informed experts vary enormously. Thus in April 1960 Alastair Buchan predicted a ratio of 150 : 50 I.C.B.Ms. by 1961. Joseph Alsop, on the other hand, six months earlier expected a ratio of 500 : 70 missiles by the same date. According to Alsop, who undoubtedly painted too black a picture of the situation, the missile gap will not be closed until about 1965-6, when the United States will put its solid-fuel missile Minuteman, now under development, into mass production. American press reports put the number of operational I.C.B.Ms. in the autumn of 1960 as 10 for the United States and 30-50 for the Soviet Union. Nobody doubts that, by about 1963, the Soviet Union will be in a position to have an I.C.B.M. force of about 500 missiles. This would enable her to carry out a decisive surprise attack against the fixed bases of the American strategic nuclear forces.

In the meantime the United States is attempting to close this gap primarily by concentrating on production of Polaris I.R.B.Ms. and by equipping its long-range bombers with air-to-surface missiles (Hound Dog with a range of about 350 miles). We cannot, however, expect that the number of submarines equipped with Polaris will rise to more than a dozen before 1963. The acceleration of the Polaris programme undoubtedly represents an effective strengthening of American missile force. We must not lose sight of the fact, however, that Polaris missiles fired from submarines are only of limited usefulness against Soviet nuclear forces on account of the limited accuracy of the system: it is primarily a weapon for the counter-city strike. If, however, the Americans wish to be able to threaten credible nuclear retaliation in the event of other than nuclear aggression, then they need in addition a considerable counter-force capability: it is precisely in this field that they have today fallen behind. The policy of massive retaliation is therefore losing much of its significance as regards the sphere of its applicability. This diminishing significance is being further accelerated by the Soviet Union's increasing ability to mount a retaliatory blow. The threat of all-out nuclear retaliation will become increasingly restricted to the case of all-out nuclear aggression and will not pose a serious deterrent to other forms of aggression. So far no satisfactory substitute has emerged. NATO and the United States are, by this token, bound to a strategic concept the military-technological foundations of which are now rapidly becoming undermined and will disappear altogether in the next few years. The subsequent closing of the missile gap will do nothing to alter this.

The dilemma of these next few years lies in the fact that a nuclear balance of increasing stability will be achieved between the two major powers, but that in face of it the West has nothing to put in the place of all-out nuclear retaliation as a deterrent against non-nuclear aggression—for the present, at any rate. There is also the fact that the West's increasing ability to strike back is meaningful only as long as the threat of retaliation which it makes possible can prevent or delay the outbreak of war. This capability would be largely pointless if, despite its existence, major hostilities were to break out. In such a contingency the West, if it did not elect to accept loss of prestige and territory, would have only the belated opportunity of wiping out millions of human lives. In the autumn of 1960 General John B. Medaris, who had shortly before retired from the post of Chief of Missile Development in the U.S. Army, made a sharp attack on the present strategy and weapons policy of the United States. In this he wrote: "At the moment we must simply accept the incoming destruction as inevitable and resort (*after* the event! H. S.) to . . . retaliation, thereby admitting that all is lost and condemning mankind to Armageddon."[1] At the present time American estimates place the probable losses in the United States homeland as a result of a Soviet strike at 50 million dead—i.e. if the attack is directed against city targets.

It is argued with some justification that to destroy cities and populations in a retaliatory blow serves no military purpose. From this it seems understandable that the U.S.A.F. should strive to acquire a twofold capability, viz. the means not only of striking back against city targets, but also of delivering a preemptive blow against the enemy's striking forces. The question is, however, whether this dual aim will not on the one hand lead to the overstretching of American technological and economic resources, or to the neglect of all other military requirements, and, on the other, whether it is not provocative in terms of external policy.

---

[1] Quoted from *Look* magazine, VOL. XXIV, No. 20, 27 Sept. 1960.

The Uncertain Trumpet

Since his nomination as Chief of Staff of the U.S. Army in 1956, General Maxwell D. Taylor has fought for acceptance of the view that the American military establishment should be prepared to fight both general nuclear war and local and limited wars. The same ideas were put forward a little later in the Gaither and Rockefeller reports. It is nevertheless true that, right up to the present time, preparations for limited, and in particular for conventional war have been badly neglected. President Eisenhower introduced the so-called "New Look" shortly after his inauguration in 1953. All four Chiefs of Staff were relieved at the same time and a campaign was instituted for an extensive reduction of the army and for a shift of the centre of gravity towards weapons earmarked for massive retaliation. The new line was formulated in 1954, and later, as the "Radford Plan," led to animated disputes in Western countries, both behind the scenes and in public. The most heated disputes took place in the United States itself and those between the representatives of the individual services were notable. The quarrels between the U.S. Army, Navy, and Air Force are a source of great concern to all who think seriously about the defence of the West. It must nevertheless be recognised that the origin of these disputes lay as much in the Administration's lack of clarity—and that of the President himself—regarding the aims of national strategy, as in the ambition, parochialism, and egoism of the senior officers at the head of the various services. As a result of this quarrel, which led to waste of time and money, not only were the conventional armaments of the United States and the West as a whole neglected, but the American lead in the field of strategic nuclear armaments was turned into a lead for the Soviet Union in the I.C.B.M. field. It has become customary since then for American generals to retire in order to air their disquiet before public opinion. All can read with profit two books which originated in these disputes, James M. Gavin's *War and Peace in the Space Age*[2] and Maxwell D. Taylor's *The Uncertain Trumpet*.[3]

[2] General James M. Gavin, *War and Peace in the Space Age*, New York 1958, London 1959.

[3] General Maxwell D. Taylor, *The Uncertain Trumpet*, New York and London 1959, 1960.

Taylor is one of the most impressive, highly cultured officers that the West has produced. Even though he puts his arguments across in a very temperamental style there can be little doubt (outside the U.S.A.F.) that his analysis and demands are basically correct. He gives firstly a detailed account of the missile gap expected to exist from 1960 onwards and then points out that the Russians have other advantages arising from their better facilities for strategic targeting, from the greater concealment of their missile launching sites, from their superior defences against manned bombers, and finally from their superior civil defence facilities. He then concludes that during this period of time the United States would lose a nuclear war if one were to break out, irrespective of which of the two major powers was the first to strike. He is of the opinion that not even with a pre-emptive attack could the West eliminate the threat from Soviet missiles. He regards it as highly illusory to think of massive retaliation as an all-weather, all-purpose strategy. He regards as equally illusory the argument that preparations for all-out warfare should have priority on the grounds that such preparations would—as is alleged—also make it possible to fight small limited wars.

The Strategic Vacuum

Taylor's views are shared by Liddell Hart, Speidel, Miksche and many others. It is to be assumed that his successor as Chief of Staff of the U.S. Army, General L. Lemnitzer, who has since become Chairman of the U.S. Joint Chiefs of Staff, will follow the same line as Taylor in this high military office. Nevertheless, the time that has been lost must be a source of concern to us. It is moreover unfortunate that there is little chance of a clear-cut decision for a strategy embracing both elements and an armaments policy to match, at all events until the conclusion of President Eisenhower's term of office.[4] The usual wordy debate is going on as to the correct strategy to be followed by the United States. The Navy advocates a strategy of limited or minimum deterrence and recommends the creation of a counter-city retaliatory capability to go with it. The U.S.A.F. continues, as before, to fight for its counter-force strategy, and between the two extremes various combinations and compromises are championed. It would appear

[4] In March 1961 President Kennedy made proposals in his Defense Message to Congress for a strategy and weapons programme embracing both elements.

that, at least for the present, the power of decision in strategic matters in the United States has been transferred from the shoulders of the political leaders to those of various competing groups of officers and officials, and of the politicians and journalists who champion their views. One thing is certain—that an active service Chief of Staff who lacks the courage to come out with his views is in the wrong job: he is just as certainly in the wrong job if he publicly criticises the declared policy of his government.

During the last decade an increasing uncertainty has developed, particularly in the European countries allied to the United States, as regards the reliability and rationality of the strategic decisions made by the American Government. Increasing doubt developed in the minds of many Europeans throughout the continent at the time of Eisenhower's Camp David talks with Khrushchev. The external political handling of the U 2 incident, the affair of the proposed presidential visit to Japan, and the American attitude towards the Common Market—E.F.T.A. question have strengthened European doubts as to the powers of leadership of the United States Government.

More than anything else it was the U 2 affair which lost the United States Government much of the confidence of its European allies. Irrespective of the general feeling that at the time of the incident Khrushchev no longer wanted the Paris Summit Conference (since he had come to see in the middle of April that it no longer offered him good enough opportunities for making gains), it was clear to everyone that not only did the United States Government, in the period after 2 May 1960, give Khrushchev a pretext for calling off the Summit Conference but it also invoked a much greater danger. In that the American President, after an initial denial, took on himself shortly afterwards the entire responsibility for the reconnaissance flights over Soviet sovereign territory, he confronted the Head of the Soviet Government with a dangerous choice. If Khrushchev were to preserve his "face" *vis-à-vis* the Soviet Union and other Communist states, and his prestige in the eyes of the world, then he was under a direct compulsion to react drastically. The world can consider itself lucky that, after all his demagogic accusations and gnashing of teeth in Paris, Khrushchev succeeded in suppressing the desire, certainly entertained in the Communist camp, to overplay his hand. We must not overestimate this single incident but its psychological consequences in the Western camp are nevertheless symptomatic. The fact that the President of the United States could first of all announce his intention of continuing these flights on grounds of military necessity only to cancel this declaration a few days later, aroused great doubts as to the sureness of touch with which the Americans were pursuing their external political aims.

The decline in confidence in American leadership, especially in matters of military strategy, has legitimate grounds. It gives rise to new and difficult problems for the formulation of American strategic plans, as is evident from the conflict with the nuclear great power aspirations of President de Gaulle. The political tensions within the alliance are in part a consequence of the dilemma of American strategy, which can offer the Western alliance no concept either persuasive or realistic as regards the present shape or size of the Western forces. This sorry state of affairs in 1960 may well lead, under the leadership of President Kennedy, to a major, concentrated and (in the end) successful effort on the part of the United States, and also to a carefully weighed strategy. But it carries with it considerable global political dangers for the immediate future. For the guiding concept of American strategy today is still that of devastating nuclear retaliation. It is, however, certain that nuclear retaliation is applicable to only a very small minority of conflict situations. Moreover it is probable that in these situations the military capabilities developed for the retaliatory mission will no longer prove adequate. Yet it is certain that, in relation to the Soviet Union, the strategic concept of nuclear retaliation is only suitable for the task of deterrence; if the latter should fail, it will be unsuitable for the task of effective defence. This is specially true of the defence of Europe.

6

Can NATO Defend us Today?

AT the end of 1960 about 400,000 combat-ready troops of the Soviet ground and air forces were stationed on the territory of the so-called "D.D.R.," and also 65,000-100,000 men of Ulbricht's "National People's Army"—in all just half a million troops.[1] This figure excludes the police units and other para-military units of the Ulbricht régime. On the territory of the Federal Republic there are at the moment about 250,000 troops of the Bundeswehr (which, within a few years, will be increased to around 350,000), about 230,000 troops of the U.S. Army and Air Force, about 45,000 British troops, 5,000 Canadians and about 10,000 French—in all a present figure of about 550,000 men.[2] These figures are approximate, especially in regard to the Air Forces. If we include those regions of Germany administered by the Soviet Union and Poland, the number of troops now stationed on German soil is probably about 1·5 million. Usable published data about the number of Soviet troops in the other countries of Central Europe is practically unobtainable.

The Situation

In view of the greater financial and material outlay required by Western troops, and in particular in view of the larger size of their supply and auxiliary units, the fighting value of Soviet troops, man for man, must be rated higher. It is therefore appropriate also to compare the number of available formations one with another. On the territory of the "D.D.R." were deployed, at the end of 1960, 8 armoured and 12 mechanised Soviet divisions (the latter fully motorised and armoured against the effects of infantry weapons) with a total of 6,000 tanks. In Poland there are 2, and in Hungary

---

[1] The figures given are subject to considerable error either way.
[2] These figures have risen considerably since August 1961: for instance, the strength of the Bundeswehr now (end 1961) stands at nearly 350,000.

4 further Soviet divisions. In the western U.S.S.R. there are 50 divisions available at short notice for use in the Central European theatre. In all we must allow for the initial employment of 75 to 80 Soviet divisions in the event of general war in Europe. Of these, 20 are immediately ready for war and would be available for operations in the first hour: this number would be doubled (i.e. raised to about 40 divisions) within 10 days. To bring up a further 40 divisions and the cadre divisions (which in the event of war would have to be filled out from the reserves) would take several weeks. To these Soviet forces we must add 13 to 14 Czechoslovak, 13 Polish, 4 Hungarian, and 4 to 6 divisions of the so-called "People's Army" of the "D.D.R." The battle-worthiness of these Satellite formations is less than that of the Soviet forces for various reasons. It is also doubtful whether they would all be at the disposal of the U.S.S.R. in wartime: we should allow for the initial deployment of at the most 20 Satellite formations in the event of war.

On the Western side there were (at the end of 1960) in Central Europe 5 U.S. divisions, 7 German divisions (one of them earmarked for the Northern European Command of NATO), 3 British, 2 French, 2 Dutch and 2 Belgian divisions. There is also one Danish division allocated to the Northern European Command, and one Canadian brigade. Only the American formations are at the moment at full strength. Almost all the others are below strength. The French divisions have shrunk to symbolic remnants. The British divisions are anything but at full strength and are little more than training units. The combat strength of the German formations is similarly inadequate but will increase in the course of the next few years. In the light of these limitations we can put the combat strength of the Western forces confronting the Russians in Central Europe during 1960-1 at the equivalent of 13 or at the most 14 divisions. It should also be noted that the West's present armament would not permit it to increase the number of its divisions and bring up its reserves for some time after the start of hostilities. Going on the present situation, therefore, we should put the ratio of military strength in Central Europe at the outbreak of war as about 3 : 2 in favour of the Soviet bloc, increasing to 3 : 1 after ten days, and to 4 : 1 (and higher) after a further period.

The ratio is similarly unfavourable on the northern flank in Denmark and Norway, where NATO at the moment disposes of at the most 2 divisions. It is better in Southern Europe, however, where Italy and Greece have at the moment 5 and 7 divisions respectively, and in Turkey where the number of war-ready divisions is at present 12.

The quality of the equipment of the Soviet ground forces, notably those in the "D.D.R.," is outstandingly good and the level of their training is plainly high. More than two-thirds of the roughly 6,000 tanks in the "D.D.R." consist of the T 54, which is a development of the T 34 weighing 36 tons and mounting a 100 mm. gun. Unlike Western tanks the T 54 has a diesel engine and its radius of action seems to be around 250 miles. As well as the T 54 a smaller number of the T 34s are still deployed in the theatre, and also the T 10, a development of the Joseph Stalin III with heavier armour, greater radius of action and a 122 mm. gun. The formations are also equipped with armoured personnel carriers and amphibious tanks. The main emphasis is clearly on the medium tank T 54. Modernisation of the self-propelled gun appears, on the other hand, to have lagged somewhat. The field artillery, however, has been extensively modernised, and the heavier calibre weapon appears able to fire nuclear projectiles. Anti-aircraft artillery has been modernised and considerably augmented: noteworthy features are the 57 mm. armoured A.A. gun mounted on a T 54 chassis, and the beginning of a conversion to surface-to-air missiles. Short-range surface-to-surface rockets are available in large numbers and are incorporated in many battalions and regiments. These are principally fired from multiple launchers mounted on trucks and tracked vehicles: it has so far been impossible to establish whether they are capable of firing nuclear warheads. In the course of the last few years the number of mortars in units has declined in favour of the rocket launcher. A far-reaching modernisation of anti-tank artillery has taken place through the extensive replacement of guns by recoilless projectors. Nearly every single Soviet gun is, moreover, suitable for the anti-tank role.

The Soviet divisions are not equipped with tactical nuclear weapons. The tactical missiles T 5 and T 7 do not appear to be directly subordinated to armies[3] and fronts,[4] but, together with the heavier, static I.C.B.Ms., appear to be organised into a separate branch of the armed forces outside the ground forces. An extensive further capability for tactical nuclear warfare is, however, vested

[3] Equivalent to Western "Corps."   [4] Equivalent to Western "Army."

in the air armies[5] which support the ground forces. The Soviet tactical air army stationed in the "D.D.R." held 700 to 800 aircraft at the end of 1960, of which perhaps a third might be equipped for tactical nuclear operations.

The equipment of the American divisions in Germany is roughly equivalent to that of the Soviet formations in the "D.D.R." It is true that the American M 48 A2 tank is not in every respect the equal of the T 54. The American divisions have tactical nuclear weapons, among which the Honest John (range 12 miles), Corporal (75 miles) and Redstone (200 miles) deserve mention. The British formations have similar equipment, while their conventional armament appears to be somewhat obsolete. The remaining Western formations (except for the tactical air forces) do not have tactical nuclear weapons, though the Bundeswehr divisions are in the process of introducing their first "dual purpose" weapons.[6] The equipment of the German formations reveals considerable weaknesses, especially in the field of armoured personnel carriers and tanks: Miksche went so far in 1959 as to describe them as "a crazy patchwork snapped up at random." There is no equivalent on the Western side to the Soviet launcher regiments and the firepower they represent. More significantly, both Allied tactical air forces (2nd and 4th A.T.A.F.) in Central Europe are numerically inferior to the Soviet tactical air formations facing them in the "D.D.R." and western U.S.S.R. About 300 front-line aircraft of the 2nd and 4th A.T.A.F. are (as at the end of 1960) equipped to fire nuclear weapons: the A.T.A.Fs. have at their disposal, in addition to their manned aircraft, the jet-propelled guided missiles Matador and Mace with ranges up to 700 miles and nuclear warheads.

Even though the formerly much-quoted figure of 175 divisions at the disposal of the Soviet Union no longer applies today (a large number of them are skeleton cadre divisions) it is nevertheless clear that the ground and associated air forces that would be available to the U.S.S.R. in the event of a war in Central Europe are quantitatively much superior to those of her Western adversary. In a long-drawn-out war, the form that the Russians think war would probably take, the opportunities open to them for sending

[5] Roughly equivalent to the former German "air fleet."

[6] As of the end of 1961 all allied divisions in Central Europe are receiving launchers for tactical nuclear weapons, the latter remaining under American control.

E

reserves into action are substantially greater than those open to the West. Lastly it must be stressed that the Soviet Union has more than 9-10 airborne divisions, and can probably find the necessary air lift for transporting two of them at once. The airborne formations available to the West are few in number even though the air transport capacity of the United States could probably be brought up to something like that of the Soviet Union after a while.

The air defence of Western Europe must be considered weak at the present time. For military geographical reasons it is doubly handicapped: in the first place it must protect not only the fighting forces but also the Western European concentrations of population and industry. Those of the Soviet Union are remote from the theatre of war. Secondly, the Western defence system is not in a position to push its warning radar well forward of the centres of population and industry. It will take many years to build up an effective surface-to-air missile belt, and to develop the manned interceptor formations of the German Air Force. A further difficulty is that the fighter bombers of the NATO air fleets have been extensively drawn into the nuclear strike plan designed to implement the strategy of massive retaliation. They would not, at the beginning of a war, be available either for air defence or for army support, but would have the initial task of co-operating in the nuclear destruction of enemy strategic targets and airfields (the so-called "counter-air" strike). Their second task would be to attack the rear communications, supply lines, and logistic support targets of the enemy (so-called "interdiction"). Only thereafter would they be available for close support of the combat formations of the ground forces. A final source of special difficulty for the air defence of Europe is the fact that the Allied tactical air fleets are to a large extent fitted with different types of aircraft and electronic equipment which require different combat methods, different forms of tactical control, and different command channels: furthermore, French resistance over many years to the integration of air defence has in the past extensively reduced its effectiveness.

Considerable differences in weapons and equipment have impeded the joint effectiveness not only of the Western air fleets but also of the NATO ground forces. Progress in the standardisation of NATO's weapons and equipment has been very limited and is subject to time-consuming procedures. The prospect is no better in the field of the joint development, testing and production of new weapons. For this reason a common logistical support organisation for NATO's ground formations is technically scarcely practicable at this stage: moreover it comes up against a variety of political difficulties and suspicions. To take an example: it is a fact that none of the five U.S. divisions can today be moved at short notice to North Germany because they would there be completely cut off from the special supply and logistic support necessary. Ten years ago NATO's armoury was, on account of its more extensive equipment with American material, much more-standardised than it is today. Today we must regard NATO's lack of a uniform supply and logistic support organisation in Europe as a dangerous weakness, especially in the event of a war lasting more than 14 days. The supply of the German forces would in particular seem to be endangered since only part of the 90 days' stockpile laid down by NATO as necessary can be maintained on German soil in a fashion that is militarily meaningful.[7]

Although Soviet superiority in an attack launched without prior redeployment would by no means be great enough to cause a rapid collapse of the NATO front, their superiority in an attack launched after careful preparation, and in the various situations that might develop in the first two or three weeks of fighting, would be so great that NATO at best would seem only able to fight a delaying action in defence of its territory.

In this context we should note the Russians' three or fourfold

[7] At all events the reasons given in early 1960 by Bonn for basing the military and civil supply of the Federal Republic on Spain are militarily unconvincing. In an emergency, how could supplies delivered by convoy to Spanish ports be transported onwards to Bavaria, Hesse or Lower Saxony? This would involve distances of nearly 1,000 miles. Overland transport would necessarily have to be concentrated on very few roads and railways in the Pyrenees. Here, and during the rest of the journey, transport would be extremely vulnerable to air attack. And, above all, enormous columns of transport would be required. Sea transport would call for an enormous fleet of small vessels which, in an emergency, would on no account be available to us in those waters. Further transhipment would, moreover, be necessary at French, Channel or North Sea ports. Air transport could not possibly handle the tonnages involved: we need only recall the effort required to supply $2\frac{1}{2}$ million Berliners during the blockade of their city. To use Spain as the German supply base would make military sense only if the battlefronts had already moved westwards across the Rhine. For supplying the Federal Republic, however, the project would be Utopian. The natural supply areas for the 50 million inhabitants of the Federal Republic and—in wartime— for the Federal German forces fighting on their own soil, are determined by considerations of military geography: in so far as Germany itself is excluded from consideration. These areas are in France, the Benelux countries, Denmark, and southern Norway.

maritime superiority in the Baltic. Compared with their Pacific, Black Sea and Northern Fleets, the Soviet Baltic Fleet is the strongest and is supported by a most powerful naval air force. The Western forces confronting them are, on the other hand, insignificant at present. We may certainly assume that the Soviet wartime objective of a thrust to the North Sea and the Atlantic would be accompanied by a "triphibious" attack against the northern flank, aimed in particular at seizing the Baltic exits and northern Norway. The exits from the Baltic are militarily NATO's weakest point in Europe without any doubt. If they were to be opened up not only would a wedge be driven between NATO forces fighting in Europe, but there would be serious consequences for the future conduct of operations in the North Atlantic; for about 100 Soviet submarines are stationed in the Baltic. NATO's maritime forces in the Atlantic, in the Channel and in the North Sea area, are however, strong enough to fulfil all the tasks allotted to them.

It must be stressed at the end of this short survey of the forces on both sides that, although the build-up of the Bundeswehr was originally designed to shift the balance of strength in favour of the West, the withdrawal of British and French troops, before the build-up started, took place on such a scale that the activation of the Bundeswehr has scarcely more than closed the gap caused by these withdrawals. Very little has in practice been done so far to increase NATO's strength in conventional troops. It is therefore illusory, if not positively misleading, to inform public opinion that NATO is now in a position, as a result of the build-up of the Bundeswehr, to develop a "forward strategy" that would be applied in the event of a European war. What in fact is more probable is that NATO would, in such a contingency, attempt to hold the line of the Rhine while attempting to fight a first delaying action on the Weser, and use delaying tactics between these two lines. No other course would be conceivable given the present balance of forces —provided, that is, that we do not abandon ourselves to delusions.

The 1957-8 decision to equip NATO forces in Europe with tactical nuclear weapons resulted from this disparity of forces and from perception of the risks implicit therein. Before, however, we proceed to investigate more closely whether further development of this process can lead to the establishment of an equilibrium of force and to effective defence we must first look in greater detail at the possible tasks of NATO's European forces.

Possible Tasks for NATO

Strategists participating in the international discussion of the various forms that contemporary war might take, have proposed the following pattern:

1. Cold War:
2. Limited War:
   (*a*) with conventional weapons;
   (*b*) with the use of tactical nuclear weapons.
3. General War:
   (*a*) primarily with conventional weapons;
   (*b*) all-out nuclear war.

Although the Soviet Union has in the past denied that 2 (*b*) is possible, and the United States has done the same for 3 (*a*), theoretical analysis must take all these forms of war into account. But they are not sufficiently sharply defined for an investigation of the various possible forms that a conflict might take in Europe. We must therefore paint a more detailed picture of the various ways in which fighting might break out in Europe and in this way provide a satisfactory basis for considering NATO's possible tasks.

Case 1. Lightning *coup de main* with conventional weapons and limited objectives (localised war). We must initially allow for the possibility that the Soviet leaders might undertake localised and limited "police" or "punitive" actions either from a desire to make a trial of strength, or in consequence of local incidents, or as a result of provocative actions by a Satellite (e.g. the "D.D.R." in relation to Berlin). It is conceivable that such actions might even remain limited to a specific locality of the country against which they are directed. They could, for example, relate to Berlin, to certain NATO airfields in northern Norway or Anatolia which (the Russians might allege) were serving the purpose of espionage against Soviet territory or the violation of its sovereignty; or they might be precipitated by possible disturbances in the so-called "D.D.R." In the latter case it is conceivable that the Russians might allege that disturbances possibly taking place in the Magdeburg area or in Thuringia were being incited or supported with personnel and material from north-eastern Lower Saxony or from northern Bavaria respectively: in such a case they might claim that it was necessary to stamp out this nest of rebellion outside the

"D.D.R.," and that they had decided for this reason to send Soviet troops to occupy certain areas of Lower Saxony or the Hof-Bayreuth area. We can imagine that such an action would ꜱe initiated to the accompaniment of an express announcement of its limitation to previously announced operational objectives and boundaries, and that it would be completed within a few hours. The Soviet leaders could initiate such an action suddenly, without any discernible preparation, and without previous redeployment of troops. It is conceivable that the Russians would expressly declare that they did not wish to employ nuclear weapons and that they would not in fact use them: it is conceivable that they would declare themselves anxious to spare the civil population as far as possible and that they would in fact hold to this declaration. It is clear that in such a case of locally limited aggression the important point would be whether NATO was able to intervene there and then with highly mobile reserves, and so restore the situation. Depending on the speed and success of the Western counter move, such an incident could lead either to the frustration of the Soviet objective or to an extension of the conflict. Such hypothetical situations could also arise if the intial aggression were to be carried out by Satellite forces alone.

Case 2. General European war arising from lightning *coups de main*. We must reckon with the possibility that a general European war might develop out of local and limited actions such as those envisaged in Case 1. This danger would be at a premium if the Soviet leaders, having initiated a local or regionally limited action, were then to miscalculate NATO's reaction. Depending on NATO's actual reactions, a general European war developing out of such incidents could begin straight away as a nuclear war or as a conventional one. It would lead to both sides bringing up their available reserves, and could—particularly inasmuch as the gradual development of the conflict might dictate only the initial very limited use of nuclear weapons or their complete non-use—develop into a long-drawn-out war.

Case 3. Nuclear blackmail. It is conceivable that the Soviet leaders might direct ultimatum-type demands at a single European NATO country[8] (or perhaps simultaneously at more than one) and back these up by missile threats. Such a demand might, for example, be directed at some such country as Belgium in connexion

[8] Sometimes referred to as "single out."

with a crisis *à la* Congo and have the object of forcing the Belgian Government to take, or desist from, certain actions in regard to the Congo. It is even more credible that reasons might be found for directing such demands at the Federal German Government. It is conceivable—and indeed, plausible—that, although the threat implicit in such an ultimatum would be regarded as all-embracing by the country in question, it might well have only an indirect (and therefore "limited") effect on the other European NATO countries: Bulganin's missile threats at the time of the Suez crisis gave us a foretaste of such eventualities. Nuclear blackmail can lead directly to total war (Case 6).

Case 4. A general attack by Soviet forces delivered without a period of preparation, limited to Europe as a whole, either with conventional weapons, or with simultaneous use of tactical nuclear weapons. This course seems unlikely at the present time but cannot in theory completely be discounted. So long as the Russians are compelled to take the threat of massive retaliation seriously in such a case, we should perhaps rather expect them, instead of taking this course, to resort straightaway to the launching of an all-out attack.

Case 5. A general assault, after careful preparation and prior redeployment, limited to Europe. The imminence of such an attack would probably be detected in good time by NATO reconnaissance. It would therefore involve the Soviet leaders in heightened risk, since to act thus would expose them to a pre-emptive strike by the strategic nuclear forces of the United States and NATO. It is therefore extremely unlikely that war in Europe would break out thus.

Case 6. All-out war. Should the Soviet leaders come to decide on a general assault on Europe, they would probably elect to embark at the outset on an all-out nuclear war, the main features of which would be simultaneous strategic nuclear strikes against the United States and conventional plus nuclear attacks on Europe. When considering Soviet strategic doctrine we saw that at the present time this contingency, too, seems extraordinarily unlikely. Nevertheless we also saw that, in the event of a Soviet first strike against the present American retaliatory forces, the military and industrial potential of the United States—and, above all, its population—would suffer such widespread devastation as might prove decisive in the subsequent course of the war. Whether or not such a decisive setback for the West were allowed to happen would be critically dependent on whether the American leaders decided in time to launch a pre-emptive strike, or on what proportion of the American retaliatory forces were activated in time to escape the Soviet surprise attack.

However serious our worries about Case 6, we can say with some conviction that, in the event of Case 4 (limited attack on Europe without prior redeployment), Case 5 (limited attack on Europe with a period of preparation), and Case 6 (all-out assault), European NATO in conjunction with the retaliatory forces of the United States should be able to give a satisfactory riposte. Or, to put it another way, the West's present armament should be adequate to deter the Soviet leaders from attempting such large-scale aggressive actions.

We must conclude differently as regards deterrence against Case 1 (localised, lightning *coup de main*), Case 2 (gradually developing general war), and Case 3 (nuclear blackmail against a single NATO country). We must certainly go on the assumption that, even if we presuppose fully rational behaviour on the part of the Soviet leaders, such cases are at the moment by no means out of the question. We can easily imagine the Soviet leaders miscalculating the reaction of the West and the latter's ability to answer in appropriate fashion. A study of United States foreign policy commissioned by the Senate Foreign Relations Committee in October 1959 states correctly that "a limited conflict in Europe could happen at any time."

The question remains: is NATO adequately prepared for such contingencies (often referred to as "piecemeal" or "salami" tactics)? The answer is certainly "No" in respect of local attacks carried out rapidly and with very limited penetration. It must be assumed that the American leaders would not, in fact, invoke massive retaliation, i.e. would not resort to a nuclear first strike, in *all* cases of this nature. On the other hand the present structure of NATO and the mobility of its striking forces do not allow it immediately to oppose such attacks in adequate strength where they occur, except in one or two places. In Europe NATO has no airborne troops at constant readiness that are worth the mention. In north Germany in particular—and specifically in Schleswig-Holstein—it might take many days before NATO forces could mount a local counter-attack that held out any hopes of success.

NATO has, until now, officially answered this question by giving an assurance that, even in such cases as these, nuclear retaliation would immediately be invoked. But Taylor, for example, counters this with the statement: ". . . there are still voices to assert the impossibility of having a limited war in the NATO area. Such an assertion means that any collision of patrols over, say, Berlin would automatically result in general atomic war. It offers no other alternative than reciprocal suicide or retreat in face of the superiority of Soviet conventional forces. Such talk does little to reassure our allies in Europe. Furthermore, it is nonsense. If men who are both sane and determined continue to direct nations, they will initially take all measures short of general war to resist aggression—regardless of the nationality of the aggressor."[9] Most independent specialists agree with Taylor. There is no doubt that European governments also think similarly.

Divided Strategy and Illogical Armament

Doubt about the automatic character of nuclear retaliation in the event of local limited actions is general. What is more, many people are of the opinion—and not without reason—that it is completely repugnant to resort to nuclear retaliation in every case of swift localised aggression: the risk of extermination to millions cannot possibly be justified on such grounds. It is clear that the Soviet leaders are not unaware that opinions of this kind are held in the West. All the more might they be tempted, in circumstances which they thought favourable, to underestimate the risks of an expressly and, in practice, strictly limited local action.

Some people—notably de Gaulle and the French military (Pierre Gallois at their head)—are similarly sceptical about the automatic character of nuclear retaliation in the event of nuclear blackmail against a single country (Case 3). It is precisely this doubt that provides the justification for the French desire to have their own nuclear retaliatory force. The official NATO doctrine (the revision of which has hitherto been only hinted at) bases itself, by contrast, on the principle that every military conflict in Europe would unleash nuclear war. It sees the task of European ground formations as holding up the advance of the Soviet army long enough for massive retaliation to have its effect. In past years

---

[9] Maxwell D. Taylor, *The Uncertain Trumpet*, p. 137.

this mission of the ground forces has been characterised by the expression "trip-wire," and Kissinger has defined the function of the British and American troops on the Continent as that of "hostages" whose purpose would be to guarantee the nuclear intervention of the United States and Britain in consequence of the inevitable involvement of their troops in the military conflict.

Doubt about the rightness of this concept is as old as doubt about the usefulness of the whole concept of massive retaliation. It goes right back to the period of the birth of the theory of limited war. But the West seems inadequately prepared even for the course which NATO assumes the war will take, i.e. for an all-out nuclear blitzkrieg. For a long time many strategists, including naturally the U.S. Navy, have assumed the possibility of a long-drawn-out "broken-backed" war if the initial nuclear exchange did not bring about the complete elimination of one or other side. It is clear that, in such a contingency, the extent of the available reserves, the logistic support organisation, and in particular, the maritime forces and general industrial potential could be of decisive importance. As long ago as 1956 Klaus Knorr showed that, whatever predictions might be made about the quick ending of an all-out war, one must certainly assume the dangerous possibility of long-lasting wars of attrition in which overall war potential might be of crucial significance. Since then, this insight has become extensively shared: it corresponds to the Soviet concept of the course of a future war. In the event of a war of this sort we should certainly have to allow for the, if only temporary, loss of Western Europe: in such a case we should certainly have to expect very extensive losses among European populations in view of the West's present intention to use at least tactical nuclear weapons on the first day of war.

In face of the variety of the six different types of war discussed above, NATO's official doctrine offers no consistent continuum of prepared strategies. The doctrine is, in any case, self-contradictory. On the one hand it takes the line that nuclear retaliation can decide the outcome in every case—and on the other it seeks compensation in tactical nuclear weapons for NATO's weakness in all forms of warfare short of the strategic nuclear. In strict logic, however, this would only make sense if we assumed that massive retaliation either would not prove decisive or would not be attempted at all. This contradiction in logic has, at least since 1952, resulted in an inconsequential armaments policy on the part of NATO—a policy that has tended in several directions at once.

As long ago as 1952, at a time when the West was still enjoying its lengthy spell of absolute nuclear superiority, it was decided in Lisbon that NATO in Europe should be provided with a total of 96 divisions, of which 35 to 40 should be deployed ready for war between Trieste and North Cape, while the remainder were to be available for mobilisation within a period of up to 30 days. In fact, nobody has seriously pursued these goals at any time. On the contrary, certain European governments deliberately set their faces against the development of a strong local defence system in order, by so doing, not to limit the American obligation to defend them by the threat of nuclear retaliation. In consequence of this, planning for the available ground forces was based on the strategic retreat, designed to slow down the enemy advance into the interior of Europe. Such a concept implied the certainty of endangering and splitting off the Scandinavian flank, and this was apparently accepted. In this connexion it should be mentioned that the Middle Eastern flank cannot in practice be protected, especially as Turkey lies to one side of the routes over which the Russians would probably advance in war.[10] In the event of a general European war it would either cost the West an extraordinary amount of time, or be quite impossible to bring in sufficient troops by air or sea to protect this flank.

Faced with the constraints of this situation, the NATO Council decided in 1954 to fight any war that might arise with tactical nuclear weapons from the very outset so as to offset the Soviet numerical superiority. This decision, by an easily understandable process of psychological feed-back, gave nearly all European political leaders the idea that henceforth there was no urgency about increasing the number of troops available to NATO. The "New Look" and the Radford Plan in the United States did the rest. Since, in the meantime, the Soviet Union also has come to dispose of large numbers of tactical nuclear weapons, this illusion has now been shattered. Nevertheless, the inconsistency of the West's armoury still persists. NATO's ground formations in Central Europe are much too large for the simple trip-wire function, but, for all that, there is a shortage of highly mobile

---

[10] The only reliable and usable pro-Western army in the Middle East is that of Israel. It is, however, tied down by the forces of its neighbours.

troops capable of going into action quickly. Despite their tactical nuclear weapons they are too weak for a long general war in Europe: they lack resources and—of critical importance—an adequate logistical support apparatus. The tactical air forces necessary for their support are earmarked for the nuclear retaliatory mission and have been withheld from that of supporting the army.

These inconsistencies, which reflect the strategic dilemma of the United States discussed at greater length at Chapter 5 above, have justifiably given rise to serious doubts as to the relevance of NATO's defensive armoury and strategic planning. The doubters are worried about the concept of nuclear retaliation by the strategic forces of the United States on the one hand, and about the concept of replacing non-existent troops by tactical nuclear weapons on the other. Both questions need close examination.

A chapter in Bernard Brodie's book *Strategy in the Missile Age*[11] bears the title "The Legacy of Douhet." World War II experience has brought about an extensive reappraisal of Douhet's theory of the decisive importance in war of the seizure and exercise of air superiority. And yet the American concept of massive retaliation by means of strategic bomber formations was a direct development of Douhet's thinking. In earlier chapters of this book we saw what problems and risks this strategy of massive retaliation has brought into being—notably the risk that the effectiveness of the retaliatory forces might be critically reduced as the result of a pre-emptive blow by the enemy, and, most of all, the risk of the loss of many millions of one's own population. Kissinger wrote as follows on this aspect: "The defense of Europe cannot be conducted solely from North America, because . . . however firm allied unity may be, a nation cannot be counted on to commit suicide in defence of a foreign territory."[12] This one sober sentence sums up all the doubts of European statesmen as to the efficacy of the strategy of nuclear retaliation. It is clear that the American "hostage" troops in Europe by no means guarantee that the United States' retaliatory forces will actually be used in the event of war: all that is guaranteed is that the United States will participate in whatever war arises—not the form of that participation. These doubts are

[11] B. Brodie, *Strategy in the Missile Age*, Princeton and London 1959.
[12] H. Kissinger, "The Search for Stability," in *Foreign Affairs*, July 1959, p. 548.

reinforced and multiplied by the fact that, in the event of a long war in Europe, we cannot count on an effective defence of Europe. Kissinger elsewhere[13] drew attention to a parallel example from history: when World War II finally broke out France's system of alliances for the defence of Poland and Czechoslovakia proved ineffective because the French strategy and armoury were defensively oriented and made no provision for actually helping the states attacked by Hitler.

American Missiles on European Soil

Principally in order to restore—or at least to strengthen—the credibility of massive retaliation in the eyes of its NATO allies, the United States Government sent its Sixth Fleet into the Mediterranean and concluded agreements with Britain, Italy and Turkey for the installation in those countries of intermediate-range ballistic missiles (I.R.B.Ms.): these were intended to supplement the forces of S.A.C. concentrated mainly in the United States, and the I.C.B.Ms. installed on U.S. territory. It was psychologically necessary to make this move, primarily because of the missile gap which, as could be seen in Europe also, began to take shape in 1957. The installation of Thor and Jupiter missiles on European soil has doubtless enhanced the credibility of the American strategy of threatened retaliation. This is true at all events in so far as what public opinion regards as an important component of the American retaliatory forces has deliberately been exposed to the risk of becoming involved in hostilities, should they break out in Europe. What gives rise to the conviction that American missile forces in Britain, Italy and Turkey would inevitably become involved, is the prospect that, in the event of a nuclear conflict in Europe, the Soviet forces would feel a compulsion to eliminate these missile bases as early as possible and whatsoever the circumstances. The installation of American I.R.B.Ms. in Europe also has the object of making it clear that NATO can defend itself against threats of nuclear blackmail exclusively and expressly directed against Europe and Europe alone.

On the other hand the military value of the seven I.R.B.M. bases already installed in Europe, or at present under construction, is very small. In the first place the Soviet Union disposes of a

[13] H. Kissinger, *Nuclear Weapons and Foreign Policy*, New York and London 1957, p. 238.

large number of I.R.B.Ms. which can cover almost every part of Europe. There is talk of a hundred fixed launching sites. The total of high-priority strategic targets presented by NATO in Europe has been put with some certainty at less than 200, i.e. about 150 NATO airfields, plus a certain number of operational national airfields (notably those of the U.K. Bomber Command) and the I.R.B.M. bases mentioned above. All these airfields and missile bases have been so far—and still are—exclusively "soft" targets: the American I.R.B.Ms. in Europe are suitable only for a surprise attack or for a pre-emptive strike, and in no way for a second strike. Nevertheless these missiles have certain advantages compared with the I.C.B.Ms. stationed in the United States, in particular their greater accuracy and the fact that their existence complicates the timing problem for an enemy planning a first strike, who must if possible strike all targets at once. These advantages are, however, very largely outweighed by the much shorter period of warning, which is one-quarter that which would be received by the missile sites in the United States. Furthermore, the Soviet Union doubtless has ample opportunity for making an accurate geodetic survey of the West's European missile sites. It is clear also that the sites are exposed not only to the fire of Soviet missiles but also to that of Soviet light and medium bombers. They are therefore vulnerable to a greater variety of Soviet offensive weapons, and weapons of greater accuracy, than are the bases in the United States. After weighing up all the military advantages and disadvantages, the conclusion must be that their limited military value resides exclusively in the fact their very presence forces the Soviet Union to focus its strategic nuclear forces on a few more targets than would otherwise have been the case. This is counterbalanced, on the other hand, by the considerable difficulties that would arise in obtaining political approval in the event of an actual decision to use them.

The slight military value of the "soft" American I.R.B.Ms. installed in Europe has long been recognised. For example, a memorandum[14] commissioned in December 1959 by the U.S. Senate Foreign Relations Committee contains the statement: "If

---

[14] *Developments in Military Technology and their Impact on U.S. Strategy and Foreign Policy*, Study by the Washington Center of Foreign Policy Research, Committee-print of the U.S. Senate Committee on Foreign Relations, Washington, D.C. 1959.

we accept the corollaries of a decision to opt for nuclear stability . . . it would be inconsistent, and be in fact self-defeating, to continue the deployment of I.R.B.Ms. on soft, unconcealed, immobile and undispersed European sites within easy range of Soviet I.R.B.Ms. Such weapons so deployed are useful only in a first strike . . . they add to the risks of nuclear instability." With regard to the destabilisation of the overall situation brought about by this deployment, it must be stressed that, if Europe continues to be equipped with I.R.B.Ms., a point will soon be reached from which no return will be possible; for this is without doubt a further temptation for the European members of NATO to go on neglecting their conventional armament. The one-sided distribution of emphasis within the Western armoury could lead to what might be, in practice, a final and absolute decision for nuclear strategic defence in all eventualities, since adequate armament for any other type of defence would be lacking. To continue to develop in this way would, moreover, present the Soviet leaders with a decidedly aggressive form of provocation, since it is a generally accepted fact that all I.R.B.Ms. installed in Europe are now suited only for the first strike role, and totally unsuited to that of second strike.

To do justice to this last problem plans have recently been drawn up for the stationing in Europe of Polaris, instead of Thor, Jupiter and other land-based missiles. These plans envisage Polaris missiles being mounted in vessels on inland waterways and in railway wagons. These plans are to be regarded with great suspicion, not least on account of the great dangers to which they expose the civil population. If, on the other hand, Polaris missiles should ever be deployed in large numbers in ocean-going ships (they need not necessarily be submarines) and maintained constantly on patrol, such a measure would represent a very considerable improvement in the West's retaliatory potential. (European press articles representing Polaris missiles as aggressive weapons are, incidentally, misleading and clearly polemical.)

It is evident that these plans have so far done nothing to restore the confidence of European governments in the strategy of nuclear retaliation by United States forces. In so far as both major powers come to dispose of hardened strategic nuclear systems, to this extent will their instinctive readiness to react by nuclear retaliation decline in cases where aggression is aimed at less than their very existence, since it will never again be possible for retaliation to eliminate the aggressor's counter-retaliatory (i.e. second strike) capability. What we assumed as our Case 3 above will become more important in future. In particular, it is already playing a big part in the contemporary strategic debate in France.

National Retaliatory Weapons?

It has been, above all, the French Government and French writers who seriously doubt whether the Americans will press the button releasing nuclear retaliation in all cases of aggression against Europe. They argue that the threat of such retaliation would appear credible to the potential aggressor only if the victim of the aggression (e.g. France) itself had a national retaliatory force. Their doubts are justified by various American admissions. The American Secretary of State, Herter, said, for example, to a Senate committee on 21 April 1959, that in the initial stages of a Soviet attack the West could not resort to the use of nuclear weapons unless the Soviets gave some sign that they were heading for all-out war: the American President would, moreover, only involve the United States in a total nuclear war once it was clear that the United States was, in fact, exposed to danger of annihilation.[15]

It is, however, doubtful whether the official French argument, for which there is something to be said, discloses the real motivation for the "force de frappe nationale" envisaged by the French. There are, indeed, weighty and positive political reasons why a country should wish its voice to be heard when the actual decision is being made to use nuclear weapons. In driving home this desire President de Gaulle has used no half measures. He went as far as compelling the U.S.A.F. to withdraw all units equipped with nuclear weapons from French territory. In view of the inadequate number of airfields at the disposal of NATO in Europe, and of the saturation of British and German airspace, this was a measure that touched NATO on the raw. It would appear, however, that it was not so much these positive reasons that were uppermost in deciding the French to create their own strategic nuclear force during the next five years, as wounded pride and the search for prestige. French pride is wounded because there were no protests when Great Britain created its own nuclear retaliatory force, whereas the protest raised over the French intention is fairly universal; because

[15] His words were: ". . . unless the facts showed that we were in danger ourselves."

the United States withholds from its ally, France, technical information long since available to the common enemy, the Soviet Union; because the United States, in so doing, compels France to spend large sums on development programmes which could be saved by American technical help.

But the chief reason for French wounded pride is that the French Government feels itself degraded by its present lack of a nuclear capability. The French President's desire for the establishment of a political triumvirate (consisting of the Heads of Government of the United States, Britain and France) at the head of NATO must be regarded as having a direct connexion with the French endeavour to create its own nuclear weapons. The nuclear weapons planned by France are, indeed, directed against the Soviet Union, but they express the important political purpose of seeking a greater freedom of action *vis-à-vis* the leading power of the Western Alliance.

An important psychological motive is to be found in France's disappointment over the withholding of American support in the Suez conflict of 1956 and in the seven-year-old war against the F.L.N. in Algeria. Anxiety lest the United States and the Soviet Union come to a bilateral arrangement at the expense of the smaller partners in the alliance also has its roots in consideration of this nature. On this point Miksche, a Frenchman by adoption, writes: "We must not expect others to risk nuclear retaliation in defence of the interests of another nation. Therefore we can scarcely hope for solidarity to develop between the Western powers in matters of global policy. . . . A country without nuclear weapons loses its freedom of action and puts itself into the unpredictable hands of the atomic powers."[16]

Miksche and other French writers likewise assert that it will be impossible to prevent other powers acquiring a nuclear capability: it cannot therefore be expected that France will stand idly by while this process goes forward. Even Mendès-France was of the opinion in 1960 that the Nuclear Club was an aristocracy among states, whereas France stood for "nuclear democracy." (No doubt this advocacy of nuclear equality for all states will cease immediately once France herself is elected to membership of the Club!)

[16] F. O. Miksche, "Die unvermeidliche Erweiterung des Atomklubs" (The Inevitable Widening of the Nuclear Club) in *Aussenpolitik* (Foreign Policy), No. 5/1960, p. 298.

F

Miksche's sentences quoted above express the main French argument in concise form. Apart from the French Government Pierre Gallois and Alan Peyrefitte are the chief proponents of this argument: it was they who developed it into a "Theory of Proportional Deterrence." According to this France should be satisfied with only a small deterrent force since France's importance to the enemy would be too small to justify the latter's running the risk of having even a few of its smaller cities destroyed. As against this, the enemy would be prepared to run a much greater risk *vis-à-vis* the United States, since the possibility of eliminating the American potential could offer advantages disproportionately greater.

Irrespective of the several arguments that can be justified in isolation, France's intention to create a striking force has its basis in ideas that are illusory. In reality no country can make war against the Soviet Union—or certainly survive one—without the help of the United States. This is particularly true of France, for whom it would be doubly impossible so long as Algeria remains her top military priority. France is under an obligation to provide NATO with six divisions but has not, in fact, made the equivalent of a single division available. France now intends to make up for this lack of "liquid military assets" by the creation of a national retaliatory force. We can see from the plans published to date that this strategic nuclear force will be of little real value. It is intended by 1964-5 to make available 50 Mirage IV fighter-bombers with a range of 750 miles and a speed of just Mach 2. This relatively small number of aircraft plus its nuclear bombs will make improbably high financial demands. It seems as though the French intend to spend annually the equivalent of roughly £200 million for each of the next five years; later on they intend to replace the Mirage by I.R.B.Ms. developed by France herself. So far the financial requirement for this five-year development period has been openly put at 6 milliard heavy francs: this is doubtless pitched too low.

In so far as France is in any way in a position to take on this additional armament burden while the Algerian war is still in progress, she will doubtless press on with her project at the expense of conventional armaments. Even the United Kingdom, which on a much broader base and with years of technical experience behind it, was pursuing a plan for the development of its own I.R.B.M. (Blue Streak) with a range of over 1,850 miles, was forced to abandon this plan for financial reasons. Modern strategic weapons cost such immense sums that it is hard to see how, for a long time ahead, other countries can compete in the same class as the United States and the Soviet Union. It was with some justification that Weinstein recently divided the world's nuclear powers into four categories: the United States and U.S.S.R. comprise the first, and Great Britain the second; France, for whom the age of nuclear weapons is only just beginning, is put in the third category; and those allied nations who are equipped with tactical nuclear weapons by the leading powers of their alliances, comprise the fourth. However much she exerts herself, it is unlikely that France will be able to attain the standard already reached by Great Britain in the nuclear weapons field within the next decade.

A number of other objections must be added to the misgivings arising from the considerable financial burdens—burdens that touch the interests of the remaining partners in the alliance because they necessarily lead to neglect of the obligation to raise conventional troops. The Suez crisis showed conclusively that small independent strategic nuclear forces are pretty useless when up against the first-class power of a Soviet Union: Great Britain's conventional forces were too weak at the time of Suez to make a rapid and successful breakthrough in Egypt by the time the two major powers made their political intervention; and her strategic nuclear armament was, on the other hand, too weak to enable her to stand up, even for twenty-four hours, to the Soviet missile threats. Moreover, the British strategic nuclear force, in the shape of Bomber Command, adds nothing of real significance to the total deterrent power of the West when weighed against S.A.C. and the nuclear forces of NATO in Europe. It is also doubtful whether the existence of Britain's national nuclear strategic force has really strengthened her influence within the alliance: the course of world politics during recent years would not support such a contention. The existence of an independent British "deterrent force" has, at all events, served to provoke France to corresponding efforts. But Great Britain's peroccupation with the creation of a strategic nuclear force, stemming from her traditional "Great Power" outlook, has produced a situation today where she is prepared for a type of war which she could certainly not survive. Twenty bombs in the megaton range would wipe out 50 per cent. of Britain's population and bring organised life in Britain to a complete standstill. Britain is no more in a position to absorb the smallest nuclear attack—let alone deliver a subsequent retaliatory blow— than is any other Western European country. The widespread inclination in Britain to give up the idea of an independent British strategic nuclear force is therefore by no means illogical. But to do this would be pointless unless the financial and economic resources thus liberated were to be put to work in the field where the alliance is today at its weakest, viz. in that of conventional troops and their equipment. But nothing can be said for the exaggerated notions put forward during 1960 by some members of the British Trades Union movement who would like not only to get rid of the British strategic nuclear forces, but also to bring about a unilateral renunciation by the West of all nuclear weapons. It would, incidentally, be useful if there could be a careful financial and economic analysis by NATO or W.E.U. of the cost to two or three European states of developing and maintaining national nuclear forces, to see whether it did not in actuality *greatly* exceed the cost of raising and maintaining ten additional up-to-date and fully mobile divisions.

Great Britain's example has not only acted as a spur to France: the first voices to speak in favour of national deterrent forces have recently been heard in the Federal Republic. If the misgivings about Great Britain apply in greater measure to France, then they apply to a very much greater degree to the Federal Republic. Whatever the course adopted by the Federal Republic, she will always remain many times the inferior of the Soviet Union in numbers of fighting troops, in future tactical nuclear weapons and in the strategic nuclear weapons after which certain German hot-heads and aspirants for world-power status now hanker. No European country can stand up alone against the Soviet Union. In the event of Soviet aggression against the Federal Republic, the unleashing of a retaliatory nuclear blow exclusively by means of German I.R.B.Ms. would be an irrational, unilateral and suicidal act: it would therefore carry no conviction as a threat. On this point Roger Hilsman wrote that if, for example, the Soviets charged Western Germany with stirring up trouble in East Germany from an area in Bavaria, and were to occupy this area in a punitive action using purely conventional forces, Germany would probably have difficulty in replying with a threat to the Soviet homeland even if it had the necessary means. For, in the first place, Germany could not hope, even with a large operational stock of I.R.B.Ms., to hit the Soviet Union as hard as the Soviet Union could hit Western Germany in return. Secondly, Germany would come face to face with the fact that this dilemma holds good for the whole of NATO. Should the West Germans retaliate against Soviet cities, this would without doubt precipitate counter-retaliation against Bonn and the Ruhr.[17] Even to instal I.R.B.Ms. in Germany would be a provocation to the Soviet leaders and would, furthermore, give them yet more and striking opportunities for making propaganda in the Satellite and uncommitted countries.

The French "force de frappe" would be as much a soft system as Bomber Command in the United Kingdom, suitable only for a surprise or pre-emptive strike. The creation of hard systems under the control of European NATO countries would, at the present time, only be possible by putting Polaris missiles into ships. But even in such a case a European country having a few Polaris missiles would at best be able to destroy several Soviet cities, whereas the Soviet Union, without difficulty and using only a small proportion of her own nuclear forces, could devastate her attacker from end to end. Independently-operated national strategic nuclear forces in the hands of European countries therefore lack credibility from the outset as a threat to the Soviet Union.

In them resides, moreover, the considerable danger that the obligation of the United States to deter the Soviet Union from aggression against European states might become weakened and finally wound up altogether. Furthermore, they diminish the cohesion of the alliance as a whole because public opinion in the countries concerned is misled into concluding that crucial significance attaches to their own "deterrent forces," and not so much to those of the United States or the alliance as a whole. They prejudice the solidarity of the alliance because its members will henceforth fear that individual governments, propped up by their independent strategic nuclear weapons, might embark upon external political or military adventures which could jeopardise not only peace but the very existence of their NATO partners. They endanger the solidarity of the alliance in particular because the United States must fear that individual governments might make use of their

[17] See R. Hilsman, *On NATO Strategy*, Military Policy Papers, Washington Center of Foreign Policy Research, Washington, D.C., December 1958, p. 9.

independent strategic nuclear forces *against* the will of the United States and so deliberately start the American retaliatory forces into motion, using their own independent force as a "rip-cord." This fear could lead the United States to make the very kind of decision that European governments fear most of all—to impose limitations and qualifications on its obligations towards its allies.

Independent strategic nuclear forces also endanger the cohesion of the alliance because, to the extent that its members became convinced that the United States would or could not risk nuclear suicide for the sake of European states acting in their own interests, and would not therefore use its nuclear forces for the defence of Europe—to this extent the governments of the European countries might avoid taking risks in the defence of other areas protected by the alliance, e.g. northern Norway, Turkey or Berlin. Should, for example, the Soviet Union threaten aggression solely against the Federal Republic, the latter might well regard the threat as all-embracing, whereas the generality of its partners might well see it as only a limited threat: if, in such a contingency, the Federal Republic had its own independent strategic nuclear forces it is conceivable that the other European governments would refuse to accept the risk of their own nuclear destruction and would leave it to the Federal Republic to master the Soviet aggression with its own forces. In the example from Hilsman, quoted above, we saw that such a trial of strength on the part of the Federal Republic would lead to its extinction.

Individual governments disposing of independent strategic nuclear forces are exposed to enhanced danger of nuclear blackmail directed solely against themselves, since a certain possibility cannot be ruled out that its allies, pointing to the independent strategic weapons of the threatened state, might go off and leave it in the lurch. It is hardly to be assumed that the threatened state would prefer—like Hitler—its own destruction to submission. As Maurice Faure so rightly said in the French National Assembly in October 1960, France's transfer from the large group of non-nuclear allies to the small group of nuclear powers will by no means solve the problem of the best structure for NATO, for the disadvantages alleged by France to be intolerable will continue to exist for the remaining twelve NATO states. "France's attitude will lead to rivalries, competition and to exaggerated demands within the alliance." Faure, Paul Reynaud and Guy Mollet drew attention expressly to what they thought could be a consequence of France's action—the possibility that it might lead to a demand by the Federal Republic for the revision of the Paris Treaties.

A special danger to the alliance must be seen in the fact that the creation of national strategic nuclear weapon systems will, as time goes by, inevitably undermine the "Shield" and thereby weaken the effective strength of NATO.

The creation of strategic nuclear forces under national control necessarily, therefore, brings into being certain psychological factors tending to undermine the alliance: these are familiar to us from our consideration of the Nth Power problem. This is why no one in the United States approves of France's intention to build its striking force. For the same reason nobody there approved when the British developed their nuclear weapons ten years ago, but at that time the principle of "interdependence" and the need to avoid rocking the political boat within the alliance compelled them to make the best of a bad job. It is an open question today whether the United States will decide to adopt a similar attitude in the case of France. Congress is opposed, as always, to giving other countries access to the secrets of United States nuclear development and production. Washington is under no illusion that the creation of an independent French nuclear force will lead Britain to continue, and to strengthen, its own nuclear capability and, what is more, will almost certainly lead Germany, Italy and possibly other NATO powers to make similar misguided efforts. It is also evident that such a process must weaken Moscow's position *vis-à-vis* Peking's desire for its own nuclear weapons: this is something that no one in the world can wish for. The fact remains, in any case, that no European state is in a position to build up an independent nuclear force without the help of the United States. If France really had to rely entirely on its own resources, this would mean that when at length the "force de frappe" became operational it would already be hopelessly obsolete. There is therefore more than a grain of truth in the French witticism about the "farce de frappe."

NATO as a Fourth Nuclear Power?

Even if there were no material difference between Great Britain's motives for its decision to create its own nuclear armament and those of France today, Britain is nevertheless very—and justifiably —concerned about France's plans at the present time. For this reason the number of British proposals has grown since 1958 for the creation of an integrated European strategic nuclear force, consisting of both American and European elements, which would be subordinated either to the NATO Supreme Commander or to its own special commander. The same idea has been ventilated to an increasing extent in the United States since 1959. The NATO Supreme Commander in Europe, General Lauris Norstad, has long been an advocate of these ideas which since the autumn of 1960 have been engaging the attention of the British and American press under the title of the Bowie Plan. It may be that specific plans will crystallise before the end of 1961. Norstad's thoughts and those of Bowie, as opposed to the nightmare of an independent French nuclear force, may have great political and even military advantages,[18] but, none the less, even they have structural implications scarcely calculated to improve the strategic position of NATO.

One of the biggest difficulties touching the effectiveness of an integrated nuclear force is the status of its Commander. The object of the creation of the force by the European members of NATO would be to make them less dependent on the American Government *alone* and on its ability to take decisions. In place of this, however, they would purchase a new dependence on a dozen European governments and their decisions. The employment of the joint strategic nuclear force presupposes that not a single government but a plurality of governments will run the risk of exposing their countries to a devastating counterblow or pre-emptive surprise attack. There is no difficulty in predicting that a unanimous decision, if it could be reached at all, would scarcely be made in time. On the contrary, many governments would, in a time of acute tension, attempt to bring under their own national control those elements of the integrated force which were stationed on their territory so as to avoid provoking a retaliatory or pre-emptive blow against their own country. This is natural enough. In an emergency, therefore, the integrated force might well lose its value and the alliance court the danger of falling apart on its account.

---

[18] They were prominent among the arguments of those opposing an independent French "force de frappe" in the French parliamentary debate of autumn 1960.

In an attempt to anticipate these difficulties, the prior drafting of a set of rules has been proposed: the idea is that the Supreme Commander should be guided by them in acting autonomously in the event of war. Such rules, however, presuppose a renunciation of sovereignty and would have most far-reaching implications: it is scarcely conceivable that they would ever come about. For a government which, in peacetime, agreed to make an advance list of the conditions and circumstances under which a joint Supreme Commander should decide, or was permitted to decide, to use strategic nuclear weapons, would thereby divest itself of its political competence and of responsibility for one of the most important decisions—perhaps the supreme decision—in the event of a future conflict. It would, furthermore, be inexpedient for the West to list in advance how it would react in all eventualities. Should the list become known, it might tempt the enemy to precipitate other situations than those envisaged in the list, or to select the cheapest risk specified in it. The list would hardly strengthen the credibility of an integrated deterrent force, but might well weaken it further.

From a political point of view an integrated force would be more likely to work if it could be laid down by a treaty beforehand that the force was limited solely and exclusively to the counter-attack role, i.e. that it should only be used after the absorption of a Soviet nuclear surprise attack. It is also argued that the Supreme Commander should be expressly deprived of the right to use the force against Soviet sovereign territory. Whereas the first suggestion would require the integrated nuclear force to take the form of a hardened system, the second would require it to have a high degree of accuracy since its object would be to attack, not concentrations of Soviet population and industry, but military concentrations outside the Soviet Union in places determined by the chances of war. In the present state of missile technology these two requirements are scarcely susceptible of combination. The second proposal would, in any event, resemble "negative deterrence" and would have only a very small deterrent effect.

For much the same reasons the question of land-based weapons scarcely arises—as, indeed, we saw when considering American I.R.B.Ms. in the United Kingdom, Italy and Turkey. Static, land-based missiles belong in Alaska, Labrador, Greenland, or

even in the deserts of Libya and the Middle East—but emphatically not in thickly-populated regions. They act as magnets to the
enemy's nuclear missiles. Anything that attracts enemy fire is
unwelcome to states with a high population density or a small
area. For this reason, too, the most suitable system would be
Polaris missiles fired from seaborne launchers. Even if it seemed
possible to build a fleet of Polaris-equipped vessels within two or
three years, big enough to maintain a continuous patrol of a dozen
such ships at war readiness, we should still need to be on our guard
against any illusions about the operational practicability of this
system. It might be suitable for deterrence against nuclear blackmail of individual NATO members, and also for deterrence against
a general attack on Europe. But it would have a very much smaller
counter-force capability than that which S.A.C. already effectively
possesses today. The weapon system would, moreover, be subject
to all the problems that we discussed in Chapter 3 when considering nuclear strategy. As a means of threatening retaliation
it would not in any way be any more credible than that already
present in the shape of the strategic nuclear forces of the United
States. Certain British suggestions envisage that American forces
should play no part in the development of an integrated European
strategic nuclear force. Should this come about, the credibility of
the force would be *very* much less even than the current credibility
of the threat of retaliation by S.A.C.

For political and psychological reasons it may very well be that
the United States Government will become convinced that it
should not altogether withhold from its European NATO partners
the opportunity of influencing the use of strategic nuclear weapons.
If, for example, considerations of this sort were to result in a
resolution to set up a European strategic force in the future, it
would make sense only if a simultaneous ban were to be placed on
efforts to create independent national forces of a similar type. But
an improvement on the current military situation in Europe
would not, in fact, be achieved. There would appear to be a
particularly great danger that two different and divergent strategies
would emerge—one for the American strategic nuclear forces and
the other for the integrated European strategic nuclear force—
which would prejudice unity of action in an emergency. We must
also take into account the fact that the European example might
lead to similar developments in other parts of the world. In the

final analysis it would be a decisive step towards the dissolution of the Nuclear Club.

The British Government, which has had an independent strategic nuclear force for a number of years, appears little inclined to integrate this fully into an integrated force. The French Government, which hopes at least within a few years to have an independent force, is similarly disinclined to surrender these prospects for the sake of an integrated force. It therefore appears decidedly uncertain whether and to what extent the governments of the European NATO powers will commit themselves to a renunciation of this kind. Bonn alone has so far expressed agreement: it is an open question whether the motive behind this resides in the hope that here is a way of getting rid of the independent and dubious French "force de frappe," or—logically associated with this hope but, for all that, self-seeking and pernicious—in the calculation that here is a way of obtaining a share in the nuclear strategic armament of the major powers. Other governments have not yet declared their attitudes: it can be assumed that by no means all governments of the smaller countries will be enthusiastic. This is why consideration has already been given, within Western European Union, to limiting membership of the integrated nuclear force to members of W.E.U. This idea should also be discouraged. The juxtaposition of NATO and W.E.U. has already caused enough chaos in other respects—quite apart from the fact that military organisations are, in principle, strikingly susceptible to the provisions of Parkinson's Law.

The setting up of an integrated strategic nuclear force in Europe cannot rid NATO of its strategic dilemma, but it diverts attention from an ancillary problem. It gives rise to the danger of a psychological "disengagement" process in the American mind, but it does not *de facto* free the United States from the responsibility for political and military leadership of the Western world. It does not reduce the long-term nuclear risk to the United States. It would be quite misleading to imagine that America could sit back and take no part in a nuclear duel between the Soviet Union and the European part of NATO. For, in such a case, should the European states sustain much greater damage than the Soviet Union—which is not difficult to foresee—then the United States would be faced during the later stages of the war with much greater risks than if she had fought against the Soviet Union from the outset side by side with her European allies. The problem of NATO in Europe is one of creating, not further retaliatory forces, but rather real possibilities of defence.

Can Nuclear Weapons Replace Men?

In the United States great emphasis has been placed since 1952-3 on the development and production of so-called tactical nuclear weapons. We shall see later what significance the adjective "tactical" might have in this context. When development started nobody put the question—people believed that by supplementing the equipment of the Western forces with tactical nuclear weapons it would be possible to compensate for their numerical inferiority on the battlefield *vis-à-vis* the Russians: furthermore the West was confident that in the development and production of tactical nuclear weapons it had a considerable lead. The NATO Council resolutions of December 1954, which stemmed from these convictions, led logically to the completely justifiable question—why, given this development, should universal military service also be necessary in European countries? Not only have the ground forces in Europe been equipped to an ever greater extent with tactical nuclear weapons since 1954, but so have in particular the air forces also. This decision contributed to the progressive withdrawal of the tactical air forces from their principal task of air defence of NATO countries and support of NATO ground forces, and to their incorporation into the "atomic strike plan," which includes also the British Bomber Command, under the aegis of S.A.C. This plan aims at joint target co-ordination in the event of a strategic nuclear attack. In the years following, weapons and equipment policies for the Western air forces have developed logically from this situation and ensure that the tactical air forces will be at their maximum efficiency when employed against operational and strategic targets; but they are largely unsuitable for wars of longer duration and, in particular, for wars of attrition. A similar development has taken place on the Soviet side, even though the tendency is less marked: but the Russians are better placed on account of their much larger numbers of older reserve aircraft.

The theory of the advantageousness of limited nuclear war (that is, of a war fought with tactical nuclear weapons) has never won universal approbation in the United States. It was propounded mainly by Edward Teller and Henry A. Kissinger. The sharp criticism which it encountered initially at the hands of William Kaufmann, Robert Osgood, James E. King, Thomas Schelling, etc., could not at first carry the day: the political and military leaders in Washington decided in favour of the theory of the advantageousness of limited nuclear war.

As time passed this theory had far-reaching consequences for the equipment of the ground forces. Conventional artillery has been extensively replaced by tactical nuclear weapons at division, corps and army level. It has also been necessary to remodel the logistic and supply system correspondingly. The progressive equipping of American divisions with tactical nuclear weapons is intended soon to bring about the equipment of every single battalion with highly mobile, recoilless projectors of the Davy Crockett type (yield up to 2 KT); it has produced a great change in the training of the tactical commanders of the ground forces. A country that has once trained and equipped its army for tactical nuclear operations will have enormous difficulties, in the possible event of conventional war, in restoring it to an appropriate posture for this type of fighting and in restraining it from the use of tactical nuclear weapons. The more that formations and commanders are conditioned by their organisation and training to the automatic and uncritical use of tactical nuclear weapons, the less effective will they be in combat situations where their use is prohibited. The greater will be, on the other hand, the temptation for them to use their nuclear weapons on their own judgment in desperate situations where they lack appropriate instructions. We have to imagine that, in future wars, commanders may have a much more restricted view of the situation as a whole than was the case even during much of the last war. Much more will depend on the powers of decision of the individual tactical commander. For example, the question of whether the enemy has already initiated the use of nuclear weapons will have to be answered in each concrete instance by many tactical commanders as individuals: possibilities for miscalculation abound, and with them the opportunities for making faulty decisions. If the present process of equipping NATO ground formations in Europe with weapons specifically intended for limited nuclear war, and of training in their use, continues for another year or so, a point may be reached from which, seemingly, there will be no turning back.

With this watershed in sight voices are once again being raised on many sides casting doubt on the validity of the whole concept. The question as to whether a "limited" war with tactical nuclear weapons is at all possible, and, if so, whether it is desirable, has recently been put again in the United States and in Europe—and put with great seriousness. In the centre of the dispute stands the theory, put forward with a wealth of detail by Kissinger in 1957, that a limited war can be conducted with nuclear weapons and that the limitation can be sustained over a long period of time. Kissinger demonstrated that it is diplomacy's task to make it clear to the enemy in peacetime that the initiation by the Americans of the use of tactical nuclear weapons would not be tantamount to the initiation of a strategic nuclear war of annihilation calling for retaliatory or pre-emptive action. Even then it was not made clear whether, in the event of war, escalation from tactical nuclear weapons up to thermo-nuclear bombs could be avoided, especially as the dropping of tactical nuclear bombs on cities within the battle area could scarcely be avoided: indeed in some cases it would be necessary.

Apart from the question of sustaining the limitation for the duration of the war, the West was from the start in two minds as to the alleged advantageousness of such a war. To answer this question one must try to form a picture of the sequence of military operations. Kissinger's original concept was that limited nuclear war on the ground would take its course in much the same way as a naval war: there would be many relatively small units which, without maintaining rigid or permanent contact with each other, would fight a highly mobile form of war, continuously changing their positions. The basic assumption was made that such a form of war would bring greater advantages to the defender than to the attacker. The latter would be forced to concentrate his forces for the offence and would thereby expose them to the tactical nuclear weapons of the defence. In order to avoid the intensity of their effects the attacker would have to disperse his troops and this would make it impossible for him physically to control the area he had occupied. The Soviet Government, in particular, would thereby lose great advantages since the Communist-dominated areas of Europe would, gradually at least, slip from the grasp of the Soviet Army, and because Soviet army units would be made extraordinarily vulnerable to attack by partisan forces. The calculations of the attacking army would be made exceedingly difficult in a nuclear war as it would be a form of conflict of which he would have had no previous experience. The argument is finally advanced that tactical nuclear weapons are the West's most up-to-date weapons and that to forgo their use would mean depriving oneself of practical advantages. The culminating argument has been that the equipping of one's relatively small ground forces with tactical nuclear weapons would save the colossal financial efforts involved in preparing for purely conventional warfare. (This argument has never, as far as I know, been carefully developed in public: it is an extremely dubious one in respect of European troops which, as is well known, cost much less than their American counterparts.) Two further arguments must be adduced for the sake of completeness. As in the case of strategic nuclear war, the side which makes first use of tactical nuclear weapons *en masse* will doubtless gain a great advantage. This advantage is particularly likely to be realised if the tactical air forces can be committed to the task of interdiction in massed surprise attacks.

In the meantime these arguments in favour of tactical nuclear defence have encountered counter-arguments of at least equal weight. First and foremost the fact has emerged that the provision of tactical nuclear weapons does not necessarily save troops. On the one hand a much higher scale of losses must be assumed since the loss of entire units will be entailed: and, on the other hand, the number of troops required will be larger because, in addition to those required for the tactical nuclear weapon units, troops will still be required no less than previously for manning the conventional weapon units. Larger numbers would be required, furthermore, for logistic support and supply units. In addition it has emerged that tactical nuclear weapons are of only limited effectiveness against attacking armoured formations. Similarly, the theory that tactical nuclear weapons favour the defence has proved to be largely wrong. The employment or even the mere presence of these weapons does indeed compel the aggressor to disperse his troops widely and to forgo major preparations for the attack: it reduces without any doubt the number of troops that can be concentrated in a given area. But this is true also of the defending side which must also disperse its troops and thereby make it no longer necessary for the attacker to concentrate, as used to be the case. The proposition that tactical nuclear weapons favour the defence is no longer valid now that both sides dispose of large numbers of such weapons. It must on the contrary be stressed that attacking armoured formations can cross nuclear-contaminated areas relatively quickly and are, in so doing, less exposed to danger than the infantry troops of the defence, tied down as these are to the defence of specific sectors, points, or obstacles. In the case of a static defence action, e.g. along a river line, the advantage lies much more with the attacker. Several types of tactical nuclear weapon, moreover, cannot be used when one's own troops are interlocked with those of the enemy. Equally applicable to the defending commander and his operational staff is the proposition that the behaviour of the enemy—of his force commanders and their tactical subordinates—is no less predictable or subject to reliable calculation under conditions of the use of tactical nuclear weapons, than are those of the troops under his own command.

Now that the theory of Western advantage in the event of tactical nuclear warfare has been undermined, a second question remains to be examined, namely: is it possible to define tactical nuclear weapons authoritatively, or, in other words, would it be possible to distinguish between "tactical" and "strategic" nuclear weapons and sustain the distinction throughout a war? Many thoughts have been put forward in recent years in the attempt to define tactical nuclear warfare. Some have attempted to define "limitation" by reference to target systems; others by reference to the destructive effect of the bombs employed; some think in terms of employment limited to the immediate combat area of the ground troops or on the high seas; and others, finally (in what was the most ambitious suggestion), in terms of employment limited to parts of the battle-field recognised by both sides as "own territory." (The trend in development—springing from other considerations—towards ever smaller, "cleaner" weapons, has its logical counterpart in this last suggestion.)

Norstad, Erler and others tell us that it is beyond the wit of man to produce a watertight definition: nevertheless, Norstad jokingly gave his opinion that to knock over the milking bucket was "tactical," whereas to slaughter the cow was "strategic." The question remains open, however, and would do so even if some convincing distinguishing mark could be found—namely, how can we be sure that the enemy, too, acknowledges the difference between tactical and strategic nuclear warfare? Will both sides be willing to reach agreement on the matter in peacetime? Or will reliance be placed on tacit agreement? In our view it is Utopian to hope for a mutually acceptable distinction that would be sustained throughout a war. Since a tactical nuclear weapon is employed because it is more effective than a classical, conventional weapon, what guarantee can there be that, for a given operational purpose, a less powerful nuclear weapon will be used instead of the one most effective for the purpose? Or, to put it another way: since nobody thinks of the dropping of a 20 KT bomb on Hiroshima as a "tactical" action, how can we expect friend and foe alike to regard the dropping of a 20 KT bomb on a troop concentration in a future war as "tactical"? Where is the threshold between tactical and strategic employment if the selfsame I.R.B.Ms. and fighter-bombers are used to strike tactical airfields in the Satellites, tactical airfields in the Soviet Union, and strategic airfields on Soviet territory also? Who will be sure that the dropping of the same megaton bomb by a fighter-bomber with a range of 650 miles will be assessed by the other side as tactical or strategic according to the geographical position of the targets? In 1960, in the Parliamentary Assembly of W.E.U., the British M.P. Mr F. W. Mulley suggested defining the difference in accordance with the range of the carrier weapon. He suggested a range of 150 miles. If this were to be accepted, such weapons as Mace and Matador, with ranges of around 650 miles, would clearly have to be regarded as "strategic" weapons. Yet, up till now, they have been classified by NATO as "tactical" weapons. Can a weapon be changed from "tactical" to "strategic" by the mere stroke of a pen? Or, vice versa, can a weapon hitherto regarded as "strategic" be redesignated as "tactical" in future by a mere declaration?

We must face the fact that it is much simpler to distinguish between nuclear and non-nuclear (conventional) weapons than between nuclear weapons of 2 KT and 5 KT yield, or between nuclear weapons of the same yield when used against different targets. The only really recognisable dividing line—one that can be accepted by everybody—is that between conventional and nuclear explosives. This distinction is psychologically deeply rooted. The single bomb on Hiroshima caused greater devastation in 1945 than the attack by more than 1,000 bombers on Hamburg two years earlier: in this lies a practical distinction recognisable to all. Every other distinction is artificial, and no one can depend on

G

its lasting more than the first hour.[19] Admiral Charles Brown, U.S.N., who was NATO C.-in-C. Southern Europe at the time, had good reason to say to an American senatorial committee in 1958: "I place no faith in the so-called controlled use of nuclear weapons. There is no dependable difference between tactical and strategic weapons. Under no circumstances would I recommend the use of nuclear weapons—no matter how small—now that both sides have the power of destroying the world."

The Destruction of Europe

Admiral Brown's testimony underlines the danger implicit in the impossibility of distinguishing between the effects of tactical and strategic nuclear weapons—that is, the direct danger of nuclear escalation. The universal and irrefutable lesson of the history of past wars is that each new weapon of offence leads to the development of a corresponding defensive weapon, that every attack provokes the desire to counterattack, and that an enemy struggling for his very existence will not willingly forgo the use of a weapon that holds out hope of success. Who will say confidently that the use of a 2 KT weapon by A will not lead to the use of a 5 KT weapon by B, and that the use of a 5 KT weapon by B will not in turn lead to the use of a 20 KT weapon by A? Who will say confidently that the use of a 20 KT weapon at a range of 150 miles will not provoke the use of the same weapon at a range of 225 miles? No one can prove that escalation would not take place.

Some people speculate that the very uncertainty on this point—or rather the relative certainty of escalation up to the thermonuclear level—would of itself deter both sides from any sort of warlike action. For example, General Panitzki, who was Deputy Chief of Staff of the Bundeswehr at the time, said in 1958 that the Soviet Union would recoil from even local aggression against NATO in Europe because the very fact that the latter was equipped with tactical nuclear weapons would *inevitably* turn an attack on NATO into an all-out nuclear war. This is a psychological specula-

---

[19] Within the broad spectrum of available types of nuclear weapon, however, there are certain weapons which must unequivocally be called "tactical" (e.g. Honest John) and certain that can similarly be called "strategic" (e.g. Thor or Jupiter). To avoid causing misunderstanding by departing from the usual terms, we retain in this book the differentiation customarily made in the past between "tactical" and "strategic" weapons. We are, however, aware that there is really no distinction between the two—as noted above.

tion and cannot be proved. It could be maintained with as much justification that the certainty of thermo-nuclear escalation, and the fear of it, would decisively weaken the defender's will to resist. Why should consciousness of the danger of nuclear escalation weaken the will of the side bent on aggression more than that of the side whose intentions are peaceful and whose only concern is with his defence? And what would be the point of clinging to a strategic concept dependent on the use of tactical nuclear weapons if deterrence could only be expected from the likelihood of escalation up to the H-bomb level?

NATO's public position today is that it will defend Europe under all circumstances with tactical nuclear weapons. In consequence NATO must expect that, in the event of aggression against Europe, tactical nuclear weapons might be used against the alliance from the start. Nuclear interdiction by NATO tactical air forces in the so-called "D.D.R.," Poland and Czechoslovakia would lead inevitably to the initiation of similar attacks by the tactical air forces of the Soviet Union against corresponding targets in the Federal Republic, Denmark, Holland and Belgium. One particular result of this would be that cities in the neighbourhood of airfields, major bridges, focal points of communications systems, and supply installations will be hit—port cities above all. This will still be the case even if the enemy does not specifically attack cities for psychological ends. If, in the event of war, the Russians were to destroy the ports of, say, Rotterdam and Antwerp for purposes of interdiction, who in the West would care to say openly that this was all a part of tactical nuclear warfare and need not lead to corresponding retaliation against Leningrad or Kiev? Or, put the other way round: would the side defending itself with nuclear anti-aircraft missiles against attacking Soviet aircraft be in a position to complain of a breach of the unwritten laws of limited nuclear warfare if the enemy air force were to try to eliminate his anti-aircraft positions with nuclear missiles, and in so doing—even though that was not his intention—were to destroy cities near by? Who could complain if the Soviet missile command, in response to destructive attacks on the Vistula bridges involving the—albeit unintentional—widespread devastation of Warsaw, proceeded similarly to destroy the Elbe and Rhine crossings and, in so doing, produced similar devastation in Hamburg, Cologne and Düsseldorf? And if we wished to lodge a complaint, to what tribunal should we take it? Nuremberg trials take place only after a "victorious" war. The only choice open to us would be between resigned acceptance and retaliation.

Nuclear escalation could arise from a thousand different causes. Nobody can be sure that the process would not begin within a few hours of the dropping of the first tactical nuclear bomb. Everyone must assume that it could lead to thermo-nuclear bombardment within a few days. Since 1954 the Russians have placed great emphasis on the development and equipment of their armed forces with tactical nuclear weapons. In particular the tactical air forces of the Soviet Union have a tactical nuclear capability. They are quantitively superior to those of NATO and are qualitatively by no means inferior.

It is still the declared policy of the West to fight with nuclear weapons from the first day. In view of its, until now, very one-sided armament the West has today scarcely any alternative. The posture of the Soviet Union, on the other hand, even in the event of a war deliberately started by its leaders, is by no means such as to compel them to use tactical nuclear weapons from the outset. The Soviet Union has the alternative of a conventional capability. For this reason she can calmly advocate nuclear disarmament all over the world. The West—and European NATO in particular—cannot at the moment, however, undertake not to be the first to use tactical nuclear weapons. This places the West in an exceedingly disadvantageous position with regard to the uncommitted world. It lays itself open to the charge of at least threatening to offend against the spirit of international military law. And the development of so-called "clean" bombs will not help it out of this fix. The employment of clean tactical nuclear weapons, rather than dirty ones, might hold out a prospect—an exceedingly brief one— of preventing nuclear escalation only if the West were simultaneously to offer its production secrets to the enemy.

Even if the use of tactical nuclear weapons did not lead to extremes of escalation, viz. to total war with strategic nuclear weapons, it would nevertheless lead to the most extensive devastation of Europe and to the most extensive loss of life amongst its peoples. Europe is the battlefield for these weapons. As long ago as 1950 Kurt Schumacher accurately characterised the strategic conception of the major powers as one of final victory to be gained by virtue of their economic, technological and human reserves, whereas (he pointed out) Germany's situation is of a completely different nature: "Germany's destiny is a different one: its destiny is that of the first encounter." The proof of this statement was furnished five years later in the first NATO exercise to be staged under the assumption of tactical nuclear warfare. NATO's exercise "Carte Blanche" in June 1955 saw the dropping of 335 nuclear bombs in the space of less than 3 days, of which 268 fell on German soil: assumed casualties in the Federal Republic were put at 1·5 to 1·7 million dead and 3·5 million wounded. A few days later in the Bundestag, discussing the outcome of this exercise, Deputy Blachstein pertinently outlined the danger "that the use of tactical nuclear weapons might develop into a war of annihilation that would wipe out the greater part of those living today."[20]

During the last few years the peoples of Europe have reacted with fear and horror to the image presented of the course of a nuclear war in their continent. And they have good reason. We do not agree with the conclusion drawn by many people from this image, viz. that there is no point in trying to defend ourselves. Despite this, we must still bring to the notice of those making military decisions—and the political decisions to which the military are subordinate—the implications of NATO's strategic conceptions to date. In Hiroshima it did not need 335 nuclear bombs, but only one of 20 KT to produce immense slaughter. The effects of a single bomb were sufficient to ensure that, in the decade following, of 32,179 children born, every sixth one—5,201 in all—came misshapen into the world. Not until generations have elapsed will it be possible to assess the genetic damage. Those who think that Europe can be defended by the massed use of such weapons will not defend Europe, but destroy it. "Fight atomic death" is therefore a justifiable slogan—what is questionable is the pertinence of the alternatives recommended by many of its champions.

The results of "Carte Blanche" led the American Professor Arnold Wolfers to the following very plausible alternative: "If it turned out that under the impact of 'Carte Blanche' and the 350-odd atomic bombs 'dropped' on Germany, the West German Parliament refused to consent to rearmament until the nuclear

[20] Blachstein's protest against the concept of limited nuclear war in Europe met with flat opposition from the Government party. This all the more justified his statement: "A Parliament that is not prepared to listen to the truth about the situation of its people, abdicates the right to decide the fate of that people."

strategy of NATO had been scrapped, our planners would have to evaluate the relative advantage of nuclear warfare minus twelve German divisions against conventional warfare plus the same divisions."[21] Neither the Federal Government nor the opposition were then able to make an adequate review of the strategic problems thrown up by the exercise. As much as three years later it was still possible for the German Federal Chancellor to make the dilletantist observation that tactical nuclear weapons are "no more than a modern development of artillery." Brodie made out a different case: "It is difficult at present to imagine our attempting to fight such a war without resort to nuclear weapons tactically, even if strategic bombing could somehow be avoided. It is almost equally difficult to imagine both sides applying to the use of nuclear weapons such controls as would prevent the devastation of the continent."[22] Kissinger said in 1957 of the United States and its ideas about strategic nuclear warfare: "There is a contradiction in conducting a war fought presumably to maintain the historical experience and tradition of a people with a strategy that is almost certain to destroy its national substance."[23] This absolutely correct statement applies without qualification to the concept of limited nuclear war in Europe.

Kissinger has himself recognised this in the meantime. In his latest book he writes: "The need for forces capable of fighting limited nuclear war still exists. However, several developments have caused a shift in my view about the relative emphasis to be given to conventional forces as against nuclear forces. These are: (1) the disagreement within our military establishment and within the alliance about the nature of limited nuclear war; (2) the growth of the Soviet nuclear stockpile. . . . While it is possible to design a theoretical model for limited nuclear war, the fact remains that fifteen years after the beginning of the nuclear age no such model has ever achieved general agreement. It would be next to impossible to obtain from our military establishment a coherent description of what is understood by 'limited nuclear war'. . . . Since disputes about targets are usually settled by addition—by

[21] A. Wolfers, "Could a War in Europe be Limited?" in *Yale Review*, Winter 1956, p. 217. Wolfers writes of 117-odd atomic bombs on West Germany: the figure of 350 atomic bombs on Germany has been substituted representing the total "dropped" on Germany *as a whole*.

[22] B. Brodie, *Strategy in the Missile Age*, p. 355.

[23] H. A. Kissinger, *Nuclear Weapons and Foreign Policy*, p. 244.

permitting each service to destroy what it considers essential to its mission—a limited nuclear war fought in this manner may become indistinguishable from all-out war. . . ." And he goes on: "If nuclear weapons become an integral part of the equipment of *every* unit, it will be next to impossible to keep a war conventional, regardless of the intentions of both sides."[24] And in a memorandum published by the Senate Foreign Relations Committee these words appear: "Heavy reliance on tactical nuclear weapons cannot be expected to compensate for the numerical inferiority of local forces against Soviet armies also equipped with these weapons. Moreover, the initiation of tactical nuclear war by 'battlefield' countries in response to non-nuclear attack assumes their willingness to bring about their own devastation."[25]

In the NATO autumn manœuvres held in Schleswig-Holstein in 1960 the total number of deaths among the civil population within 48 hours of the initiation of tactical nuclear warfare was put at between 300,000 and 400,000. What must astound any unprejudiced critic faced with the results of such manœuvres, is the fact that German critics are so extraordinarily tactful and restrained towards the NATO concept. Here, too, we may once again refer to Kissinger. The decision to use nuclear weapons in all cases in limited war in Europe was evidently taken in too much of a hurry by the political and military leaders. There is no doubt whatever that no adequate analysis of the problem preceded the decision. To persist with this decision would mean that every conceivable instance of military conflict in Europe would automatically lead to the decimation of Europe's civil population—that of Germany in particular. That this concept should remain in force is inconceivable. So long as it is not changed, however, and so long as a change of concept is not reflected in developments in the actual weapons field, it cannot be assumed that Europe is defensible in war. On the contrary, we should all assume that Europe will be destroyed. And the peoples of Europe would not care whether it was tactical nuclear weapons or strategic missiles that brought about their extermination.

Who Controls the Use of Nuclear Weapons?

So far as it is possible to tell from published information NATO

---

[24] H. A. Kissinger, *The Necessity for Choice*, New York 1960.
[25] *Developments in Military Technology* (see note 12, p. 78).

has made no serious study of the implications of a limited war in Europe. The governments represented on the NATO Council have so far scarcely grasped the problem. The so-called Generals' Memorandum[26] published in the summer of 1960 at the instance of Defence Minister Strauss, with its lapidary demand that the Bundeswehr should have the same weapons as the forces of its allies, also fails to go to the roots of the matter: so, too, does the maxim enounced by the majority of the Bundestag on 25 March 1958, that "the Armed Forces of the Federal Republic should be equipped with the very latest weapons." Deputy Kiesinger did, it is true, declare on the same day on behalf of the Government parties that the term "very latest weapons" should not include thermo-nuclear weapons: in so doing, he disassociated himself from those who, infected by "Great Power aspirations," maintain that the Federal Republic should have the same weapons as the Soviet Union. But Kiesinger's explanation by no means gives one to understand that the Federal Government's wish to equip the Bundeswehr with nuclear weapons was based on any profound strategic analysis. The declarations of the Federal Government since that date show that it has no very clear idea either of the consequences of a war fought with tactical nuclear weapons, nor of its necessary prerequisites.

The Federal Government has, therefore, not committed itself to exploring who will have the political responsibility for ordering the use of tactical nuclear weapons in an emergency. Current arrangements suggest that the decision will, in practice, be made by the NATO Supreme Commander in Europe (SACEUR). What is unclear, however, is whether the NATO Council or the President of the United States will carry the political responsibility for such an order. It is also unclear whether the Federal German Government will have the right to protest against the employment of nuclear weapons either from German soil or against targets on German territory. President de Gaulle has explicitly demanded that the order for the use of nuclear weapons stationed in France should be made dependent on the agreement of the Government of France. The veto right which he has demanded—a corollary of his insistence on positive participation in the decision to use American tactical nuclear weapons—reflects the example of the Anglo-American arrangements for the stationing of American strategic

[26] Cf. Chapter 10, section headed "Germany is not a Major Power" (pp. 168ff.).

nuclear weapons in the United Kingdom and the voice the latter is permitted in any decision as to their actual use. De Gaulle's demand seems justified. The same problem exists for the Federal Republic—even though Bonn may not yet have recognised it. For if nuclear weapons are to be fired from the territory of a country, there will always be the risk of retaliation against that country even though it was not its own troops who actually fired the shot.

If the Russians were to be the first to use nuclear weapons in war, the question of where lay the competence for a corresponding decision by the West would matter less. But we must allow for the fact that its great strategic flexibility permits the Soviet Union to shift this decision to the shoulders of its enemy—this has been the case up to the present at all events. As in the case discussed above of political competence and responsibility for the decision to initiate the use of an integrated strategic nuclear force, so in the present case of the initiation of the use of tactical nuclear weapons it is clear that the drawing up in peacetime of an advance list of conditions or prerequisites would create the danger that the enemy might use his knowledge of the list to put us at a disadvantage. It is, furthermore, doubtful whether the European governments could ever agree on such a catalogue.

The process of equipping components of NATO's armed forces with so-called dual-purpose weapons has in the meantime led to the boundary line between conventional and tactical nuclear warfare becoming ever more blurred in the minds of the military. At the present time what seems to be envisaged is that the nuclear warheads now under American control will pass into the hands of the troops of the allied forces in Europe at the outbreak of hostilities or immediately thereafter. This arrangement can mean, in practice, that in the event of conflict each divisional commander and, later, even commanders subordinate to him will have direct access to nuclear weapons. It is doubtful to what extent they will be able to resist temptation, should their troops get into a desperate situation, even though they had no instructions to use nuclear weapons. It would, at all events, be quite unrealistic to extend the American control of nuclear warheads down to anti-tank companies and Davy Crockett troops. The danger that such weapons might be used as a result of a miscalculation of the situation by commanders on the spot, or of enemy provocation, and also the danger of nuclear escalation, becomes infinite. Mulley was right, in his capacity as *rapporteur* to W.E.U., to express fear lest the introduction of nuclear weapons for tactical use in Europe should lead to a situation which could strikingly increase the danger of unintended global war.

In view of the predictable consequences of defensive operations conducted with tactical nuclear weapons, it is a dereliction of responsibility to place the power to decide on their use in the hands of the military. We cannot escape from recognition of this fact even by preventing the further dissemination of nuclear weapons within NATO. When Mulley recommended this latter course to W.E.U. in 1960, a French source proposed something of a precisely contrary nature, viz. that provision should be made for the equipment of all European members of NATO with tactical nuclear weapons. This proposal was rejected by a great majority and, as the vote was taken, the representatives of the German Government parties found themselves in a state of remarkable isolation. It is doubtful whether the measures proposed by Mulley stand any chance of acceptance in the short term. It would be the more important to ensure:

1. that the power to decide to use available tactical nuclear weapons should rest with the political leaders;
2. that no practical arrangements should be permitted within the military machine that could lead, in the course of a battle, to the short-circuiting of government responsibility or the prejudicing of governmental decisions;
3. that nevertheless it must be possible to take decisions quickly.

The present structure of European NATO would seem to rule out any early fulfilment of these demands. So long as the present armaments structure of NATO, the inordinate weight it places on nuclear weapons, and the criminal neglect of its conventional armament persist, the decision to use mass destruction weapons in an emergency—a matter of life or death for the country concerned —will in all probability be taken by the military.

In theory the problem could be solved if one day a United States of Europe with a responsible all-European Government were to be brought into being. We must all agree, however, that such a solution is extremely remote; though we may wish it well, such a development must remain Utopian during the lifetime of the present generation. Let us rather recognise that, instead of pursuing this Utopian vision, the various European states have, in step with their progressive economic recovery, chased ever more rapidly after their separate national foreign policy goals. Examples of this process are legion. We need only remember the Suez crisis, the extraordinary difficulty in finding a common Western platform for disarmament negotiations whenever the opportunity arose, the various different positions towards the German and Oder-Neisse questions, the different attitudes towards Summit diplomacy, the estimate made by the European allies of the U 2 incident. The different attitudes towards the Algerian war and French nuclear armament opens up yet again the permanent cleavage within the alliance over its political strategy.

Who Leads the Alliance?

The political conception of NATO is, by its nature, defensive and "reactive." NATO pursues no offensive aims. Public opinion in the allied countries takes little interest in the problems of common defence. The peoples of Western Europe will only become more conscious of the need for a real defence capability than they have in the past, when the Western powers submit to Moscow agreed global political proposals that are clear to everyone—only to have them rejected. Moscow itself could also provoke such a reaction through a high-pressure policy of aggression. Public opinion in the European countries is today too much inclined to place exclusive reliance on the trip-wire theory of the function of the United States troops in Germany. The wish to see these troops in Germany, furthermore, springs in many people largely from the wish to keep Germany—their partner in the alliance—under observation and control.

Public opinion in the United Kingdom can be worked up against Germany by a handful of newspapers on almost any pretext. And in the Federal Republic the same effect can be produced. A new and growing distrust of the Federal Republic is arising in both Great Britain and France (mainly in the former, but underground in the latter) and is caused by the progressive build-up of the Bundeswehr. At the same time those concerned refuse to recognise that the build-up of the Bundeswehr is an absolute necessity for the overall purpose of the alliance as long as Great Britain and France—the latter now more than ever—fail to make conventional forces available to the alliance in significant numbers. Other members of the alliance also distrust one another. The differences over the relationship of the European Common Market with E.F.T.A. inflame public opinion in Britain and France. The United States has hitherto failed, from short or medium-term commercial interests, to pursue a policy of mediation between the Six and the Seven such as might help to establish harmonious future relations between them.

Certain European states cannot get used to the idea that they no longer rank among the first-class major powers. In 1956 the British and French Governments together tried to open the Suez Canal, to guarantee the oil supplies to Western Europe, to undermine Colonel Nasser's position, and to stop Communist penetration in the Middle East. They were defeated on all counts, and to some extent, indeed, achieved the opposite of the effect intended. But for all that Paris failed to learn its lesson from this catastrophic débâcle. For seven years France has been fighting a guerrilla war in Algeria and has been unable to bring it to a victorious conclusion. She also lost her war in Vietnam. France's intention is to offset the damage done by these calamities to her prestige and great power status, on the one hand by building up her nuclear armoury and, on the other, by her leadership of the Common Market countries. Regardless of NATO and its military needs, France has withdrawn a great part of her Mediterranean Fleet from the alliance, has resisted for years the establishment of a co-ordinated air defence system in Western Europe, and has forced American air squadrons to leave French soil.

The Federal German Government is also guilty of serious errors. The insistent demand for nuclear weapons, repeated with clockwork regularity, serves only to diminish the trust of Germany's partners in the alliance. The Federal Government's Spanish adventure evoked cool amazement, and to some extent indignation, within the alliance. Not only Germans have been outraged by the inept use of such phrases as "mortal enemy" and "exterminate."[27]

NATO's chief weakness lies in the absence of clear and convincing political and military leadership from the United States. This lack has contributed substantially to the disappearance of confidence in the feasibility of defending Europe. It remains, nevertheless, true that no European state can today entrust its

[27] For fuller details of these reproaches see Chapter 10, section headed "Germany is not a Major Power" (pp. 168ff.).

defence solely to its own forces. Not even the two major powers can do this. Nevertheless, European governments to an increasing extent wish to become independent of the alliance and its authority. NATO's threat of total retaliation leads, in every case of extra-European political conflict between the two major powers, to attempts by the European members of the alliance to impose moderation and restraint on Washington. Western Europe hopes to wring the last drop from deterrence—not least to enable it to keep down its own defence efforts. But should deterrence fail, then there must be no war. This latter wish is all too justified, not least because Europe is in no way armed to fight such a war. In the strategy of exclusive nuclear retaliation, however, lies one tremendous risk. So long as it is effective, peace may well be preserved. But if in a single exceptional case deterrence should fail in its object, our completely one-sided reliance on nuclear strategic forces would lead us straight into complete catastrophe.

Retaliation or Defence?

A ten-year sequence of cause and effect has led NATO into its present impasse. It started with the doctrine of nuclear retaliation and this led to neglect of conventional armaments. An attempt was made to restore the resulting unbalanced situation by the addition of tactical nuclear weapons: this led to further neglect of conventional armaments. From this followed the decision to equip the European members of NATO also with tactical nuclear weapons: this engendered a desire on their part to dispose of their own nuclear weapons. The leading power of the alliance negatived this desire, and this stimulated members of the alliance to divert their financial resources to the development and production of their own nuclear weapons instead of the means of conventional defence. The latest twist in this sequence is the plan to give European members of NATO shares in a joint Polaris force. As we saw at the beginning of this chapter, the weapons structure acquired by NATO as a result of this process fits the organisation for the satisfactory discharge of one solitary mission in Central Europe— deterrence of, or retaliation against, general Soviet assaults on Europe or on the West as a whole (Cases 4, 5 and 6 above). From this it is clear that, should such cases materialise, the present structure of NATO makes it extremely probable that it would have to accept the responsibility for the first use of nuclear weapons. In face of other limited, or gradual, forms of aggression by the Soviet Union, exemplified above as Cases 1, 2 and 3, NATO can only hope that the threat of nuclear retaliation will prove adequate to deter.

In all cases where the threat of retaliation fails to prevent aggression, NATO is confronted with three alternatives:

1. To attempt, contrary to the strategic concept hitherto in force, to parry the aggression with purely conventional weapons. Given the present weapons structure of NATO this could be tantamount to defeat.

2. To offer no resistance to the aggression. This would be tantamount to the disintegration of the alliance and a decided weakening of the Western position.

3. To retaliate with nuclear weapons. This would be tantamount to committing collective suicide.

We know that the third alternative leads to full-scale devastation of Europe and simultaneous strategic withdrawal. Even if the West's nuclear strategy should lead in the final outcome to "victory" and the subsequent "liberation" of Europe, there would be little object in first incurring the devastation of the continent. But if the nuclear strategy should not lead to the final victory of the West, and should the Soviet invading forces become established, this, together with the devastation preceding the invasion, would make the subsequent state of Europe even more frightful.

The prospect of such a development in the fighting would without doubt cripple the fighting spirit of European troops within a short period. Japan capitulated after two nuclear bursts, yet it would appear to be the intention that the allied troops in Europe should only begin to fight after the dropping of many more equally terrifying weapons.

"For a soldier, a hopeless fight is a senseless fight. A good man will be on his guard against bringing his subordinates into the position of making pointless sacrifices. Something that our policy must provide for in all circumstances is the preservation of the human, social and economic substance of our people. If we come to the point where we have to call upon our nation to defend freedom we must tell it that it is also defending its own fatherland with a degree of probability bordering on certainty, that it is keeping war away from its territory, and that it is not squandering the last shreds of its substance." The present arms structure of

Western Europe makes it out of the question for us to give our peoples an assurance similar to this one demanded by Schumacher in 1950. The so-called NATO "Shield" is only suited today to the task of winning a few days' grace by means of a defensive delaying action. Mulley was right, in April 1960, in maintaining that the line from the Thuringian Forest to Lübeck—the most suitable area for a Soviet surprise attack and rapid advance by Soviet mechanised divisions—is practically undefended. The task of the "Shield" in Europe today is no more than to prevent a safe drive westwards and a rapid *fait accompli*: it is not suited for lasting out a conventional war. At the most it can bring about a pause for breath or for counsel while nuclear strategic decisions are made. But, contrary to popular notions that have prevailed hitherto, it is today no longer an automatic rip-cord or trip-wire for initiating nuclear retaliation in response to all forms of aggression.

The conviction entertained by many observers, that every future war will be fought with nuclear weapons, or that every military conflict in Europe must lead to thermo-nuclear war, is plain stupidity. But it finds some support in what was once the official doctrine of responding with thermo-nuclear bombs in the event of an armoured brigade attack. One must agree with Brodie who says that "total nuclear war is to be avoided at almost any cost." Professor Klaus Knorr was right to put the following question as long ago as 1956: "Suppose the Soviet army suddenly advanced across West Germany, employing only 'conventional' weapons, and replying with the use of atomic weapons against tactical targets only as the Western powers applied them. How might the United States react? Would the United States unleash S.A.C. even though this meant the devastation of the large metropolitan areas of the United States and probably death to tens of millions of Americans? . . . Yet if the United States were unwilling to accept its own destruction as the price of stopping a westward eruption of Soviet divisions, might not the Kremlin proceed on this very assumption?"[28] A year later Kissinger also put the very reasonable question: "What if the Red Army attacks in Europe explicitly to disarm West Germany and offers to the United States immunity from strategic bombing and a withdrawal to the Oder after achieving its limited objective? Is it clear that France would

[28] K. Knorr, "Military Potential in the Nuclear Age," in *Military Policy and National Security*, ed. W. W. Kaufmann, Princeton 1956, pp. 147-8.

fight under such circumstances? Or that the United Kingdom would initiate an all-out war which, however it ended, might mean the end of British civilisation? Or that an American President would trade fifty American cities for Western Europe?"[29] Equally justifiably Liddell Hart wrote in 1960: "To aim at winning a war, to take victory as your object, is no more than a state of lunacy . . . for the sword could not be *used*, actually, without producing mutual suicide. It is like the old ceremonial Japanese sword dedicated for committing hara-kiri."[30]

If the outbreak of war is tantamount to the destruction of one's national existence, as the above writers have shown it to be, it must be supposed that in a war the will to fight will be crippled from the very outset and that all defence preparations will be ineffective. This fact makes utter nonsense of the attempts of certain politicians to reassure people with the chestnut that the United States has many more nuclear bombs than the Soviet Union. If the Clausewitz renaissance of recent years is to have any effect whatsoever, then it is to be hoped that it will serve to remind politicians that statesmanship must give the lead to the military planner. In other words, military strategy must be consistent with rational political aims, and the technical and material aspects of military policy must be consistent with the strategic aims. Today it is rather the reverse. Having taken refuge in the technology of nuclear warfare, we have given rise to a new bastard form of Maginot psychology. In war this could lead to quick defeat or annihilation—perhaps to both. We cannot therefore even be sure that Weinstein was right to postulate in 1955 that "there can be no winner in war."

Many readers may think these conclusions overdrawn: they may even be wrong. Prediction is as risky a business in military questions as in horse-racing. Nevertheless, we believe it to be a matter of urgent necessity to express our conviction that NATO in Europe has prepared for the wrong war. If this is true, it must result in attempts to take our fate into our hands again. It is by no means impossible for the 450 million people in Western Europe and North America to defend themselves effectively. But to do this great spiritual efforts will be required and equally considerable political efforts must accompany them.

[29] H. A. Kissinger, *Nuclear Weapons and Foreign Policy*, p. 244.
[30] B. H. Liddell Hart, *Deterrent or Defence*, p. 66.

7

The Challenge of the Sixties

WE have assumed above that Khrushchev's "peaceful co-existence" slogan can only be taken seriously in so far as it demonstrates a belief in the non-inevitability of World War III. It is, however, at the same time used by the Russians as a psychological smoke screen for obscuring the intention of the Soviet Union and world Communism to use all methods beneath the level of actual war for extending its power, and the fact that—viewed globally—Khrushchev thinks of it only as an outward armistice in an all-out revolutionary epoch. Co-existence as the Russians see it has room neither for the idea of balance nor of respect for law. It does not rule out Soviet support for or exploitation of the revolutions in Asia, Africa and Latin America which are partly in progress and to some extent still to come. It also by no means disavows the efforts, which are continuously being made, to undermine the old continent spiritually and politically by infiltration of Communism ideology and Communist propaganda. Khrushchev acknowledges expressly and pathetically the necessity for "wars of national liberation," but in admitting this he takes a splendidly one-sided view of things: he did not, at all events, see Hungary coming into the category of a "war of liberation." Khrushchev's co-existence ideology is the equivalent of a one-way street: changes are only allowed if they benefit the Soviet Union; revolutions in the West are permissible and historically inevitable, in the East they are a crime against the people.

Cold War on Three Levels

In the decade ahead of us the West must come to grips with Moscow and Peking's Communism on three different fronts: on that of economic and technical competition; on that of the ideological and spiritual debate; and also on that of mutaul military

H

threats, deterrence and counter-deterrence. So long as an equilibrium can be maintained on the front of military threats and deterrence—and only so long—the real confrontation will take place first and foremost on the technical and economic front.

At the same time, however, the world situation will be changed by newly emergent factors on which the Western powers will be able to exercise no fundamental influence: by the emergence of new states and new aspirant forces, above all by Asia's "demographic explosion" and the prospect that we shall be faced by a China 800 million strong by 1970. There is no certainty whatsoever by what date and in what way China might become a danger to Soviet policy. It is equally doubtful whether such a development might be beneficial to the West or, on the other hand, whether it might not create an additional threat to peace by forcing on the Soviet Union policies which it does not at present basically endorse. To make prognostications like those of Starlinger[1] is a dubious exercise—but for this very reason we Europeans must consciously keep the problems of East and South Asia before our eyes. In this area, at all events, the United States is several steps ahead. New forces will similarly radiate outwards from Africa and Latin America. Whereas until recently the African members of the United Nations mustered only about an eighth of the total votes in the General Assembly, the number of African members has grown from 10 to 26 in the course of a few years, and will probably before long rise to a total of 33. The African countries will then comprise about a third of the votes in the United Nations. It is questionable whether the African countries will form their own bloc in world politics—but it is by no means certain that they will not do so. The compactness of the bloc of 22 American votes so far maintained under United States leadership is beginning to crumble. The social, economic and political structure in Central and South America is inherently unstable. The example of Fidel Castro and its influence on other Latin American leaders shows that the paternalistic form in which Washington has hitherto exerted its influence cannot be maintained. If the West wishes to prevent the undermining of its position in South and Central

---

[1] "The question for the Soviets will soon be, not whether they will be able to overrun Europe at no great risk, but what they must themselves do in the Far East to provide the rearward protection which *alone* (my italics, H. S.) can protect them from the threat of being overrun (*sic!* H. S.) from the East." W. Starlinger, *Grenzen der Sowjetmacht* (Limits of Soviet Power), 1955.

America, an extensive change in Washington's policy towards this area will be necessary. In this Western Europe can be of only limited assistance.

It is high time that the West acquired the art of making genuine friends in the under-developed countries. That of making enemies requires no further refinement. It befits us Germans little to presume to criticise the former imperialist and colonial powers: we also have by no means fully utilised our opportunities of cultivating friendly relations with the newer peoples and states during the decade just ended. The younger nations are carried along by the general movement towards neutrality. The West would do well to recognise and to allow for the fact that if ultimately India or Africa turned neutral, this might benefit the West: this goes also for Japan. But to attempt to manœuvre new nations into accepting military assistance which they do not want through the agency of politically corrupt régimes, is to do the Western cause only an illusory service. Western political collaboration with régimes hated by their peoples can produce long-lasting adverse effects. Hatred of the government of a Syngman Rhee or a Kishi can easily be switched to their allies.

The Ideological Vacuum

In combating Communism in the spiritual field and in opposing its ideological infiltration it will be indispensable to analyse more extensively than we have done hitherto its ideological processes and the social realities it has created. And we must bring far greater intellectual energy to the task. Marx and Lenin analysed the problems of their time and the social system of the world in which they lived: they also attempted far-reaching predictions of future developments. In the meantime, however, the actual political, economic and social developments in many parts of the world, notably in the Soviet Union itself, have advanced well beyond the stages envisaged by Marx and Lenin. Where the declarations of Marx and Lenin no longer apply, "Marxism-Leninism" attempts to answer the new questions for them. In so doing it inevitably involves itself in contradicting the ideological fathers. The scientific, technical and economic achievements of the Soviet Union, the modern development of an industrial society and the rise of the standard of living of the masses pose unexpected problems. The Communist parties are forced constantly to realign their ideology

116   THE CHALLENGE OF THE SIXTIES

to the changed realities. In this process the ideology, proclaimed
in all its scientific trappings, becomes more and more exposed to
criticism and the revelation of internal contradictions. The Soviet
Union is bringing into being a new and extensive intelligentsia.
Whereas in 1914 there were only 100,000 students at higher
educational establishments, there were 500,000 in 1933 and well
over two million in 1960. It is questionable whether the C.P.S.U.
will succeed in enclosing this new intelligentsia, which is growing
up with no real transcendental ties, for ever in the chains of an
ideology subject to constant change and realignment. We can
assume that a spontaneous tendency to scepticism and enlighten-
ment will keep breaking through in this sector of the community.
Such a trend can prove a long-term hindrance to a Communism
that exalts ideology to the status of religion. It is doubtful whether
such exaltation will prove possible in view of the all-pervading
Soviet preoccupation with material things and the associated
constant need for manipulation. The more strongly the intellectual
strength of the West is joined in the battle with Communist
ideology, the more difficult it will be for the Communists in the
long run to substitute ideology for religion and philosophy in the
minds of their peoples. Their task will doubtless be facilitated by
their ability to put up "quarantine barriers" against intellectual
influences from the West.

All the more cause has the West to engage in positive struggle
with Communist ideology, at least in its own sphere of influence.
That familiar type of trite anti-Communism, so often encountered
in the Federal Republic—and also in the United States—can do
little to further this task: indeed it can do long-term damage to the
Western cause. The same would apply if the West tried to build
up a counter-ideology, as is done amongst others by the movement
for so-called Moral Rearmament. One of the substantial advantages
of the Western concept of freedom, as against the ideals of Communism, lies in the very fact that we do not wish to—nor can—
impose a uniform ideology or even a uniform religion upon all
men. But a bold advocacy of the so-called "pluralist society" helps
just as little as a formal appeal to Christianity or to so-called
Western values. One of the most important tasks of our generation
is for our intellectual leaders, historians, philosophers, teachers
and ministers to inculcate in the consciousness of us all the common spiritual foundations and the religious affinities of the West.

Only in so far as this succeeds shall we be able to join aggressive battle with Communism from a standpoint peculiarly our own. The great effort being made by the American administration under Kennedy to equip the nation for the struggle with Communism—an effort which may be taken up by the Western states as a whole—will only bear permanent fruit if it simultaneously strives to create superior principles of social order and to promote higher moral and spiritual performance.

There exists in the West at present a motley collection of competing ideologies, which in sum add up to something resembling an ideological vacuum. This vacuum is a heaven-sent opportunity for Communist aggression—especially where it happens to coincide with economic difficulties, built-in political conservatism, or incongruous and unjust social systems. This vacuum cannot be filled by a uniform ideology: in its place a common consciousness of commonly accepted ethical and socio-ethical basic values is required. The question as to how far individual freedom is possible in industrial society and how it can be brought about, the question of how far democratic organisation is possible in the society of today, the question of social justice and how it is to be achieved, the question of the basic rights of the individual and of nations and how they are to be realised—these are the questions that will decide the outcome of the struggle. The West's opportunity lies in making social democracy a live force with which the popular masses can identify themselves. If the West is not able to make democracy a live force in all areas of society, its economic growth and technical achievements—however high—will be of no avail. The West must not forget that it is not fighting for the technological or economic perfection of capitalism, but for the establishment and defence of the right of self-determination of individuals and peoples.

Economic and Technological Competition

The West can contemplate with equanimity the competition for higher living standards. Even if the present imbalance, favourable to the Soviet Union, in rates of economic growth were to continue for some time, the enormous lead of the United States in this field would make it quite impossible for the Soviet Union, during the whole of the coming decade, to lift the standard of living of its people to anything like that of the American. The same is true, with some qualification, of the comparison with the Federal Republic, with France or with Britain. Despite this, their consciousness of the steady growth of their standard of living from its initial low level will be a great psychological prop to the Communist leadership. The West must ensure that, in its area, not only the average standard of living, but also that of all social classes constantly increases: it must in particular advance the standard of living to the general level in all areas where there is distress on account of political or economic backwardness. Its particular task will be to guarantee that the advance towards a fuller measure of social justice engages all its attention and does not slacken. No structural rebuilding of Western economies is necessary for this, but rather an economic and financial policy that makes full and determined use of all its potentialities. Those who proclaim the ideals of freedom in areas where misery and want prevail and where unemployment is a permanently recurring feature do not have a leg to stand on. No one can live for long upon ideals: only very few can live for them for long.

In view of the epoch of competition in productivity between East and West that clearly lies before us, the West's domestic rivalries in the economic field between the Six and the Seven has the air of an historical anachronism. The West needs the highest degree of division of labour; manifestations of national and regional egoism are bad. Moscow has long recognised this fact in its direction of the Eastern bloc: the degree of economic integration, of international division of labour and international direction of investment in the region of the Council for Mutual Economic Assistance exceeds that of the West by a wide margin. For all that opportunities are still open to the Eastern bloc for further increasing its effectiveness—the possibility of introducing multilateral clearance of accounts and currency stabilisation on the model of the European Payments Union, the opportunity for the creation of an international "capital market" within the Eastern bloc, and above all the possibility of creating competitive markets. The process begun by Khrushchev's policy of economic decentralisation within the Soviet Union provides an entirely suitable basis for building up competition and markets within limited areas, particularly in the consumer industries. We must certainly assume that traditional Marxist ideology will not prevent the Soviet leaders from discovering the superior rational basis and effectiveness of the market system. At all events we need not doubt the cold determination of the Soviet leaders to raise the living standard of their masses by all practicable means.

Competition for superior technology and higher living standards necessarily entails competition for better education of potential leaders in the technical, administrative and economic fields. The Soviet efforts in this area are enormous and are superior to the comparable efforts of the Federal Republic. We must learn from the Russians in this field, particularly as regards the mobilisation of the resources of the state. In this connexion, the West's basic convictions cannot but lead to encouragement of education generally as well as just technical training.

Economic competition is not restricted to the sovereign areas of the two major powers and the powers directly allied to them. It is being extended at a rapidly growing tempo to the area of the so-called under-developed countries. The new states, which have arisen all over the world in the place of former colonies, are naturally enough attempting to bypass several generations of capitalist development in order to catch up with the standard of living of the "old" nations as quickly as possible. This goal can only be achieved if the countries with well-developed economies support them by word and deed, by assistance in training programmes, and by help in the field of investment and trade policy. In this a new field in economic competition between the major powers has been opened up that only came to the consciousness of world public opinion through the débâcle over financial aid for the Aswan Dam. In this competition the Soviet Union suffers from a twofold handicap: she shares, in the final analysis, the colossal responsibility for the economic development of China; her financial resources are limited in comparison with those of the United States, Great Britain and Germany. In consequence the development assistance provided by the Soviet Union to date comprises only a small fragment of that provided so far by the United States and the West European countries. Nevertheless they have achieved a political effect by means of credits which are to some extent short-term but are at all events well aimed, through the despatch of experts and by means of their trading policies in Asia, Africa and Latin America: this political effect is out of all proportion to the Soviet share in the total of effective economic assistance. The economic assistance granted to date by the Western countries has been without doubt much greater, but it has by no means achieved a comparable political effect. One of the reasons for this relative lack of success is to be found in the fact that the United States has up till the present linked economic aid with political conditions and acceptance of obligations under its various military alliances: it is also to be found in the inadequate heed given to the peculiar political and economic conditions in the under-developed countries.

It is important to recognise that economic aid *without* political conditions is a political weapon. The governments of many undeveloped countries, following their basic line of political neutrality, will coolly accept development assistance from either side. It is important for us to understand that even in such cases Western aid cannot be dispensed with. The manner in which the West's development aid is organised, especially when this is determined by purely capitalist considerations, is often inferior to the Soviet form. Here also new efforts are necessary. The West's mission towards the undeveloped countries and the import- ance of its political outcome for the future development of the world situation cannot possibly be overestimated. "We can only compare it all with the situation that challenged us during the first half and the middle of the present century—the domestication of capitalism within the framework of the modern social and welfare state. Whatever one's attitude to this development, there should be no contesting the fact that Marx's analysis of a hundred years ago is not wholly wrong: and it should be recognised that, after its great crisis, free society only succeeded in finding the strength to provide for its common sustenance and welfare—and finding it in conditions of equality, stability and progress—when Keynes succeeded in stealing Marx's thunder. For it was the combination of welfare state and market economy, and this combination alone that—despite all the internal problems with which it still confronts us—brought the free world the immense advances in production that mark the period since World War II. But we are also aware that, in relation to the undeveloped countries, there is an equally radical rival doctrine with its gospel of 'Imperialism is the highest stage of Capitalism' taken from Marx's proclamation of a century ago in respect of the conditions governing economic production in the old industrialised countries. It is up to us to show whether, in the field of 'therapy,'

we can again get the better of Marx and Lenin." There is almost
nothing to be added to this statement which is taken from a
lecture given in 1960 by Professor Karl Schiller of Hamburg.
Assistance to the under-developed countries in the development
of their economies will be a major theatre of conflict in the cold
war during the coming decade. This theatre of conflict will call
for the highest degree of political tact and ability to project oneself
into another's position: it will also make very considerable demands
on our economic production. We shall only be able to meet the
latter by withdrawing resources that will slow down the further rise
in the standard of living or the general rate of economic growth.
It is therefore desirable to restrict armaments in order to increase
development aid.

The Arms Race and the Danger of War

Hopes for the ending of the arms race have, nevertheless, not
risen in recent years. The undeniable sterility of all past disarmament negotiations, even in so narrow a field as that of ending
nuclear tests, has led to a deep sense of resignation in which there
is much food for thought. It is doubtful whether we shall succeed
during the next few years, by means of disarmament and arms
control agreements, in diverting financial resources and a share in
the social product from arms to development aid. Furthermore,
the United States is faced by the necessity of making extra efforts
to close the missile gap as soon as possible, and European NATO
as a whole is faced by the necessity of embarking on an extensive
remodelling of its armaments.

Whether or not the arms race can be stopped, "canalised," or
at least damped down, the West must at all costs preserve an
equilibrium on the front of military threats, deterrence and
counter-deterrence. If this equilibrium were allowed to lapse the
main weight of the real confrontation with Communism might
very quickly shift from the economic and technological front to
that of naked threats backed by military power. If, therefore,
disarmament and control elude our grasp, the West *must* do
everything to preserve a stable situation, both in the conventional
field and at the awesome level of thermo-nuclear armaments. If
today or tomorrow Washington or NATO were to fail to preserve
the military equilibrium *vis-à-vis* Moscow and the Warsaw Pact
countries, we should then need to worry acutely about the freedom

of Berlin. And Berlin is only a symbol of many points of possible danger to peace. The Soviet and Communist threat of aggression is many-sided: it is not confined to ideological, internal and external political warfare; it extends beyond boastful promises of higher technological achievement and a higher living standard; it does not reach its limit with the attempt to secure a political following in the undeveloped countries by means of economic assistance. The threat of aggression remains, as before, also military in character. Peace is threatened not only in Berlin, Laos and Vietnam, but also in South-East Asia as a whole, in the Middle East, in Africa and in Latin America. There will be a particular danger of aggression by the methods of power politics possibly accompanied by the conscious acceptance of the risk of military conflicts so long as the United States does not close the missile gap and NATO as a whole does not adapt its armaments structure and policy, so little fitted for its defence, to the needs of the present situation. But even if such an adaptation were to be accomplished within the next few years, we could not even then completely rule out the danger.

The West has at least two decisive motives for seeking to conduct the struggle on the ideological/spiritual and economic/technological fronts: the wish, grounded in its moral convictions, to preserve the present "armistice"; and the superiority of its spiritual foundations and economic base. But it must, for all that, take into account—and be militarily prepared for—the possibility of serious disputes and risks on the third front also.

It is natural enough, when considering the short-term prospect, to see a particular danger in the conflict over the freedom of Berlin. Taylor's book repeatedly draws attention to this point. It is here that the influence of the present Soviet superiority in conventional weapons under the "umbrella" · of the strategic nuclear balance of terror is felt at its strongest. We may doubt if President Eisenhower was very well advised to answer at a press conference in the spring of 1959 that to go to war over Berlin was impossible. Willy Brandt, the Mayor of Berlin, gave no reply to the same question when it was put to him in public, and this seems more sensible. For "without the *ultima ratio* of military defence it may not be possible to uphold the status of Berlin" (Eschenburg). The West, which has committed itself to the military defence of the freedom of Berlin, must carefully watch the political and juridical position there, so as to preserve it against Khrushchev's and Ulbricht's attempts to stifle it piecemeal. It was therefore to our great sorrow that we heard President Eisenhower's statement, made after his Camp David meeting with Khrushchev, that the situation in Berlin was "abnormal." For this is what the Soviet leaders have always asserted, and it was on this assertion that they based their proposal for "free city" status—a proposal aimed, as they alleged, at the normalisation of the situation. In view of the risk of war arising from the Berlin conflict, of which the other side is also aware, we must be principally on our guard against indirect aggression here. Berlin will certainly remain one of the chief danger spots for world peace during the coming years precisely because its geographically isolated position invites indirect aggression and makes defence against it extremely difficult.

Berlin is, at one and the same time, the Achilles heel and a test case for NATO. The possibilities of compromising with Khrushchev (so as to help him save face) are almost completely exhausted. Berlin will therefore remain during the sixties a challenge to the West—and to the East as well, in whose eyes a free Berlin symbolises the Western claim for the termination of the Soviet occupation of Central Europe. The West cannot, however, enter into isolated negotiations over the question of Berlin since there is almost no more room for negotiation on the matter.

This will probably remain the case during those years in which the competition between the Six and the Seven and the question of an integrated strategic nuclear force for European NATO will be finally settled. The West would do well to look at the continuing struggle with Communism that lies ahead of us in its chronological perspective. We have grounds for hoping that the West will survive without war the dangerous period before the closing of the missile gap and the creation of an effective defence capability in Europe. We have grounds for hope that a stable equilibrium of military power can be created and preserved between East and West. But we must recognise that, precisely because of this, the spiritual and psychological battle with Communism and the struggle for the under-developed countries will gain considerably in importance.

Well before the end of the coming decade we shall have to think of China as a major power with an effective military capability. Summit conferences on the destiny of the world will then cease to make sense without China—if this does not become the case earlier. It is true that advanced industrial societies within the Eastern bloc, such as those of the Soviet Union and its German satellite, might by then have become a factor for stability; but the revolutionary leadership would then go over to other powers. There is no *status quo* in world politics; not even—indeed, especially not—in the co-existence proclaimed by Khrushchev. The West must have no fear of this prospect. In fear there lies just as great a danger of war as in the excessive deployment and parading of military power.

Given unanimity and determination on the part of the West, nobody need fear that, even if the arms race continues, it will be unable to maintain a continuous military equilibrium with the Eastern bloc. But we have also come to see clearly that, given the continuation of the arms race, the destabilising factors could gain the upper hand: we need only think of the danger of the further spread of nuclear weapons. The arms race is a consequence of political tension, but it is also the cause of further tension. It is hard to imagine how world peace can be preserved through the sixties if the arms race continues. Arms limitation and control on a global scale are therefore a crucial, perhaps *the* crucial, historical imperative of the sixties.

Those who have grasped the overall prospect for the decade ahead of us will agree with John F. Kennedy: we are confronted by the challenge of the century. We have no alternative but to take up the challenge.

8

Arms Limitation and Control

JULES MOCH, who has for years represented France at the various disarmament negotiations, has pointed out that up to 1945 sixty million bombs would have been necessary to destroy France, whereas today only twenty bombs would be required, i.e. twenty aircraft over their targets. The development of modern air forces, of nuclear bombs and long-range missiles, has immeasurably increased the destructive powers of modern warfare. Although humanity has thousands of years of experience of warfare and its consequences, it may nevertheless be that we do not yet have a good enough idea of the horrors of a future thermo-nuclear war. The desire of millions, perhaps billions, of human beings, white, yellow and dark skinned, for disarmament is some-thing completely justifiable: it needs no further motivation. The governments of all these many peoples, however, have not so far been able to realise their aspirations. This has not happened through any want of seriousness: the main reason has been, rather, a sense of responsibility towards their own peoples. None of the governments participating in disarmament negotiations and none of the governments affected by future disarmament agreements can be sure that total disarmament will come about. Each one must, on the contrary, proceed on the assumption that even disarmament down to small arms would not make war impossible; and that even in this extreme case, the distribution of the remaining small arms throughout the world would have to be such as to preserve an equilibrium. No government can be sure, without extensive controls, that all the others are really retaining only small arms. It would require no more than quite small secret stocks of heavy bombs to threaten world peace and hold out hopes of lucrative blackmail of peace-loving nations. Any attempt to conclude arms limitation agreements that do not provide for the establishment of a controlled balance of military power is therefore doomed to failure.

Attempts to bring about such agreements on a voluntary basis are historically of quite recent date, and are, practically speaking, confined to the twentieth century. There are only very few positive examples, such as the Washington Naval Treaty of 1922 between the major maritime powers. This lasted only a few years. The disarmament negotiations under the aegis of the League of Nations, like those under the aegis of the United Nations, were a succession of failures. These failures have led many to the conclusion that disarmament is a dangerous illusion. But this goes hand in hand with another equally extreme notion—that disarmament is possible because it *must* be possible. The Soviet Union has twice, in the history of disarmament, come forward with proposals for comprehensive disarmament—in 1927 and 1959-60. Both proposals bore the marks of incomplete seriousness: anyone who proposes total disarmament, just like that, either suffers from delusions or is a plain propagandist. The less disarmament negotiations in the years after 1945 seemed calculated to lead to a practical outcome, the more both sides used them for propaganda purposes. The misuse of foreign policy for propaganda purposes is, indeed, no new phenomenon peculiar to the twentieth century. Nevertheless, this misuse has been stepped up and perfected to a horrifying degree during the last fifty years. In many ways it has obscured the real tasks of foreign policy. The concept of arms limitation and its control is, on the other hand, so new that it has not yet sunk deep enough into the consciousness of responsible statesmen; nor has the intellectual and institutional apparatus necessary for its realisation yet been adequately developed. Nevertheless, we need not doubt that many governments are very seriously striving for disarmament agreements. This is right and necessary. International arms control is a categorical imperative.

In view of the global nature of contemporary strategic relationships the problem has become much more complex than it was in the nineteen-twenties. Agreement between a few major powers would no longer suffice: there are more than two or three states that could start World War III. A disarmament treaty without China no longer makes sense, and the exclusion of other smaller states is equally impermissible. Arms limitation must lead to an equilibrium between the rival military powers. But this equilibrium can neither be limited to specific regions of the earth nor to specific weapons, neither to Europe nor the Pacific, neither to maritime warfare nor to the means of waging nuclear war. It is a question of a comprehensive world-wide system of balance. This makes things much more difficult than in the days of the League of Nations in Geneva.

None the less, the United Nations has succeeded in taking a step which was denied to the League of Nations—the setting up of U.N. police forces for the prevention or settlement of military conflicts. It is true that it can only be effective in conflicts in which the major powers are not themselves direct participants, since otherwise it would be up against a veto in the United Nations Security Council, should it be sent into action.[1] The first experiment with an international U.N. police force in the Israeli conflict (after the Sinai campaign) proved successful, just as did—with some qualifications—its predecessor, the U.N. Armistice Commission. Whether the current experiment in the Congo will be equally successful depends on the attitude of the major powers.

For practical disarmament purposes the U.N. police force stands for the establishment of an international control organisation with its own limited weapons complement for carrying out its tasks. If the United Nations could resolve to set up a police force in the form of a highly mobile fire brigade, composed of national contingents and constantly on call, able to intervene at any time to prevent outbreaks of fire, then this force could one day become the nucleus both of a future disarmament control organisation (which would, of course, have to be equipped quite differently) and of an international force for the preservation of peace. It would be even better if a permanent U.N. international police force could be composed, not of international contingents, but of "denationalised" individuals, integrated into a joint force under the exclusive flag of the United Nations. It is doubtful whether the Soviet Union would agree to a solution with such far-reaching implications; but an attempt at something of this sort might be useful. The formation of a permanent U.N. police force would, however, by no means bring what are today the central problems of disarmament any nearer to a solution. These central problems must first be settled between the world powers if there is to be any chance whatever of a general settlement.

---

[1] The U.N. resolution to defend South Korea against indirect aggression from the Soviet Union with a U.N. force was an exceptional stroke of luck brought about by a Russian diplomatic error.

The popular notion of disarmament is often of something concerned exclusively with nuclear weapons. A military balance effected by treaty can, in fact, only be achieved if the so-called conventional weapons are also included. Only in so far as an equilibrium can be brought about in this field also will it be possible to resolve the disarmament equation. Armament policy and disarmament policy have the same objects in view—security against surprise attack, security against qualitative military inferiority as a result of technological breakthroughs on the part of a potential enemy, and security against quantitative inferiority. In aiming at these goals governments have up till now put more trust, despite the colossal risks involved, in the present system of deterrence and counter-deterrence than in the possibility of creating new systems through mutual understanding—systems whose overall risks have not yet been adequately worked out. They act in accordance with the principle: what we have, we know; what we might have is uncertain and obscure. This attitude has had the result that all governments participating in disarmament talks have been too strongly influenced by short-term so-called "military necessities" and too little by long-term political necessities. Despite advancing understanding on the part of the community of its interests in the field of disarmament policy, there is still inadequate understanding of the identity of aim of both armament and disarmament policy. This is the reason for the hitherto widespread failure to put the problem in its correct light.

Parallelism of Interests

The hope that, despite all previous failures, it might yet be possible to reach disarmament agreements can only be ascribed to recognition of the community of interests which the major powers have in this field. Both major powers are interested in making a total nuclear war impossible. Both are therefore equally interested in eliminating the possibility of surprise attacks and the initiation of nuclear war against the will of either ("catalytic" war); both are interested in eliminating the possibility of war by accident as a result of false alarm or of misinterpretation of intelligence; both fear arbitrary action on the part of their allies and are therefore keenly interested in closing the doors of the Nuclear Club to further comers. Both powers, finally, have a common economic interest in reducing their expenditure on armaments.

It is doubtful whether agreements designed to provide security against surprise attacks will be reached before both major powers have "hardened" their strategic nuclear forces: on the other hand the necessity for agreed measures against nuclear surprise attacks will probably diminish *after* this point of time, provided that it is possible to prevent nuclear weapons spreading into the hands of further powers. It is therefore logical to put the prevention of the spread of nuclear weapons to further powers first on the great powers' agenda in their efforts to reach understanding on arms limitation: since it would scarcely be possible to control[2] a general ban on the production of nuclear weapons (at least in respect of the great powers who dispose of large easily concealable stocks of fissile material) this aspect of the matter becomes focused on an agreed ban on nuclear testing. This question of ending nuclear tests also shows very clearly that, in matters of disarmament policy, the interests of the major powers do not always coincide with those of the smaller powers.

Within the Western bloc, by contrast, both the United States as a major power and the other allies certainly agree that arms limitation must lead to a general balance or equilibrium made up of a series of partial balances at the levels of the various forms of possible warfare. There has so far been no sign that the Soviet Union would accept such a formulation of the goal of disarmament policy. She has no interest in giving up what are advantages as regards both strategy and disarmament policy, i.e. in the quantitative superiority of her conventional armaments. Nevertheless, that it might also be in the West's interest to conclude limitation and control agreements with the Soviet Union in limited fields of armaments only is by no means to be ruled out. The West, however, will not be interested in "neutralisation," by means of arms limitation and control agreements, of the nuclear weapons available to both sides, so long as it remains inferior in the field of conventional arms. Nevertheless it will be able to proceed on the assumption that a strategy of deterrence and some form of control against surprise attack do not need to be mutually exclusive or to interfere with each other.

[2] Except for new production of nuclear warheads from new fissile material produced in future. Since the reactors needed for producing new fissile material take up a large area, they can be hidden only with difficulty and are thus easy to control. In consequence the subsequent utilisation of the material produced in these reactors is also easy to keep track of and to control.

I

The history of disarmament negotiations since 1954 shows that both major powers—and Britain and France also—resisted measures which might have led to reductions in fields in which they had achieved a lead. They also set their faces against agreements which might have prevented them catching up a lead on the other side. When the Soviet Union rejected the Baruch Plan in 1946 with the argument that it would permit no derogation of its right of veto in the United Nations Security Council, her real motive was the wish not to be deprived of the chance of catching up the American lead in the nuclear field. The resistance of influential Americans today to a nuclear test ban springs from their wish to maintain their lead in the development and production of small nuclear weapons.

The Disarmament Roundabout

If one follows Anthony Nutting's account of the disarmament negotiations we can see that these resolve themselves into several different episodes. The first episode, centred mainly on the Baruch Plan, came to an end with the outbreak of the Korean War. The second began in 1952 with the re-establishment of a Disarmament Commission by the United Nations. The Soviet Union demanded a prohibition in principle on all nuclear weapons from the very outset: she opposed inspection and proposed a relative reduction of one-third in armed forces strength. The West, on the other hand, emphasised the establishment of fixed ceilings for the armed forces and a balanced equilibrium between them. The negotiations produced no tangible results. The third round took place in 1954 in the U.N. Disarmament Subcommittee which had been revived as a result of the Foreign Ministers' conference in Berlin, and was equally unfruitful. A further episode took shape in May 1955 in connexion with the Geneva Summit Conference which was to take place in July of the same year: the Soviet Government made new proposals which, in respect of the controls always maintained by the West to be necessary, came very close to the Western proposals. At this point, however, the United States and the West drew back and, for the first time, by withdrawing the majority of their proposals, went unmistakably over to the defensive. Before doing this they put forward at the Geneva Summit Conference the Eisenhower "Open Skies" proposal, and the vague Eden proposals for reducing forces in a European zone (Eden Plan, second version): both proposals were limited to specific geographical sectors.

During the fifth round, which was marked by the initiative of Harold Stassen, it looked in the spring and summer of 1957 as though the U.N. Disarmament Subcommittee in London might reach agreement on a partial disarmament treaty. Stassen was recalled by Washington, however, and in the autumn of the same year the Soviet Union abandoned the negotiations with the demand that they be referred back to the full United Nations General Assembly. The sixth round was marked by the exchange of notes in 1957 and 1958, by the Rapacki Plan, and by the Soviet declaration of their intention to renounce further atom bomb tests unilaterally. This was preceded by a very intensive series of tests within the Soviet Union. The United States and Great Britain were compelled to follow the Soviet example. No tests have been carried out by any power, except France, since 3 November 1958.[3]

The seventh round was marked by the parallel conferences started in Geneva in 1958—one on a nuclear test ban, and the other about prevention of surprise attacks: the former has, with several interruptions, continued its work up to the present and has made some progress in the shape of draft treaty articles.

The eighth round was introduced by the Geneva Foreign Ministers' conference of May-June 1959. The "Peace Plan" tabled there by the West combined a solution of the German question with world-wide disarmament with the creation of a zone of limited armaments, the latter to be reached by parallel simultaneous steps. It was after the collapse of this conference, in September 1959, that Khrushchev made his spectacular proposal of total disarmament within four years. The West allowed itself once more to be put on the defensive, and in March 1960 a U.N. Disarmament Committee of Ten was set up on which the East and the West had equal representation. China, on the other hand, continued as before to take no part in the negotiations. In April 1960 the West tabled at this conference a three-stage plan without time limits, which stressed numerical limitation of conventional troops and the establishment of international control. The Soviet Union stuck to its plan for total disarmament within four years

---

[3] The Soviet Union resumed the testing of nuclear weapons in the atmosphere in September 1961. Shortly afterwards the United States resumed underground nuclear weapon tests. (Trans.)

announced in 1959, which sharply limited the possibility of inspection and control and allowed it to become fully effective only at the moment when "total disarmament down to small arms" had been reached. In the summer of 1960 the Soviet Union walked out of these negotiations in order to attend the autumn sitting of the U.N. General Assembly in New York and there indulge in propaganda, boorishness and high-flown oratory.

Only a few experts can keep in their heads the course of disarmament negotiations during the last fifteen years; but they are of only secondary importance for the future. We need only note here that all participants, in accordance with their short-term appreciation of the situation, have considerably varied their proposals and demands in the course of these fifteen years. At times the Russians have maintained that nuclear disarmament and troop reductions can only be negotiated jointly; at other times they have taken the position that prohibition of nuclear weapons must come before all else; and at yet other times they have gone so far as to demand that nuclear disarmament should be excluded from consideration on the grounds that it is too difficult to accomplish. As regards nuclear disarmament the Soviet Union has at times confined itself to a ban on nuclear tests without linking it to a ban on production; but at other times it has demanded a complete ban on all nuclear weapons. As regards manpower the Russians have on occasion refused to accept absolute figures, and have envisaged only percentage reductions in actual forces' strengths: but on other occasions they have wished to impose absolute ceilings varying from between 1·5 and 1·7 million for the United States, the Soviet Union and China, to 650,000 for Britain and France. As regards inspection and control, the Soviet Union initially took up the position that this was the cardinal point of any disarmament agreement; but since then it has equated the general Western desire for control and inspection with a desire to carry out espionage. At times it has made concrete, if limited, concessions.

A survey of the Western proposals of the last fifteen years gives a similarly confused picture. At times the West has taken up the position that disarmament is only possible if control and inspection are introduced simultaneously: at other times it has demanded that controls should be set up first and followed only later by disarmament. Within a short period of time the West has maintained both that effective international control of a nuclear test ban is possible and is not possible. On occasion the West has accepted a military manpower figure of 1·5 million for the major powers and 650,000 for Britain and France, but its latest demand is that the limit should be placed at 2·5 million and 750,000 respectively. The West's position has frequently shifted as regards the political context of disarmament: sometimes it has maintained that disarmament agreements are a prerequisite of far-reaching political settlements, and at other times that disarmament agreements are only possible given simultaneous political settlements (e.g. of the German question); at other times the West has gone back to putting disarmament first again.

The Federal Republic's position has similarly varied: at times it has taken the view that disarmament would be impossible so long as Germany remained divided. At other times general and controlled disarmament was laid down as a necessary precondition for the relaxation of tension and solution of the German question; and the Federal Republic has sometimes taken the view that any disarmament scheme must proceed by stages and be linked to step-by-step solutions of the German question.

This roundabout of shifts in basic positions on both sides only becomes understandable if we recognise that no consistent strategy has underlain the negotiating position of either side. The Soviet Union was interested in nuclear disarmament only for as long as she felt herself inferior in this field. The West, *per contra*, later developed reservations as the Soviet Union became more ready for discussions in the nuclear field, because it was conscious of its conventional inferiority. Every initiative taken by either side in the disarmament field has left open an escape route advantageous to that side. Both sides have wished to represent any possible disarmament as a victory for themselves, and have geared their various initiatives in the field of disarmament policy to propaganda and prestige considerations of this sort.

This attitude, and the simultaneous continuation of the arms race, have seriously damaged the confidence of each side in the seriousness of its negotiating partners. Some Western observers believe there are reasons for thinking that the Soviet leaders really act on the assumption that the West has no serious intention of disarming because the Pentagon is against it. It is in every way conceivable that in all disarmament negotiations the Soviet Union has assumed—and will continue to assume in future—that "capitalist states" have an inevitable propensity towards wars and that therefore a serious desire for disarmament cannot be expected from them. The undermining of Soviet confidence in the loyalty of their Western negotiating partners lies, at all events, in their fear of a thermo-nuclear surprise attack (whether precipitated by calculated decision or misinterpretation of intelligence); in their hysterical aversion to every sort of inspection and control (which they equate purely and simply with espionage); in their fear of a reunited Germany; and, finally, in their conviction that they cannot expect fair treatment in the United Nations because of the minority position which they must long occupy there.

The lack of confidence on the Western side has similar causes: fear of numerically superior Soviet ground forces; fear of possible military action by other Communist states possibly supported by the Soviet Union; fear of military technological breakthroughs within a closed Soviet society which cannot be observed from outside; and, not least, the conviction that the Communist leaders are undeviatingly determined to put an end to Western society (if necessary by force), and fear that for this reason the Russians might launch a thermo-nuclear surprise attack. When we recall that in the Soviet Union the word "capitalist" counts as one of the worst terms of abuse, while to be called a "Communist" is one of the most damaging insults to an American, we really need not wonder at this mutual lack of confidence. Furthermore, each side's distrust of the other is fed by his lack of confidence in his own loyalty to negotiated arms limitations.

However we interpret the progress made to date and the results achieved in fifteen years of disarmament negotiations, "perhaps the principal lesson to be learnt from all the long frustrating exchanges between the Soviets and the West has been that the three central issues—disarmament, Germany and European security—are inseparably interlocked; no agreed solution can be found for one without the others."[4]

There is no need to lose hope, however. We must recognise that disarmament agreements can be reached even without mutual confidence. Robert Bowie had good reason to stress the fact that the criterion for any promising disarmament agreement is to adjust it in such a way that it is to the advantage of both sides to adhere to its provisions: "the Soviets can be trusted to pursue

[4] A. Nutting, *Disarmament. An Outline of Negotiations*, London 1959, p. 50.

their own interests as they see them. Hence measures for arms control should be reliable if they can be so devised that compliance will be more in the Soviet interest than evasion or violation."[5] On the other hand, no agreement on arms control will remain reliable and effective so long as it does not serve the national interest of both parties. Professor Bowie adds the interesting suggestion that every agreement should make provision for the possibility that a signatory might withdraw from it at short notice. The threat of withdrawal of a signatory might possibly induce the others to think twice about any treaty infringement they might themselves have in mind. There is probably a good deal of scope for future negotiations in gearing our own disarmament initiative to the vital interests of the other side. It is clear that every disarmament measure has two aspects: it can lead to certain improvements in one's own security—perhaps only after some time; but it will lead equally to a weakening in one's own security—again possibly only after the lapse of a considerable period of time. Consideration of the question—"to what extent do possible infringements by the other side of rules we have made between us leave me worse off than I am now?"—is thirdly a necessary step towards weighing up these two aspects.

All or Nothing?

Defence and disarmament strategy have correctly been referred to as Siamese twins. Paul Nitze has said that the aim of a policy directed at arms limitation and mutual control is to make mutual deterrence more reliable, stable and secure, and it is clear that the aim of defence strategy could be defined in the same words.[6] Arms control and deterrent—or defence—strategy have indeed the same goal: to maximise stability, i.e. to maximise one's own security while avoiding a military posture that is provocative because suitable for preventive attack. (One's posture must therefore be as little dependent as possible on the need to respond immediately

[5] R. Bowie, "Basic Requirements for Arms Control," in *Daedalus* (Journal of the American Academy of Arts and Sciences), Special Issue on Arms Control, Fall 1960. Later since republished as *Arms Control, Disarmament and National Security*, New York 1961.

[6] Nitze's nomination by Kennedy, since this book went to press, as Assistant Secretary for International Security Affairs in the U.S. Department of Defence can perhaps be regarded as a sign that the new U.S. Administration will make greater efforts than its predecessor to achieve a unified disarmament and defence policy.

to the imminence of enemy attack.) Such a posture is of inestimable value from one's own unilateral standpoint; but it is the more so when one's enemy disposes of a like posture.

Measured against the noble, but Utopian, objective of total disarmament, the aim of achieving a stable equilibrium may seem in every way a modest one; but when one measures it against the growing danger of thermo-nuclear war, it is seen to merit our very greatest efforts. The greater the detail in which the various separate objectives are presented, however, the greater the probability that the interests of the other side will be impaired, and the greater the likelihood of making negotiation of an agreement difficult or impossible. Comprehensive proposals that include not only a ban on nuclear tests but also both a simultaneous ban on the production of nuclear weapons and the destruction of existing weapons, that aim at bringing all these measures under far-reaching and watertight control, at controlling long-range missiles, heavy bombers and satellites, at setting up a global inspection system for protection against surprise attack, and finally at fixing the relative strength of conventional land, sea and air forces under a system of reciprocal controls—such proposals have clearly as little prospect of accomplishment as the Soviet proposal for short-term total disarmament. Even if agreement were to be reached on such comprehensive plans, there would necessarily be very little confidence from the outset in the general intention or ability to adhere to the agreement: lack of confidence would secretly tempt the participants at best to honour the agreement in the letter rather than in the spirit, and to cast about for means of evasion not specifically ruled out by the treaty. Nobody today doubts that it is out of the question to subject the, perhaps, 200,000 nuclear war-heads in existence at the end of 1960, to a comprehensive system of control. Assessment and control of existing fissile material is at this stage even less possible. The preparation of an inventory of long-range missiles is, at all events, a theoretical possibility in view of the relatively small number now extant. But in view of the enormous difficulties facing the conclusion of a satisfactory agreement on inspection, this too seems in practice to be ruled out.[7]

One does not have to agree with Anthony Nutting's conclusion[8]

[7] What is more, control of all I.C.B.Ms. is of doubtful utility because this would be to throw away the advantages of "hard" systems.

[8] A. Nutting, *Disarmament*, p. 51.

that there is no hope of making even a *start* on disarmament so
long as there is no agreement on four minimum demands:

  (*a*) a ban on nuclear tests under appropriate controls;
  (*b*) the establishment of a nuclear-free zone in Central Europe
       in conjunction with measures for the "thinning out" of
       military forces in Germany and neighbouring countries;
  (*c*) the status of Berlin; and finally, if possible,
  (*d*) some measure of progress in solving the German problem
       "such as the setting up of an all-German commission to
       make proposals for reunification by stages."

Disarmament initiatives are only politically relevant if they are
so concrete and limited that they are acceptable to both sides, that
it seems to be to the advantage of both sides to keep to them, and
that their effectiveness in preserving the peace (even given the
expected changes in the field of military technology) cannot in the
foreseeable future be questioned.

There is no prime necessity for linking in a "package deal"
disarmament objectives in more than one field, or disarmament and
other political objectives. On the contrary, it would seem not only
possible but even desirable to deal with certain disarmament steps
on their own. Indeed, these are some disarmament objectives that,
to everybody's advantage, could be achieved through unilateral
initiatives and not through specific agreements. An outstanding
example was the cessation of nuclear tests on the part of the major
powers between 1958 and 1961, brought about by the unilateral
declaration of the Soviet Union.[9] A unilateral peacetime declaration
by the West renouncing the first use of nuclear weapons in war
could hold out similar prospects of success. But such a declaration
would presuppose a satisfactory level of conventional armaments
in the West, which does not exist at the moment. Both examples
show that, given certain assumptions about disarmament, unilateral
actions can serve a useful purpose, in so far as they are carefully
calculated and carefully limited. The extreme "unilateralism" of
certain British trades union leaders is of a quite different order.

[9] This example serves to show at all events that observance of a disarmament
agreement depends on the self-interest of the participants. The French Government was not interested and has not been restrained, despite the U.N. resolution,
from carrying out tests. (H.S.) Similarly, the Russians claimed that the nuclear
tests carried out by them in 1961 were necessary for their defence, i.e. were in
their self-interest. The tests also were carried out despite a U.N. resolution
which sought to restrain them. (Trans.)

Let us agree that there is no question of the morality behind it. But unilateral nuclear disarmament on the part of the West would certainly be a mistake: if the West were to espouse such a concept, the door would be wide open to Soviet aggression and nuclear blackmail. Instead of this unilateralism we should exhaustively investigate the possibilities open to us of unilateral action of the type described above.

Thomas Schelling points out[10] the interesting fact that disarmament agreements are, moreover, attainable by tacit agreement between the major powers. Such tacit agreements can be reached through unilateral initiative and education of the other side in the end and the means of such initiatives. An outstanding example of the effectiveness of such methods is the refusal of the major powers up till now to pass on either nuclear weapons or production know-how to other powers. (In making this point we must specifically draw attention to the fact that a breach of this tacit agreement, such as might be brought about by placing Polaris missiles at the disposal of the NATO allies, would lead to similar results in the East—at any rate as regards China.) A tacit agreement seems also to exist as regards armed aircraft keeping to prescribed patrol areas, if we disregard the as yet unexplained case of the RB 47 aircraft shot down off Murmansk. It is conceivable that tacit agreement might in future permit mutually unrestricted operation of inspection and reconnaissance satellites by both sides. It is also conceivable that the major powers, in any future conventional conflict in which they might participate, might tacitly agree not to use nuclear weapons. It may be imagined that such agreements would not be reached if attempts were made to negotiate them officially. (Indeed it is conceivable that they would be less effective in the form of a negotiated treaty, which would inevitably be susceptible to interpretation, than in the form of a tacit agreement.) We are here up against the principle, stressed above, that both sides will only conclude or keep such agreements when they have a greater interest in keeping them than in breaking them.

Unilateral actions and tacit agreements, it is true, only yield limited results. They cannot therefore be regarded as something that makes other forms of disarmament negotiation superfluous. The question is, however, whether future disarmament negotia-

[10] T. C. Schelling, "Reciprocal Measures for Arms Stabilization," in *Daedalus*, Fall 1960 (see note 5, p. 135).

tions must continue to be conducted in the same spectacular, public setting as in the past. Their public character has been a disadvantage to them, and has necessarily made them into an arena for world-wide propaganda. It therefore seems desirable that disarmament negotiations should in future be conducted through normal diplomatic channels. If disarmament negotiations were to be switched back on to the level of traditional diplomatic intercourse between the United States and the Soviet Union, the question would naturally arise as to how far the two partners could rely on the allies of either falling into line with their major power. The Soviet Union will ask itself to what extent Germany or France will follow the United States, and the United States will have to ask itself how far China will follow the Soviet Union. A disarmament agreement which excludes China is of as little value and as dangerous as one which excludes France or Germany.

A comprehensive disarmament agreement is at the moment improbable, because NATO's high degree of dependence on its nuclear weapons decisively circumscribes the West's freedom of action in the field of disarmament policy. Because of the present imbalance between the conventional forces of the East and those of the West, any percentage reduction, or pegging, of their present size would be calculated to freeze the difficulties now besetting disarmament. The West cannot embark on comprehensive nuclear disarmament unless simultaneous steps are taken to equalise the disparate levels of conventional armed forces' strength. It is also out of regard for the imperatives of disarmament policy that the West must terminate its one-sided dependence on nuclear weapons: instead, it must work out a newly oriented strategy and a re-modelled armament structure, and place decided stress on an adequate conventional defence capability. On this crucial point of armaments disparity between East and West it once again becomes clear that defence and disarmament strategy go hand in hand and are subject to the same basic considerations. We must not regard arms control—a cherished, but so far unrealised objective—as a substitute for additional efforts in the conventional field. "If the disparity in local power becomes too great, the Soviet Union will lose any incentive for responsible negotiations. No scheme of arms control will then seem to enhance its security as much as its existing (conventional) superiority."[11] On the other hand it would

[11] H. A. Kissinger, *The Necessity for Choice*, New York 1960, p. 94.

be an expensive, dangerous, and (because of the time element) perhaps fruitless course to pursue, if NATO were to raise its conventional armament to the level of that of the Eastern bloc in order to bring about the compulsory limitation of conventional arms. Nevertheless, a firm decision by the West to strengthen its conventional forces would act as a considerable incentive to the Soviet Union.

The Problem of Inspection

Public opinion has seen clearly during the last few years that the focal point of the efforts devoted to what is popularly called disarmament is the bringing about of arms limitations and their inspection. Thus there is little hope of the complete elimination of nuclear weapons since there is no sort of control to which even the approximate determination of stockpiles would be susceptible: there is no question of devising and (particularly in times of stress) operating control machinery which could not be circumvented. Each side will suspect the other of evading the controls, since as few as twenty H-bombs could decisively alter the world situation to the advantage of the power having them. If fighting broke out, inspection and control might cease at once, and the production of nuclear weapons would then presumably start afresh. Every major power is, therefore, under the strongest stimulus on no account to give up all its nuclear weapons or to submit to controls. The well-worn phrase "general and controlled disarmament" therefore needs, particularly in the minds of politicians who make daily use of it, close substantiation if it is to ring true. Specialists know well that it is the setting up of mutual controls guaranteeing against surprise attack that should be the focal point of general "controls."

The setting up of reliable inspection facilities is the key to the general problem of disarmament. A relatively simple means of affording protection against surprise attack is the setting up of overlapping radar stations able to penetrate well into the territory of the other side and give relatively early warning of the launching of missiles or the take-off of bombers: but it is obvious that this would not be an adequate degree of protection against surprise. Inspection machinery is most effective when it is set up on enemy territory, and this is possible both on the ground and in the air. Taking this further, such inspection machinery can comprise systems designed either to survey the entire territory at the disposal of the other side or merely part of it, or systems specifically excluding part of the enemy territory (particularly, for instance, those areas where he has installed his strategic nuclear retaliatory weapons). So far as it is a question of ground-based inspection systems, these can be either stationary or mobile.

The idea of inspection as a safeguard against surprise attacks was first given concrete expression in 1955 in Eisenhower's "Open Skies" proposal. It is true that, at the time, intercontinental missiles did not exist: inspection from the air is of only limited effectiveness against surprise attacks carried out by this means. At best it can provide a warning period of 25 to 30 minutes against a nuclear strategic surprise attack, provided that the inspectors have the technical means to communicate their reports to their own capitals. Inspection systems of all kinds are, furthermore, particularly unproductive in periods of tension; in the event of conventional war each belligerent government would be able to circumscribe or to cripple the enemy inspection system installed on its territory, in order to conceal its own troop movements. In this way the other side would be prevented from recognising whether and when its adversary was about to extend the struggle to the strategic nuclear dimension. But, looking at things from the reverse viewpoint, each of the two major powers might for this very reason be interested in having inspection personnel of the other major power at hand in times of crisis, so as to be able, with their help, to leave the other major power in no doubt that one had no intention oneself of making a strategic nuclear attack and thereby provoking a pre-emptive blow. All such considerations strike one as very artificial and carry little conviction. On the assumption that dissemination of nuclear weapons to further governments can successfully be prevented, a better and more convincing guarantee against strategic nuclear attack than complex and—when all is said and done—unsatisfactory inspection schemes is offered by the hardening of the major powers' strategic nuclear weapons systems.

The Soviet rejection of airborne controls over the territory of the Soviet Union is absolutely logical and distinct from the traditional Russian xenophobia and the specifically Communist suspicion of foreigners on the territory of the Soviet Union. Such controls could give the United States enormously important intelligence of the location of strategic targets in the Soviet Union and, in particular, make possible an accurate geodetic survey of Soviet missile sites. With such intelligence in the hands of the United States the American nuclear strategic surprise attack so much feared by the Russians would seem substantially more dangerous than hitherto. On the other hand the Russians know already today the location of all strategic targets within the United States: they have made a geodetic survey of these targets and, to this extent, have an important edge over the strategic nuclear power of the United States. Why should they give up this great advantage without some return? Even the conclusion of an agreement on the relatively harmless machinery for supervising a test ban— machinery involving fixed control stations—has encountered tough opposition from the Soviet leaders. Experience makes it seem quite improbable that the Soviet Union will agree to measures of inspection on its sovereign territory that go significantly further. We should mislead ourselves if we were to see in this only the expression of ill-will: it is more to the point to judge this question exclusively from the standpoint of Soviet interest. For this reason the recent French proposal for concentrating inspection on the relatively small number of I.C.B.Ms. now in existence has no prospect whatever of acceptance: it would, furthermore, give rise to the danger that the hardened strategic nuclear systems of the Western powers might subsequently be "softened" again and the situation brought about by the "hardening" might thereby be destabilised.

In view of the colossal difficulties facing the institution of reliable systems—difficulties arising from the manifold interests of the participants—there would seem to be little hope that the major powers will be able to agree on measures for mutual inspection: let us face the fact that there are many far less important matters on which they have been absolutely unable to agree. It would therefore seem desirable initially to contemplate more modest steps towards arms limitation. The less these affect the vital sensitivities of the major powers—and in particular their sovereign territory—the more likely they are to have some prospect of success. Such partial solutions may be limited either as regards area, or as regards substance. A limited regional agreement was recently concluded regarding Antarctica. The value of this treaty as a legal precedent cannot be overestimated. Central Europe has for years been the focal point of all discussions about limited regional agreements. The focal point in discussions about limited substantive agreements has been the proposal for a general ban on nuclear test detonations.

Cessation of Tests as a First Step

The idea of a general ban on nuclear test detonations has grown primarily out of the world-wide concern over the genetic effects of nuclear fall-out. In the meantime it has acquired an additional and extraordinary psychological importance because public opinion throughout the world would see the achievement of a ban on tests as the first recognisable step on the road to disarmament and, to this extent, as a contribution to the relaxation of tension: such a ban could represent a starting-point for the restoration of a minimum of confidence in the readiness of the partners to negotiate seriously on disarmament. Above all, however, the serious negotiations between the major powers on the question of an end to tests have acquired a high strategic and political importance because the conclusion of a universal and binding test ban would for the first time hold out the prospect of imposing a restraint, backed by international law, on the further spread of nuclear weapons.

The Americans have been slow to embrace this idea because they believed that a ban on test explosions would deprive them of the advantage which they possessed in the development of the so-called "small" nuclear weapons and which they wished to consolidate through further tests. From the point of view of the theory of the advantageousness of tactical nuclear warfare (developed since the mid-1950s) it seemed desirable to press on seriously with the development of tactical nuclear weapons; and for this purpose it was necessary to be able to test them. Had the Americans endorsed the Soviet proposal for a ban on tests in 1956, when the Russians first suggested it, they would probably have retained a considerable technical superiority in the field of thermonuclear weapons also. Up to that time the United States had tested about six different types of H-bomb, the Soviet Union only one. But American rejection of an agreed end to tests enabled the Soviet Union after 1956 to carry out live tests of a fairly large number of newly developed weapons. The Russians have thus been able to go a long way towards catching up the American lead in the field of weapons development. From this historical experience we can see that agreement on a general cessation of tests would not jeopardise the maintenance of the present American lead in the development of small nuclear weapons, but would rather stabilise it. Nevertheless, the cessation of tests has at all times had influential opponents in the United States, Edward Teller at their head. They argue that the test ban not only affects small weapons, but also prevents the perfection of the process of hardening strategic nuclear weapons, since it makes impossible experiments in the nuclear bombardment of blast-protected or mobile missile launching sites, warning systems, etc. Furthermore, very great importance is attached to the argument that the number of control measures and control stations so far conceded by the Soviet Union—a number alleged to be on the low side—would not prevent the Russians from carrying out secret underground test explosions in the future.

The negotiations between the United States, the United Kingdom and the Soviet Union on a test ban agreement are for the present held up by the question of the control of underground explosions. The American attitude on this matter has not been without its contradictions. A bitter debate is now taking place in the United States on the advisability of a cessation of tests. It is nevertheless hard to see how the risk run by the Americans can be as great as Teller and others allege. For the Russians would run an extraordinarily great political and psychological risk if they were to fly in the face of a treaty and embark on underground testing. If one single person were to defect, his disclosures would be enough to put the agreed control machinery on the track and to lead them to concrete evidence of Soviet infringement of the treaty. The Soviet Union, which sets itself up before the whole world as a peaceloving nation, can scarcely afford to stand thus convicted of a flagrant infringement of negotiated disarmament agreements.

In the negotiations over a test ban the Russians have made relatively far-reaching concessions regarding controls. This contrasts with their initial rejection of every sort of control on Soviet territory. The conclusion of an agreement on an ending to tests would be something of inestimable value, if only to have this legal precedent in favour of mutual controls written into international law. Furthermore, such an agreement and the experience to be gained from it for future disarmament negotiations would be a valuable experiment in the keeping of disarmament treaties in one's own interest. A global ban on nuclear tests, locking the door against the independent development of nuclear weapons by further states, would be something of quite unusual importance and would statisfy one material precondition of the stabilisation of the strategic nuclear equilibrium in the world. It is naturally uncertain whether China and France would enter into a world-wide agreement.[12] Peking's admission to the United Nations would probably be the minimum price for China's accession to such a treaty, even if other security considerations do not make her admission seem ever more necessary. Should no test ban agreement be reached, however, China would at all events soon become a nuclear power, and her acquisition of long-range means of delivery would then be of only secondary importance. The courses that the other powers would adopt as of natural necessity, in consequence of such an eventuality, would be of the first importance and would have a profoundly adverse affect on the global system of nuclear strategy.

What of the Future?

Up till now we Germans have learnt very little about the extremely complex question of arms limitation, inspection and control.[13] We know next to nothing of the motives and the objectives of the political strategy underlying the disarmament negotiations between East and West. We are not, of course, alone in our ignorance: throughout the world the levels are unsatis-factorily low both of research into this partly academic, partly technical field of study, and of the education of public opinion in its implications. Almost nowhere does the necessary unity of defence and disarmament strategy seem to exist. Disarmament and control systems become rapidly obsolete in face of the current tempo of progress in military technology. Space travel is just round the corner and will introduce quite new perspectives. Arms limitation systems must, therefore, in future be devised to antici-pate future conditions, and they must take into account future developments in enemy psychology as well as our own. At least it

[12] Unless they had achieved a given degree of technical progress as regards their own nuclear weapons by the time the question arose.

[13] This lack of information is particularly marked in the field of bacteriological and chemical warfare, and as regards the control problems arising from them. At the time of going to press the writer can make no judgments on this score.

K

can be said that the correct principle underlay the Baruch Plan of 1945-6: new military inventions which give rise to new dangers, and are therefore in particular need of international control, are easier to master in the initial stage than after intensive development at the hands of several states. For this reason every effort should be made *now*, at the initial stage, to regulate space travel and bring it within the ambit of international agreement and regulation. A joint space research programme on the part of the major powers might, furthermore, have great technical and political advantages.

The most widely read books on the subject deal mainly with the necessity for disarmament and with its past history. For this reason we must now draw attention to a book which gives perhaps the best available survey of the present state of Western insight into the complex problems of arms control, and also refers to many authoritative works in the same field. This is the special (Fall 1960) edition of *Daedalus*, the Journal of the American Academy of Arts and Sciences, which brings together under the title *Arms Control* more than twenty essays by leading American specialists from Bowie, Kissinger and Kahn to Edward Teller.[14]

It is the writer's view that the prospects of international arms limitation will be at their most hopeful as long as the doors of the Nuclear Club are kept shut and its membership is not enlarged even by such indirect methods as the transfer of nuclear weapons to allied powers. Whether anything comes of this opportunity will depend first and foremost on whether we are prepared, instead of making a big propaganda and diplomatic display in the name of total disarmament, to embark on a relatively small measure of partial disarmament, which as a first step will encourage the growth of confidence necessary for taking further large steps. Perhaps one could coin the phrase "graduated disarmament." Agreement on the cessation of nuclear tests would be helpful as a first step and should be approached purely for its own sake without attempts to link it to other agreements. Agreement on a Central European zone of arms limitation, and a system of mutual control in this regionally limited area, might also prove useful as an early step: for this reason we will develop this idea in greater detail in the next chapter.

To end this chapter, let us draw attention to three general aspects of a disarmament strategy for NATO:

[14] See note 5, p. 135, and 10, p. 138.

1. In order to ensure peace through arms limitation we must know above all how future wars might arise and subsequently develop. Defence and disarmament strategies must interlock.

2. The Soviet Union will be encouraged to negotiate seriously on disarmament only if, and for as long as, NATO can convince the Soviet leaders beyond any doubt that it is able and willing to put its military strategy of posing a threat for purposes of deterrence actually into practice in an emergency.

3. If Western unity is not to be split in the course of future negotiations, the West's disarmament strategy must be approved by all the individual allied powers and must do justice in equal measure to their separate interests. If the price to be paid for this is that we put forward proposals which are liable to prejudice the universal imperative of military equilibrium and so harm the West, or leave open escape routes to our own advantage, then the old sterile disarmament roundabout will start up once again.

If the Soviet Union, despite its highly-coloured and strident disarmament propaganda, were in fact not interested in arms limitation, it should be possible to bring the fact to the notice of the world by means of a disarmament policy specifically calculated to this end. We do not, however, know whether the Soviet leaders' approach is in fact purely negative; and even if this were the case today, we cannot be sure whether this must always be the case. Even Moscow's missile euphoria will one day evaporate; even Moscow's interests are subject to the law of change. The West need not therefore shape its disarmament strategy to serve propagandist ends, even though it must constantly calculate the psychological and political effects of its initiatives. The problem of disarmament is probably the most difficult problem of contemporary politics. But this need not cause anyone to lose heart: on the contrary, modern armaments technology is imposing new political forms on us, and we ignore this at our mortal peril. These new forms may not arrive today or tomorrow. But we shall be compelled to adopt them sooner and more quickly than most political and military leaders appear to realise.

9

Disengagement Misunderstood

THE idea of easing the intractable situation in Central Europe by means of military readjustments and thereby making real progress towards the reunification of Germany was first put forward in 1952 by Dr Pfleiderer, formerly an F.D.P. representative in the Federal German parliament and later German Ambassador in Belgrade. The idea attracted little notice at the time though its stock rose a few points a little later during the discussions on the so-called Bonin Plan. It was not until the Berlin Conference of 1954, when Sir Anthony Eden came out with the idea of a Central European zone of arms limitation and control, that the idea first assumed international importance.

From Eden I to Rapacki III

It would be a waste of time to make a detailed survey here of the historical evolution of the disengagement concept. Those wishing to take a closer look at the matter should read Eugene Hinterhoff's book[1] or Michael Howard's shorter essay.[2] The fact that these two most important books on the problem of disengagement should have been written by Englishmen shows clearly that there has always been a special interest in the idea in Britain—and, moreover, that there still is. One must agree with Sir John Slessor, who writes in the foreword to Hinterhoff's book: "But the author is perfectly right in suggesting that adherence to the *status quo* (which, anyway, is constantly changing), talk about German reunification in freedom, liberation of captive peoples, relaxation of tension and so on are no substitute for a practical, constructive, long-term master plan for a political solution."

The proposals for working towards a Central European settlement which public discussion has grouped together under the

[1] E. Hinterhoff, *Disengagement*, London 1959.
[2] M. Howard, *Disengagement in Europe*, Penguin Books, Harmondsworth 1958.

popular title "disengagement" have suffered from association with
a phrase that has impeded their understanding. It has widely—and
erroneously—been assumed that they aim essentially at a political
solution accompanied by the complete withdrawal of the Americans
from the European continent. George Kennan's proposals are to
some extent responsible for this. For the most part, however,
disengagement proposals emanating from Western sources, particularly those coming from Britain (from Eden, through Gaitskell,
to Healey) have confined themselves expressly to the Central
European area and never dreamt for a moment of including withdrawal of U.S. troops. Eden later submitted a variant of his
proposals to the Geneva Summit Conference of 1955. His idea
was to ascertain whether there was any chance of a demilitarised
zone between East and West inside Europe, stationing of troops
within this zone to be subject to mutual agreement.

When, two years later, the Russians seemed for the first time
to be ready seriously to pursue these ideas, further consideration
of them was obstructed by the Federal Government. In the same
year Hugh Gaitskell made a set of very far-reaching proposals, and
stressed the explosive nature of the Eastern European situation—
something that had become clear enough through events in Poland
and Hungary. This proposal was later worked out in detail by
Denis Healey. These proposals related to Germany, Poland,
Czechoslovakia and Hungary (and—if possible—Rumania and
Bulgaria). Healey gave this concept the title "A neutral belt in
Europe."[3] The British Labourites laid down three conditions:
Germany should accept the Oder-Neisse frontier; NATO should be
preserved; U.S. forces should remain in Europe. Eisenhower and
F. J. Strauss made remarks in the spring of 1957 which—assuming
that German unity could be achieved—could be taken to imply
concurrence with the idea of neutralisation. In the same year
George Kennan gave the brilliant Reith Lectures which have since
become famous: these appeared to have the intention of putting
up for debate the idea that American troops should be withdrawn
and that the United States should thus disengage itself politically
from Europe. These ideas, no more than hinted at by Kennan,

---

[3] Even Healey's use of the word "neutral" in his title has made it more
difficult for the general public, so far as it is politically aware, to heed his
arguments. In fact, the neutrality or neutralisation of the states included in the
zone is by no means a prerequisite.

have largely contributed to discrediting the whole idea of disengagement and the very word itself. The proposals of Gaitskell and Healey have become the official policy of the Labour Party. They have also, after a lapse of time and with certain modifications, become an ingredient of the German Social Democratic political platform. Fritz Erler was their chief advocate: it was not least for this reason that they were brusquely rejected by the Federal Government. In America also they evoked a hostile response, with which Dean Acheson was conspicuously associated. It was evident from his criticism that he had not troubled to reach a careful understanding of the matter and was clearly influenced by the political and military failure of the "disengagement" experiment he had instituted in Korea in 1950: this experiment, of course, took place in circumstances that were in no way comparable.

In the autumn of 1957 the so-called Rapacki Plan was made known to the world. This at first confined itself to the creation of an atom-free zone in Central Europe and in the next twelve months was twice altered and expanded by Rapacki until, in its final version, it appeared to bear some resemblance to the British ideas. The Rapacki Plan in all its versions was rejected by the West, the decision being chiefly influenced by Bonn and Washington. The impression had gained ground in these capitals that, because these proposals were of Communist origin, they would confer military and political advantages on the Soviet Union. Although the Western rejection of Rapacki was bolstered up primarily by military arguments, the Western governments never seriously worked out just what precisely the implications of general Central European "disengagement" would be for the military confrontation in the area. The flat, uncompromising rejection of the Rapacki Plan and the refusal to contemplate any negotiations on proposals of a like nature must be regarded, even today, as a diplomatic failure on the part of the West. The German Social Democrats once again took up the idea of a zone of arms limitation and control early in 1959, and made it the subject of an independent and detailed presentation in November of the same year.[4]

[4] In the form of a comprehensive speech by the writer to the German Bundestag: the points made in the rest of the chapter constitute a shortened, but in essentials unchanged, version of that presentation. The military analysis of the writer's proposals which the Federal Chancellor commissioned from the Operations Staff of the Bundeswehr has unfortunately not been published in any of the versions said to exist: nor has it been made available to the writer.

Arms Limitation and Control in Central Europe

In April 1959 F. J. Strauss stated: "The demands of military equilibrium in Europe must be met. By military equilibrium is meant not arithmetical equality but broad comparability of the forces needed for defence on the one side with those of the other." This statement is certainly correct. No matter in what way the military or political situation in Central Europe may be modified, a balance of power must be maintained between NATO and the Warsaw Pact. Any regional arms limitation in Central Europe must have as its aim a rough parity as regards:

(a) the populations concerned and their economic strength;

(b) the number of troops remaining in the area and their weapons;

(c) the area to be affected by the regional arms control arrangements; and

(d) the military obstacles in the area.

In short, a zone of arms control must not be allowed to alter the present tactical or strategic situation to the advantage or disadvantage of either of the participating military blocs.

It is clear from this requirement for parity that there could be no question of any zone of arms limitation which, for example, included only the two zones of Germany. Nor would there be parity if the zone were to embrace the area, say, from the Atlantic coast of Europe up to the Western border of the Soviet Union. Parity would only exist if the zone were to embrace the Federal Republic on the one side, and the so-called "D.D.R.," Poland, Czechoslovakia—and possibly Hungary—on the other. One of the most interesting points in Rapacki's proposals—and one that we must cling to in any future negotiations—was his express implication that East Germany, plus Poland, plus Czechoslovakia would be regarded as the equivalent of the Federal Republic for the purpose of negotiations.

The establishment of a zone of arms limitation and control in the area outlined above would by no means be conditional on the Federal Republic's leaving NATO or the Eastern states leaving the Warsaw Pact; any other treaty ties would also remain unaffected.

In the first stage mutual international controls would be necessary on the ground: these would comprise both fixed (notably at ports and airfields) and mobile controls. Mutual aerial observation would also be required. In addition a ceiling would have to be placed on foreign troops within the zone and on those of the states included in it. Assuming, to start with, a Bundeswehr strength of 300,000, the numerical ratio between the Bundeswehr and the Polish army might be fixed at 3 : 2, that between the Federal Republic and the "D.D.R." at 3 : 1, that with the Czechoslovak army also at 3 : 1. This would produce an overall ratio of 3 : 4 between the forces of the Federal Republic and those of the Satellite states within the zone, or—if Hungary were to be included —one of 3 : 4·5. These troops would have to be limited strictly to conventional weapons, and their arms would have to be subject to international and reciprocal control: this control would naturally have to apply also to the paramilitary formations which exist in several of the states.

For the next step it would be necessary for both alliances to establish forward radar stations along the opposite boundary of the zone, i.e. the Warsaw Pact countries along (say) the Rhine, and NATO along (say) the Bug. In the next phase the agreed reduction of foreign troops would take place by stages, under mutual controls, after which small residual detachments, in about brigade strength, would remain as symbols along the dividing line. The symbolic occupation of Berlin would, of course, have to be maintained.

The military and political advantages of such a solution would be as follows:

1. The task of the NATO shield—that of fighting delaying actions so as to win time for deciding whether to use nuclear weapons—would be eased. The West would no longer be compelled to pose the implausible threat of immediate and universal nuclear response to every sort of aggression. Should a zone of control be established containing only the very minimum of foreign troops, an attempt to launch a general offensive with conventional forces would require a long period of time to mount. This would permit NATO to take its time over the decision to launch its counterblow. The danger of the "accidental" outbreak of total war between the major powers would be considerably reduced.

2. The process of easing tensions in Central Europe by means of military readjustments might make it possible to take steps towards a solution of the German problem. This would seem impossible as long as the military *status quo* is maintained.

3. The establishment of a zone of arms control in Central Europe and the experience of the manipulation of mutual international arms controls which it would make possible, might serve as a test case for general disarmament. It could create enough confidence to encourage the powers to proceed with arms limitation and control elsewhere than in this Central European zone.

The requirement for parity stressed above, would be generally statisfied. The West/East ratio of the areas affected would be of the order 1 : 2 (namely, 96,500 square miles of the Federal Republic as against 120,000 square miles of Poland, 42,500 square miles of the "D.D.R.," and 50,000 square miles of Czechoslovakia: this totals 212,000 square miles on the Eastern side—with the possibility that Hungary might also come in). In breadth the affected area would extend for 200-250 miles to the West of the dividing line, and 500-625 miles to the east of it (with reductions at the northern and southern extremities where salients would be formed by Soviet-controlled East Prussia and Hungary should the latter not become part of the zone of control. The ratio of the depth of the areas to be given up between the dividing line and the forward military positions would also be of the order 1 : 2. The ratio of the populations affected, namely about 53 million on the western and 58 million on the eastern side (plus Hungary), would be about 1 : 1. The imbalance between the greater area to be evacuated by Soviet troops and that of West Germany, would be compensated for by the fact that the economic power of the Federal Republic is much greater than that of the four above-named Eastern bloc states.

Objections and Counter-objections

The military objections raised in the West against the ideas put forward hinge almost entirely on spatial requirements. Some people, for example, maintain that there would be too little room for NATO's strategic nuclear weapons to be adequately deployed or, alternatively, to be provided with sufficient area for forward protection. This objection smacks clearly of dilettantism; for, as far as Western Europe is concerned strategic weapons are stationed exclusively in the United Kingdom, and there is so far no intention of deploying them on the European continent. The creation of a zone of control in Central Europe would not make the U.K.-based strategic weapons any more vulnerable than they are now. There is also no force in the general argument that NATO could not give up the 200-250 miles broad Federal Republic because the area available for manœuvre would lose critically in depth. The Soviet army stands today 60 miles from the Kiel Canal and 75 miles from Frankfurt. In future it would be 500-625 miles distant from these vital points: its tanks would not be stationed just across the Elbe but away to the east of the Vistula and the Bug. Whereas today the Soviet army need cross only one river in order to move forward into the Federal Republic, and whereas the exits from the Baltic are immediately exposed to attack by the Soviet ground forces, these would in future—together with the bases for their naval forces and seaborne troops—be stationed very much further to the east. The Soviet army would have, in the event of war, *three* major rivers to cross, at each of which it would be exposed to the full force of interdiction at the hands of the Allied tactical air forces and medium-range missiles. By contrast the troops of the other NATO powers stationed in the Federal Republic would have to cross only one extra river, viz. the Rhine.

As part of the spatial argument the objection is sometimes raised that NATO's flanks would become exposed in Scandinavia and southern Europe. This objection stems from the theory that a Central Europe emptied of troops would become a vacuum into which the Russians could pour and thence proceed to roll up the flanks. To this it must be stated that before Soviet troops, advancing across the Bug into Central Europe, could regain the positions they occupy today, NATO forces would have crossed the Rhine to reoccupy *at least* its present-day positions.

The vacuum argument is, furthermore, completely misleading in that, as should be plain to all, the forces of the Bundeswehr would continue to be stationed at the centre of Europe. The objection raised by the German military in this connexion, that NATO would be unable effectively to counter a Soviet move to reoccupy the Central zone previously evacuated by the Soviet army (the so-called re-entry problem) is equally misleading. The Soviet ground forces would, in fact, require a good deal of time to cross Poland and the "D.D.R." and to reoccupy their "take-off" positions in the latter territory. This would give NATO a longer warning period and more time for forward deployment to the east of the German western frontier (and possibly to the east of the control-zone dividing line); in any case NATO troops would, as has been pointed out above, reach the positions they now occupy much sooner than the Russians would reach theirs, particularly as transportation facilities are better in the Federal Republic than in Poland.

The objection will next be raised that NATO would be critically weakened if it did not have tactical nuclear weapons in the front line area on the territory of the Federal Republic. The answer to this is that the present role of NATO tactical nuclear weapons in the Federal Republic is, as publicly announced, to compensate for the superiority of the massed Soviet conventional troops. Should, however, these Soviet troops be withdrawn eastwards from the frontier areas, there would be no need for NATO to deploy tactical nuclear weapons inside the zone for the former purpose. Should, however, Soviet troops re-enter the zone, then the West's tactical nuclear weapons could without hesitation be reintroduced into the Federal Republic from across the German western frontier. Even in such a contingency NATO forces would have an advantage over the Soviet troops similarly engaged both as regards distance to be travelled and, in consequence, the time that would be taken. Furthermore we must point out that what are, at present, the West's most important tactical nuclear weapons, namely the fighter-bomber squadrons in the Eiffel and Hunsrück, would only have to be moved a few miles further west in the event of the setting up of a zone of control, whereas the Soviet squadrons at present based in the "D.D.R." would have to be moved back very considerable distances to the east.

To the objection that a so-called small war might arise between the forces of the states within the zone, one may reply that, given the ratio of military power outlined above, the Bundeswehr would always be able to hold and defend the frontiers of the Federal Republic against the joint forces of the "D.D.R.," Poland and Czechoslovakia. The Bundeswehr would also be able to bring to a halt, or repel, limited local action carried out by the forces of these states. Since, in the same breath, the fear is often expressed that the Soviet Union or the Satellites might have reason to fear that the Bundeswehr would, under these conditions, go over to the attack, we must refer back to our suggestion that small detachments of foreign troops should remain deployed along the dividing line.

Let us now consider three objections concerning the control of nuclear disarmament within the zone. It is said, for one thing, that the establishment of a zone of control could not, in an emergency, prevent the bombardment of the zone by nuclear weapons from outside. Bombardment with nuclear weapons would, however, be a most manifestly belligerent action on the part of the nuclear power concerned: its action would immediately invite retaliation from outside the zone by the allies of the state attacked. The possibility of this would compel the aggressor to make an early attempt to eliminate the bases of his victim's allies. In other words, bombardment of the zone from outside would mean general war in Europe. In such a case, however, the resultant situation for the West would be no different from what it is today. We must, of course, agree that non-deployment of nuclear weapons within the zone does not rule out the possibility of such bombardment: but should nuclear weapons be deployed inside the zone, as is the case today, any outbreak of fighting would be more likely to lead to an exchange of nuclear blows. The next objection, that warheads for so-called dual purpose weapons (above all for fighter-bombers) would be easy to conceal within the zone and so elude control, is certainly correct: but it applies not only to the proposed Central European zone of control but to any attempt whatever to enforce international or general arms control. Finally, it will be maintained that it will be possible, despite all controls, secretly to introduce warheads for dual-purpose weapons into the zone. This objection also has force. On any occasion, however, on which actual use was made of nuclear weapons by one side, the other would receive corresponding help from its allies.

It is primarily in the Federal Republic that criticism—which has there become public and vocal—of the proposal for a Central European zone of arms limitation and control is decked out in the guise of military argumentation. We have seen above how valid these arguments were. But against them can be ranged the supporting testimony of a number of independent military authorities, such as Liddell Hart, Field-Marshal Montgomery, Sir John Slessor (who has many times championed the cause, the latest occasion being his detailed statement of November 1960), and General Eddelman, who as Commander of U.S. Army, Europe, supported the proposals in May 1959. So long as General Heusinger remains in the active service of the Federal Government his public statements on this subject cannot count as those of an independent authority: we must wait and see, however, whether he will one day emerge as an independent commentator and, if so, what he will say. It has leaked out in Bonn that he holds by no means so negative a position towards the Rapacki Plan as the Federal Government, although the Rapacki Plan must be regarded as no more than a preliminary step towards the proposals outlined above —and a step that, in itself, is not yet acceptable. General Norstad also spoke in 1959 on behalf of the creation of a Central European zone of control. He put special stress upon inspection by overlapping radar screens. Since his remarks at the spring 1960 sitting of the NATO Council in Istanbul failed to secure unanimous agreement, he extended his proposals to cover an area between the Dneiper and the Atlantic.

Of particular interest in this respect, however, is Defence Minister Strauss's statement of October 1959: "We do not wish to appear obstructive towards the cause of disarmament: we also believe disarmament to be essential to the easing of tension. It would, of course, be dishonourable to say that inspection and control might take place anywhere in the world—only not in Germany. But we Germans must give a good example, and we have said that we are prepared to make the Federal Republic, either as a whole or in part, into a zone of inspection or control. This does not mean that the zone of inspection and control is identical with the limits of the Federal Republic, but it means making the Federal Republic, either wholly or in part, into a component of a zone of control and inspection in accordance with proposals agreed between the major powers. If the major powers cannot agree among themselves, any proposals that Germany might make would not be of world-shaking importance. But if they do agree, then there are no particular German wishes in the matter which would stand in the way of such agreement. . . . There is no point in arguing that the disarmament zone should extend as far as the Urals if the Russians were against it. The inspection zone, which might perhaps be the first phase of more comprehensive disarmament, must extend as far to the east as the Russians are prepared to agree. . . . The West would have to offer something of equal value in return. That is why I have been at pains to use this very careful expression 'as a whole or in part.' The 'as a whole' allows for the possibility, however, that if equivalence were to be forthcoming, the whole of the Federal Republic could of course form a component."

It does not detract from the value of Strauss's concession that he later attempted, for political reasons, to water down his remarks. For the sake of accuracy, however, we must point out that Strauss was against a Central European zone of control for its own sake: he would not agree to it unless it were the first of a number of simultaneously agreed further steps.

The establishment of a Central European zone of arms limitation and control would naturally have military and political consequences. At the moment it would entail the transfer of about four American and two British divisions, plus some smaller formations of the other Western allies, to behind the German western frontier. The cost of this transfer would inevitably be considerable, and large sums would have to be invested in re-creating the logistic support facilities that had been given up. The Federal Republic would have to play its part in meeting these costs. On the Soviet side, however, the costs would be no less—indeed, they would be substantially higher. In other respects, however, the area between the German western frontier and the Atlantic is completely adequate for the additional storage space and deployment of the forces mentioned above. Under the scheme adopted by the Lisbon resolution of the NATO Council this area ought to have been maintaining military forces several times larger, whereas in fact almost no NATO units are today situated there.

We do not suggest that the American, British and French forces deployed in Europe—apart from the "symbolic" detachments remaining in the zone—should give up their so-called tactical nuclear weapons. The "symbolic" detachments in Berlin today have no such weapons. It is not therefore clear why the U.S. ground forces and tactical air fleets, or the Sixth Fleet in the Mediterranean, should—as is alleged—think that such a scheme would discriminate against them rather than the Soviet forces, or why this scheme should cause the Americans to think of abandoning Europe. The U.S. Senate Foreign Relations Committee, no less, has several times discounted the repeated assertions of the Federal Government that such an eventuality might encourage the Americans to think of leaving Europe. There will, of course, have to be some new thinking about the roles of the various members of NATO. But this is clearly inevitable anyway, given the present situation, and does not depend on the setting up of a Central European zone of control.

Political Implications

As against the alleged military objections and difficulties which are in reality political in origin, there are real problems to be faced in the matter of financial outlay (referred to above), but most of all in the problem of public opinion in the countries to which NATO forces would have to be redeployed. Here indeed, is one of the main reasons for the negative attitude of the French, Dutch and other Governments. It is not the military, but rather the politico-psychological reasons—particularly in Bonn—that are the chief obstacles to serious pursuit by the West of a zone of arms limitation in Europe. Michael Howard listed these reasons after exhaustive discussions with a group of British specialists.[5] He puts the following questions: Would not the new political and military structure of Europe make Germany into a more formidable economic competitor? Would not the unstable character of the régimes in Eastern Europe be an additional threat to peace once Soviet troops had withdrawn? Would not settlement of the German frontier question be a necessary prerequisite? And also a settlement of the frontiers between Hungary and Rumania? Since the establishment of a zone of military limitation would doubtless have political repercussions, which in the so-called "D.D.R.," Poland and Hungary would result in the ousting of the present Communist régimes, would not this process be accompanied by internal chaos? And would the Communists passively accept the defeat of their comrades? Might not the result be an area just as dangerous and turbulent as the Middle East is today, without our being able to assume that the Communists would not scruple to exploit every difficulty? He writes: "If we neglect all considerations of morale and politics and look at the question in a purely military light, the reply must be favourable."[6] One cannot but agree with this judgment. But this does not dispose of all our worries on political grounds.

It is evident that Russian evacuation of East Germany could and should have political repercussions there. This is, after all, the whole object of the proposal from the point of view of Germany as a whole. For this reason any optimistic estimate of the chances of the Russians accepting such a proposal would be misplaced. But

---

[5] M. Howard, *Disengagement in Europe*, p. 50 and *passim*.
[6] *Op. cit.*, p. 64.

such proposals would, at all events, be eminently suitable as a concrete gesture designed to leave the Satellite populations in no doubt as to the West's—and the Federal Republic's—will to peace and disarmament. After the Rapacki initiative by the East an out-of-hand Soviet rejection of such proposals seems improbable. None the less it would be in the West's own interest to take seriously the anxieties that exist lest Soviet withdrawal be followed by political explosions in the countries in question. The withdrawal of foreign troops should therefore take place by stages and be extended over a longish period of time in order to reduce such chances to a minimum. This would create the opportunity for similar step-by-step adjustments of the political structures. But when all is said and done, the West can neither take up the position that the presence of Soviet armies in Central Europe is desirable as a factor making for order and stability, nor maintain that the Russians should stay put for fear that they might return later on. A good deal of Federal German criticism ran on these lines: in so doing, however, it ran counter to the logic of a further objection springing from the same political considerations, viz. that a Central European zone of arms limitation cannot but lead to "a freezing of the division of Germany." In fact, nothing is better calculated to perpetuate the division of Germany than the continued presence of Soviet troops on German soil.

One thing remains certain—that from the point of view of the overall interest of Western Europe there is no over-riding military objection to "military thinning out" or to a zone of limitation and inspection in central Europe. Even Kissinger agreed at the end of 1959 that this was so. Alastair Buchan had every reason to write: "At the moment any suggestion for a zone of arms limitation in Central Europe would mean a bigger sacrifice for the Soviets than for NATO" and "The point is to revive Soviet interest in disengagement by less dangerous means than frightening them with the sight of a Federal Republic armed with nuclear weapons."

Such proposals undoubtedly do not go well with Dr Adenauer's preoccupation with the *status quo*. Nor are they in harmony with the nuclear capability sought by Dr Adenauer for the Federal Republic's armoury. It is, however, illusory to think that there can be a policy of the *status quo*. However slim the chances may seem to be, in view of the international climate during 1960, of the major powers getting back to negotiations on Central European questions, it will remain essential that they do so, for solution of the Berlin question is not possible along any other lines. But there will be no grounds for hope as long as the West is compelled to fear that Soviet tactics in such negotiations will split the West into different camps, and as long as the West fears the eventual re-establishment of German hegemony in Central Europe. What will be decisive in all this is the political leadership that the new American Administration can give to the West. It must reanalyse the idea of a Central European zone of inspection, separate and distinct from the now outmoded catch-phrase of "disengagement."

There were a number of similar objections before the Austrian State Treaty which neutralised Austria and removed it wholly from the Western bloc in the military sense. Then, too, the objections were advanced in the guise of military arguments. Nevertheless there can be no doubt that the Austrian State Treaty was an exceedingly important step towards the consolidation of the freedom of the Austrian people and in no way jeopardised world peace. Our proposals are in no way concerned with neutrality or neutralisation, as was the case with the Austrian State Treaty, but with a redistribution of tasks—from the military standpoint—*within* the Western alliance. The West must stop thinking it has a clear choice between the fulfilment of all its demands and the preservation of the *status quo*.

Let us stress in concluding that: ". . . some protection against surprise attack is better than none. I would like to see a prototype pilot scheme of control and inspection set up in a limited area . . . with the object of putting into operation at least a model of real arms control."[7] Today it is somewhat unrealistic to believe that a universal and comprehensive system of control can be brought about. It is all the more desirable for a beginning to be made at least with a regional system—even one excluding Soviet national territory.

To sum up, an effective system of arms limitation and control between the German western frontier and the eastern border of Poland would at least rule out the dangerous possibilities of local *coups de main* by the Russians discussed in Chapter 6. To achieve this would be very much in the German interest.

[7] Marshal of the R.A.F. Sir J. Slessor, "Where East and West can Meet," *Daily Telegraph*, 18 Nov. 1960.

L

10

Germany's Interests

IT will be clear to everyone that the defence of the Federal Republic cannot be conceived of outside the wider framework of German foreign policy. The direct connexion between German reunification policy and German defence policy has been manifest since the summer of 1950. It was the inevitable consequence of the world situation prevailing after the end of World War II, when a beginning was being made with the task of rebuilding an independent German political will, that conflict should arise between German political aims in the fields of reunification and defence policy respectively, and that this conflict should culminate in the question as to which of these two aims should have priority. The opinions of the Federal Chancellor, who has held office since 1949, decided the Federal Government from the outset to opt in favour of the primacy of defence political aims. In Dr Adenauer's view the following are the most important tasks of German foreign policy:

1. To regain state sovereignty and autonomy in the field of foreign policy;
2. To protect the Federal Republic from the danger of a Communist attack from outside and of a Communist *coup d'état* directed from outside;
3. To restore German unity;
4. To achieve the political and economic unity of Western Europe;
5. To ensure world peace through general controlled disarmament.

During the last decade the restoration of German unity has ranked at best fourth in the actual policy of the Federal Government, i.e. has had a lower priority than Western European integration. This was contrary to the above priority list which was drawn up by one of Adenauer's closest advisers on foreign policy.[1] Active German participation in the general effort to secure controlled disarmament has been minimal and unformulated.

Nor have the Western occupying powers and later allies of the Federal Republic regarded the reunification of Germany as a major objective of their foreign policy. More than once during this period, candid friends among Western politicians have been heard to say in conversation: "Of course, we all want the reunification of Germany, but some of us clearly want it more than others." Not only in Germany itself, but elsewhere in the Western alliance also, there were considerable differences in the priority given to the solution of the German problem. In particular there were considerable differences between solemn declarations on the one hand, and day-to-day foreign policy decisions on the other. In July 1959 Kissinger summed this up in the following highly equivocal way: "It is said by some that nobody really wants German reunification. But surely it is within our control to set our own goals. If the West understands its interests, it must advocate German unification despite the experiences of two world wars and despite the understandable fear of a revival of German truculence. The West may have to acquiesce in the division of Germany, but it cannot condone it. Any other course will in the end bring on what we should fear most: a militant, dissatisfied power in the centre of the Continent. To strive for Germany unification is not a bargaining device but the condition for European stability."[2] Reading between the lines of this formula, what it amounts to is this: "We Americans are bound to *speak* in favour of the reunification of Germany and to keep the matter alive: what we *do* about it is another matter." In the early fifties similar considerations had already suggested to the West that it should make its policy for German remilitarisation palatable to the Germans by presenting it as a means of making progress towards reunification. Dr Adenauer set himself up as the leading exponent of this doctrine.

There is no doubt today that this policy—if it ever was one— has led nowhere. The Federal Government's assertion, constantly

---

[1] Wilhelm Grewe, *Deutsche Aussenpolitik der Nachkriegszeit* (German Foreign Policy since the War), Stuttgart 1960. Grewe is Federal Germany's Ambassador in the United States and has been a member of Dr Adenauer's brains trust on foreign policy since the early 1950s.

[2] H. A. Kissinger, "The Search for Stability," in *Foreign Affairs*, July 1959.

repeated in the years 1952 to 1954, that Western integration and the Federal Republic's membership of the Western alliance would compel the Soviet Union to enter upon serious negotiations for the reunification of Germany, has turned out to be a thoroughly bad bet. To this extent those who criticised the Federal Government's policy at the time have been justified by the march of events. It remains an open question, however, whether the alternative political courses advocated at the time—in particular by Georg Pfleiderer, Paul Sethe and the German Social Democrats—would have been successful had they been tried. There is no point today in bemoaning the failure to take advantage of the real or imaginary opportunities of those years: it will not bring them back. Everybody now knows that no solution of the German problem is possible if a reunited Germany is to belong, as an entity, either to NATO or to the Warsaw Pact; and that likewise no solution is possible if the question of the alliances of a reunited Germany is to be left to an all-German government, as has for years been demanded by the West in its official dealings with Moscow on the German question.

It is equally clear today that, given present power political relationships, the mere settlement of the question of a reunited Germany's military or political alignments will not necessarily make it possible to reach agreement on German reunification by negotiation. The period is long past in which it was possible for the Swedish Foreign Minister, Östen Ünden, to say that the door to German reunification could be opened by the twin keys of free elections and the settlement of military status. Both keys are still certainly needed, but they are no longer enough in themselves: further barriers have in the meantime been erected which require further keys. The so-called "Germany Plan" of the Social Democratic opposition has taken these factors realistically into account. The writer, who took part in the preliminary work which later led to the drawing up of the above document, has in the meantime come to the conclusion that even this very far-reaching conception came too late in view of the increase in Russian power of which the Soviet leaders were already conscious in 1958.[3]

[3] It was, of course, only possible for an opposition party to publish this conception which represented an extreme range of Western concessions. Publication meant running a considerable risk, especially as the title and several sections of the contents—despite their, to some extent, striking similarity to the contents of the "Peace Plan" of the Western Powers published in Geneva a few weeks later—were unhappily phrased and not drafted with sufficient

Aims of German Foreign Policy

Whereas, up to the end of the fifties, the Federal Republic could feel secure under the military protection of the United States and its capability for strategic nuclear retaliation, and to this extent had ample scope for shaping its own defence policy, the subsequent shift in the military and power political balance between East and West has today led to a situation where a substantial contribution by the Federal Republic to the defence of the West has become an inescapable necessity. At the beginning of the new decade we are faced with the major task of preserving peace and ensuring freedom for the Germans in places where that freedom exists, i.e. in the Federal Republic and Berlin. This task can only be accomplished if the German nation, having won the confidence of the West, can retain and strengthen this confidence, and can loyally fill the place taken up by the Federal Republic within the framework of Western defence as a whole. The fulfilment of this task will be jeopardised if political factions within the Federal Republic begin to accuse one another of a lack of loyalty to the alliance and thus diminish the confidence of our allies. "In the interest of Western freedom of action and of the internal stability of the Federal Republic, which is essential to the conduct of German foreign policy, we must put an end to the misuse of foreign policy for the purpose of carrying on internal political disputes."[4]

No one can today claim that the German contribution to the common defence of the Western alliance is a political means to the end of achieving German reunification. The preservation of Western readiness for defence through deterrence is, however, a *sine qua non* of any policy directed towards freeing that part of the nation living in servitude and uniting them with us in freedom and security. The reunification of the nation can only be achieved if our policy is "a balanced combination of the military efforts necessary to preserve freedom, a foreign policy aimed at reducing the danger of war, and sound internal institutions conducive to freedom and social justice" (F. Erler). At the same time, however, this combination

---

clarity. As a result of the failure of the Geneva Foreign Ministers' Conference in early 1959, at which the "Germany Plan" was aimed, the concept round which the plan was drawn up has become an epitaph to a whole epoch.

[4] Herbert Wehner in November 1960, to the Congress of the German Social Democratic Party.

presupposes "the confidence of Germany's eastern neighbours in the establishment of relations that will be peaceful, correct and—it is to be hoped—one day even friendly." The outlook at the beginning of the sixties is therefore not a good one. It can but be hoped that these conditions can be created in the course of time: every German government will have to bend its utmost efforts towards these goals.

In the meantime not only the defence of the Western position in Berlin, but the creation of a satisfactory defence capability for the West as a whole is a condition of our very existence. "At the threshold of the second decade of the Federal Republic's existence no acute observer can be blind to the fact that we are just about to enter upon the period of our greatest trials . . . and that nothing could be less called for in looking back over the difficulties we have transcended and the distance we have travelled, than self-satisfaction. There is no doubt that in many respects the world situation has deteriorated for Germany rather than improved. The situation has grown more precarious in proportion to the extent that the world balance of forces has shifted against the West, to the extent that the U.S.S.R. has achieved parity with the West, and to the extent that the U.S.S.R. boasts of its superiority. Anyone wishing to assess the prospects for our foreign policy over the next decade would do well to drop facile optimism. The Germans have abandoned themselves to illusions in the past far too long already and have been far too much inclined to give a ready ear to anyone offering hopeful remedies. The coming decade promises to be a period of fateful decisions. The Western world disposes of sufficient energy and resources to survive the battles ahead. The crucial question is whether it will find the moral courage to renounce its comfortable illusions and accept the hardships, deprivations and demands on its strength that will be called forth by these battles." We cannot but agree with this estimate of our situation at the end of a decade of Adenauer foreign policy made by the German Ambassador in Washington, Wilhelm Grewe.[5] In much the same words it could have come from the pen of Willy Brandt, or—*cum grano salis*—of John F. Kennedy.

The crucial area in this "period of trials" will be Berlin, as it has been since November 1958. The West has scarcely any

---

[5] Grewe, *Deutsche Aussenpolitik der Nachkriegszeit*.

psychological, political or juridical scope for making concessions in the Berlin conflict if it does not wish to hazard Western confidence in its own inner solidarity. Isolated agreements on Berlin, if they were to be made, might at one and the same time invite the Soviet Union to resume piecemeal tactics against the city and expose the weaknesses of the West. Great care is therefore necessary in negotiations over Berlin to avoid these pitfalls. It would seem that the Berlin conflict can only be solved as part of a general solution of the German problem, and that the German problem can only be solved as part of a general solution of the Central European question. Solution of Central European questions presupposes in its turn far-reaching previous or simultaneous agreement on measures of arms limitation and control. Without the setting up of arms limitation and inspection on at least a regional basis, a solution would hardly appear possible.

In the meantime it is of urgent importance to Germany that no political developments should take place that might tempt the West to make concessions over Berlin. The West's success to date in maintaining its position in Berlin testifies to the fact that, in face of a determined Western attitude, the risk of war arising from the Berlin conflict has seemed unacceptable to the Soviet leadership. On the other hand we need only think of the Berlin Blockade of 1948-9 to recall that the Soviet Union and her German satellite dispose of a wide variety of non-military means of aggression against Berlin.

Liddell Hart tells us that, in Soviet eyes, the argument best calculated to prop up the West's position in Berlin might be that people who, in 1945, could blindly take up so disadvantageous a position, could equally well be "crazy enough" to fight a suicidal war in defence of this position, rather than submit to Soviet threats and abandon their position in Berlin. However that may be, the fact that the Soviet Union must, despite its lead in missiles and its consciousness of military superiority, assume that in the final analysis acceptance of the risk of war might lead to mutual destruction—this fact must urge caution on the Russians in their attempts to eliminate the Western bastion of freedom in Berlin. They have, in fact, been much more cautious since the handing over of the so-called Berlin ultimatum in November 1958 than might have been feared. They certainly realise that serious incursions into the Western position in Berlin would inevitably lead to the economy of the United States being placed on a war footing, as it was during the summer of 1950. To compete in an arms race with a United States working at full blast, and with its economy vectored on to the rapid build-up of armaments, would however lead the Soviet Union into serious difficulties. Alongside the spiritual powers of resistance of the Berlin population, therefore, the American undertaking to support the city is the most important factor in preserving its freedom. Only because—and only as long as—the Soviet leaders see a mortal risk in the military power of the West poised to implement its undertaking to defend Berlin, will they be deterred from aggressive incursions against Berlin.

It is, therefore, of outstanding importance to Germany that the West's ability to defend itself (and therefore its power to deter) should be restored beyond any doubt in the present period, and thereafter be preserved. The Federal Republic cannot, therefore, support moves to make Western Europe into a "third force." We can just as little take it for granted, however, that all new ideas on defence policy that come out of the United states will necessarily be in line with Germany's interests.

We cannot be interested in a Western defence structure predicated on the eventual liberation of a Germany devastated after a "final battle." Nor can we be interested in a NATO defence structure calculated to convert every military conflict automatically into a nuclear war. Lastly, we cannot be interested in a Western defence structure that might be regarded by the Soviet leaders as provocative and so give rise to a Soviet preventive or pre-emptive attack. Therefore in present circumstances Kurt Schumacher's dictum of 1950 cannot be upheld: "Only if the forces of democracy are strong enough to be able to meet attack from the East with prompt counterattack and so decide the war beyond Germany's frontiers—only under such circumstances can the German people make a military contribution to the defence of freedom."

Germany is not a Major Power

Soviet-directed Communism in Europe will inevitably look on the Federal Republic as the "breakwater" of Western defence and call it the vanguard of Western aggression as long as its own aims remain expansive and aggressive. The Federal Republic will not be able to escape such charges. Nevertheless the Federal Republic must not play the part of—or feel itself cast in the role of—the military or political spearhead of the West, lest it run the risk of arousing the Soviet Union to preventive aggression. Since German reunification is only attainable by negotiation, the German people cannot interest itself in the establishment and cultivation of a state of enmity between themselves and the Soviet Union. We Germans must, on the contrary, be interested in establishing a working relationship as things develop, while preserving our ability to defend ourselves. Negotiation of an agreed settlement of the German problem is quite inconceivable other than on the basis of partnership between East and West. The optimum goal of German defence policy and strategy would therefore be the creation of an armaments structure clearly unsuited for the offensive role yet adequate beyond the shadow of a doubt to defend German territory. From this point of view a territorial (or militia) system based on general conscription might in every way be preferable to a standing army maintained on the same basis. To what extent such an "ideal" combination might be realisable in practice remains still to be worked out.

Under no circumstances should the Federal Republic create the impression that it cherishes the ambition of becoming the "decisive" military power of continental NATO. Even less permissible would be any move to acquire armament, which in itself gave rise to the impression that Germany was claiming parity with the Soviet Union. No government of the Federal Republic should therefore demand that the Republic needs "the same weapons as the Soviet Union." It is plainly absurd for the Federal Republic, looking over its shoulder at the Soviet Union, to demand strategic mass destruction weapons. For the Federal Republic to be equipped with nuclear missiles capable of devastating Moscow or Leningrad would inevitably provoke the Soviet Union in just the same way as the supply of nuclear missiles to Cuba would provoke the United States. Moreover, as we have pointed out in Chapter 6, to equip the Federal Republic in this way could only adversely affect NATO's strategy.

The Federal Government has of late rightly been concerned to find out how important is the criticism made by public opinion in several allied countries charging the Germans with "aggressiveness" or "restlessness." It is true that the governments of these countries meet these fears by pointing out that the military integration of the Bundeswehr into NATO has made it impossible for the

Federal Republic to resort to acts of violence. Arguments of this nature are, however, stimulating latent distrust of Germany. Thanks to Hitler it will probably be a long time before countries abroad come to look on the Germans as a normal people once again. The question is—are we really doing all we can to help them correct this opinion?

Many official speakers in the Bundestag would do well, in discussing military and strategic questions, to recall the saying of Graf Schlieffen: "Be, rather than seem." In recent years many Germans have seemed to be anxious to flex muscles which they did not, in fact, possess. A somewhat less noisy military policy would do the Germans nothing but good: this is specially true in relation to our allies. The Spanish adventure of the German Defence Ministry not only put valuable ammunition into the hands of the Communist propaganda machine, it also seriously undermined the confidence of many of our Western allies and for a while manœuvred us into a somewhat frightening isolation in the public opinion of many countries. For many foreigners it suggested—though without good reason—Hitler's attempts to work with Madrid. Belated attempts to hush the matter up could not blind the world to the fact that, as regards Germany's allies, the diplomatic preparations for this project were of strikingly poor quality. We Germans must clearly understand that, throughout the world, Franco is regarded as a relic from the time of Hitler and Mussolini: there are particular reasons why we Germans should be ultra-careful to avoid giving the impression that we are in any way intimate or have any affinities with Franco's Spain. For this reason it is one thing if the President of the United States were to speak out in favour of admitting Spain to NATO, but quite another if the Federal Chancellor were to do so.

The publication six months later of the so-called—and wrongly called—"Generals' Memorandum" by the Defence Ministry was a political blunder of similar psychological ineptitude. This, too, handed the Communists a propaganda weapon which they proceeded to use to great effect all the way from Tokyo to New York. This incident, too, created uncertainty in the minds of our allies as to the internal stability of our German democracy. The less people abroad knew of the actual state of affairs in the Federal Republic the more inclined they were to take this as real evidence of the existence behind the scenes of a conspiracy by the generals for taking over power.[6] In a democracy functioning on the basis of the division of responsibility it is no part of the army's business to direct "military demands" at the political direction of the state. The Bundeswehr as such has no constitutional status, moreover, and is not an autonomous entity with power to act independently and with its own responsibility to parliament or constitutional court. It is, on the contrary, subordinate to a department of the executive: the inspectors and commanders of the Bundeswehr must submit their proposals and counter-proposals to the responsible minister or to the Defence Council of the Cabinet through the prescribed channels. If their views are not endorsed at this level they are free—as are all officials—to resign and *thereafter* to put their case to the public.[7] German officers should not regard as a model the bad example set by the French generals in the last stages of the disintegration of the Fourth Republic and in the crisis of the Fifth. Instead they should recall certain excellent old Prussian traditions and do their utmost to avoid giving others grounds for harking back to General Schleicher's lapses from political discipline which undermined the authority of the Weimar Republic.

The Bonn Government's constant public advocacy of nuclear weapons for the Bundeswehr must be criticised for much the same reason. The manner in which NATO's forces are armed is something for the NATO Council to decide. No doubt democratic governments need the sanction of their parliaments for their co-operation in such decisions: it was therefore right for the German Bundestag to devote its attention, in the spring of 1958, to the question of nuclear weapons. But what gave strongest grounds for disquiet was the vociferousness with which nuclear arms were called for on this occasion. The lack of any ability to discriminate in the basic strategic and political issues shown by

[6] This was really a case of the political abuse by the Defence Minister of the powers of the senior commanders of the Bundeswehr. The Minister believed that he could win greater authority for his policies in the eyes of the German people by means of a public vote of his generals. Strauss is therefore more sharply to be taken to task than the officer who allowed himself to be misused by providing his signature. In fact, the so-called memorandum contained no thoughts that had not already been expressed in public by the Federal Government or the Minister. It was definitely not the work of a team of top military officers, but rather of a political team in a ministerial backroom.

[7] Before this is possible there is a practical requirement to be met: the military officer or civil servant who sends in his resignation because of a political disagreement should be allowed to receive the pension due to him.

many of our politicians was similarly a cause for concern. Questionable, too, were the oversimplifications to which this gave rise in the ensuing public debate; this showed that the charge of oversimplification applied to many opponents of nuclear weapons for the Bundeswehr also. Instead of this the one side has got to understand that the categoric demand for equipping the Bundeswehr with nuclear weapons is only calculated still more to increase the present-day inadequacy of NATO's armament and strategy:[8] the other side has got to understand that the question of nuclear weapons for the German armed forces is not one of pure ethical principle,[9] but—like every political issue—one of responsibility. The question of the possible consequences, which every political decision-maker must ask himself on moral grounds, opens up the whole field of enquiry as to the justifiableness of the ends, the expediency of the means, the unavoidability of the side-effects, and the interrelationships of the ends, side-effects and means. Of such questions there is no end. In brief, anyone faced with making political decisions on matters of nuclear armament *must* first, in calculating the effects to be aimed at and those to be avoided, employ both political and military analysis in order to identify the ends, means and side-effects; thereafter he should evaluate these from the ethical standpoint, and weigh them one against the other.

We do not have to wait for the Bundeswehr to be equipped with nuclear weapons to court the danger that Germany and its neighbours might be overwhelmed by "atomic death"—the danger exists here and now, at a time when the Bundeswehr disposes of not a single nuclear weapon! The characteristics of the organisation of British and American nuclear-equipped units on German soil, and the tasks now assigned to them, contribute in no small degree to this danger. We went in some detail into the

[8] Contrary to all sorts of nebulous assertions, the arming of the Bundeswehr with nuclear weapons has never, as at the time of writing, been debated in NATO. Up till now it has only been a question of the delivery to the Bundeswehr of weapons *without* their nuclear warheads. Cf. the detailed treatment of the matter in Chapters 6 and 11.

[9] This concept is taken from the still impressive lecture of Max Weber on "Politics as a Profession," Munich 1919. The passage in question reads: "It is not just that the principles of Christian ethics amount to irresponsibility, or that a responsible attitude is tantamount to a denial of Christian ideas. But there is a world of difference between acting in accordance with the maxim—'The Christian does what his religion prescribes and leaves the rest to God'—or in accordance with the prescription of the maxim of responsibility—'Everyone is accountable for the (foreseeable) consequences of his actions.' "

problems arising from this component of the present NATO concept in Chapter 6, and in Chapter 11 we shall be making some recommendations for the solution of these problems.

The fact must be stressed at this point that the hue and cry for nuclear weapons for the Bundeswehr, raised by many ill-briefed German politicians, has damaged us Germans not only as regards our internal politics but also in the field of foreign policy. It has not only frightened our Eastern neighbours and presented the Soviet Government and its propaganda machine with a splendid opportunity of strengthening its alliances with the allegation of a direct and dangerous threat from Germany (and of terrifying the neutrals with allegations of a resurgence of "furor Teutonicus"), but it has caused real anxiety within the Western alliance. Alastair Buchan showed characteristic English courtesy when he wrote: ". . . a Western Germany that participated in a purely European nuclear deterrent must abandon all hope of reunification."[10] Klaus Knorr had this to say on the question of strategic nuclear weapons for the Germans:[11] "Another problem worth mentioning is that the U.S.S.R. would probably interpret transfer of control—to West Germany, for instance—as a move so hostile that the host country[12] would thereby assume the immediate risk of a pre-emptive Soviet strike." Professor Knorr, one of the most cool-headed of the American academic strategists, was one of the authors of the so-called Bowie Plan: without doubt he has access to a very wide range of information. Anxiety over the possible consequences of placing strategic nuclear weapons at the disposal of Germany could therefore become the seed of the collapse of the alliance. Early in 1960, as a counterblast to the official demands coming out of Bonn, the Parliamentary Assembly of Western European Union approved a report which contained the following sentence: "We should do everything possible to prevent nuclear weapons from spreading to more and more countries."

It is also in Germany's interest to limit the further spread of nuclear weapons. The Federal Republic would be well advised to follow Sweden's example in its statements on nuclear weapons. During the winter of 1959-60 the Swedish Government postponed

[10] A. Buchan, *NATO in the* 1960's, London and New York 1960, p. 70.
[11] In *Bulletin of the Atomic Scientists*, September 1960.
[12] A "host country" is one in which United States strategic nuclear weapons are stationed under American control.

for five years the decision to go over to nuclear weapons so as to give support during this period to the general efforts to close the Nuclear Club. The Swedish Government will only make a final decision if, by the end of the period, there is no prospect of closing the doors of the Nuclear Club and halting the further spread of nuclear weapons. The intention is that, in the meantime, it should continuously observe and examine the premises, consequences, advantages and disadvantages of such a decision. Such a policy would be to the advantage of the Federal Republic also. It would not by any means prevent the Federal Republic from making an authoritative and professional contribution to NATO's consultations and decisions on matters of nuclear organisation and strategy.

Hopes of rationalising the Central European problem will certainly recede still further if, during the coming decade, things progress in such a way as to make it appear indispensable for the middle-range and smaller powers to go over to nuclear weapons and for the Federal Republic to do likewise. Great Britain and France already display anxiety at the numerical ratio that will clearly soon be established between the Bundeswehr and the forces of the other European NATO countries. The relevance of this ratio to the implications for the alliance of the French adoption of a nuclear posture were pointed out on a number of occasions in the French National Assembly, and the reactions of speakers of *all* parties were particularly instructive. The Soviet Union cannot seriously feel itself to be threatened by the armament of the Bundeswehr so long as the Bundeswehr remains an integrated component of the overall defence of the West, and so long as the Bundeswehr does not constitute the decisive mass of NATO's continental forces. But the danger of the Soviet Union's being provoked to preventive aggression will grow from that moment on when the Federal Republic appears able, if need be, to conduct an independent and autonomous foreign policy backed by the power of nuclear weapons. Recognition of this fact should not be obscured by the use the Soviets will make of *any* Federal German arms policy whatsoever as a propaganda pretext for the maintenance of Soviet troops in the so-called "D.D.R.," for the maintenance of its military grip on Poland, and for military support of the Ulbricht régime.

The Federal Republic has hitherto been ill-prepared for participating in the strategic decision-making process within NATO. It has at its disposal no adequate organisation for the analysis of strategic problems. Study and criticism of, and collaboration in, NATO projects is reserved at the moment almost exclusively for the Defence Ministry: and here, naturally, it is conducted behind locked doors. No discussion takes place in the Federal Republic of the basic problems: no discussion takes place even in secret where defence problems can be put in an essentially wider perspective than is possible in the Defence Ministry: there are no competent organisations that might be commissioned to undertake scientific analysis. The setting up of scientific institutes where research into the complexities of politico-strategic problems can be carried on, is a necessity in the Federal Republic as elsewhere.

Defence and Reunification

In collaborating as it does in NATO planning, the Federal Republic is confronted by a fateful contradiction. In order to create a meaningful defence capability it must work for extensive integration within NATO; but it cannot lose sight of the fact that, as integration proceeds, the Federal Republic's scope for conducting a foreign policy directed towards reunification, which is slight enough as things stand now, will be further attenuated. It is conceivable that a time will come in the process of fusing the Federal Republic into Western Europe when the point of no return will be reached and the division of Germany into East and West will become permanent. The much more far-reaching fusion of the "D.D.R." into the economic organisation of COMECON[13] and into the military bloc of the Warsaw Pact is leading to similar results, but in the opposite direction. The longer the orientation and integration processes of the two parts of Germany continue, the narrower will appear the room remaining for agreeing on reunification.

"After eleven years of German foreign policy the situation is more serious than ever. . . . No one can guarantee that joint efforts will be successful in re-establishing the unity of the State, but we can be certain that, unless we prosecute our foreign policy in solidarity and determination no solution to the German problem will be found" (Willy Brandt in November 1960). The "joint stock-taking" demanded by Herbert Wehner in the name of the German Social Democrats in June 1960 remains therefore—quite

[13] COMECON = Council for Mutual Economic Assistance.

independent of the 1961 elections to the Bundestag—a constant necessity. This stock-taking must embrace an analysis of the foreign policy and military situations, and must look into what openings there are for the exertion of German influence in both spheres. Before any attempt is made to exert German influence a careful assessment and evaluation of German interests will be necessary. Germany's contribution to the grand strategy of the West presupposes membership of the North Atlantic Alliance, but this contribution must not on any account be regarded as a mere secondary function of our membership of the alliance. Our fellow members can expect us Germans to make our contribution to the formulation of the political, military and disarmament strategy of the West from the point of view of our own interests. And we ourselves must see to it that whatever German Government is in power is kept aware of this expectation.

It is inconceivable that German collaboration in the task of solving the West's strategic problems should be left exclusively to the secret discussions of experts in the Federal Defence Ministry and in the Federal Chancellor's office on the one hand, or to the military dilettantism of German politicians' week-end speeches on the other. The question of what is the most appropriate role for the Federal Republic within the Western alliance in the interest of German reunification policy calls urgently for penetrating scientific analysis and informed political discussion. This has not only a quantitive but also—and above all—a substantive application with regard to the military tasks to be taken on by the Bundeswehr. This latter question has been brought home to public opinion in the Federal Republic only vaguely and with reference to only a few of its specific applications—as regards the contruction of destroyers and the larger types of warship, as regards the German Federal Government's right to consultation and veto in the event of NATO's using nuclear weapons on German soil, and as regards the question of the wartime supply of the Federal Republic which became the subject of public debate after the Spanish episode.

The Federal Government and its Defence Council seem so far to have worked out no coherent overall concept for the German role within the framework of Western defence. The incomprehensible lack of any ideas in the field of civil defence—incomprehensible considering the constant emphasis on defence preparedness

—speaks for itself. At the present time only 2 per cent. of the total defence budget is devoted by the Federal Government to the protection of its civil population. It refuses to allow a commission to be set up to study the urgent problems of civil defence—and this despite the fact that everyone knows that civil defence is by no means a matter that can be glossed over in the event of war. The fact-finding tours of a Bundestag committee which, in the autumn of 1960, visited Sweden and Switzerland with the object of studying the extensive civil defence installations in those countries, have thrown as yet no light on the matter. The Federal Government's propaganda—conducted hitherto in most polemical fashion—in support of its plans for emergency legislation cannot conceal the fact that they have not succeeded in reaching a consistent civil defence concept nor an overall defence concept—not least because of the continuing conflict between the Minister of the Interior and the Minister of Defence regarding their respective spheres of competence.

Politicians can make appropriate decisions only after the most careful preparation of the relevant materials by competent professionals, but in doing so they should not become completely dependent on their advisers. In this respect the field of strategy is no different from that of transport policy or social security legislation. Military advisers throughout the world tend to underestimate the imperatives of disarmament policy or quite simply to regard the goal of arms limitation as illusory and to pay it only lip service. Overall conceptions can be worked out only by the political leaders specifically charged with the task, and only they can accept the responsibility for so doing. And only if we have such overall conceptions does a policy of attempting to influence our allies become meaningful. We are neither a major power able to impose our will on others, nor are we a satellite with no alternative but to adapt ourselves to the will of a major power. We do not have the right to allow our peoples' existence to become the passive object of the strategic decisions of other states. We have, on the contrary, a duty to make our own contribution. The better we are able, soundly and impartially, to put forward conceptions that carry conviction through their inner logic and consistency with the overall interests of the West, the greater will be our success.

Soundness and rationality are also called for in our relations with the East. We have reason enough to regard the policies of the

M

Soviet Union as threatening: we have good reason to arm ourselves against them together with our allies: but we do no good either to our own cause nor to the world in general if we brand the Soviet Union as the "arch enemy" or call in our speeches for "the nuclear extermination of the forces of evil."

The urgent necessity for embarking on a more profound discussion of our defence problems must not obscure or drive into the background the overriding national goal of reunification in conditions of ensured peace and freedom. There are political forces in the Federal Republic which abet this tendency. For example, a sterile controversy is being conducted as to whether the creation by the Federal Republic of a defence readiness is the result or the cause of tension in Europe. It is obvious that both answers contain an element of truth, and that a completely satisfactory answer, which embraces both answers, can only be given at a higher level. For obviously the process takes the form of a spiral: the division of Germany, which was decreed during a state of latent tension between the allied powers of World War II, has in the course of time given rise to new tensions. These in turn have intensified the division and necessitated the creation of a defence capability: this has given rise to further tensions, and so forth. To interrupt this process is now a world problem.

Yet more dangerous are the attacks, which to some extent go hand in hand with the necessary stress on the creation of a defence capability, on those who with the best will in the world can see nothing final and definitive in the Federal Republic and its provincial capital, Bonn. Instead of joining these attacks we should all impress on our minds, and those of our children, the words of the fundamental law:[14] "The German nation as a whole is called upon to bring about the unity and freedom of Germany in conditions of free self-determination." No doubt the development of a state consciousness oriented on the Federal Republic is desirable: but there is no doubt that it is every bit as much a matter of life and death to preserve a national consciousness oriented on the nation as a whole. Unity, justice and freedom for the German Fatherland![15] The Federal Republic is, however, only part of the German Fatherland. It makes no sense to attempt to obscure, in the sacred name of Western European integration, the immense chasm

[14] i.e. the Constitution of the Federal Republic.
[15] First line of the German national anthem.

between Federal German state consciousness and the German nation as a whole. One day we shall all see that the German generation now growing up will not for ever be prevented by its preoccupation with professional success, television, football and cars, from taking thought for its national destiny. We ourselves, our allies in the West, and the East also, must not be allowed to forget that the perpetuation of the division of Germany represents a conspicuous threat to world peace. Precisely because, despite all protests to the contrary in both West and East, the reunification of Germany was by no means the prime objective of the global policy of the powers concerned, it behoves us to remind them of this threat from time to time. "There is only one motive . . . for seeking a solution of the German question in the sense of overcoming the present division: the fear that perpetuation of that division will result in war" (F. Erler). If the German people or the German Government were to give the impression that they were content to come to terms with the division, this motive would lose all its force.

For this reason the Federal Republic and its Government must in the future constantly be concerned to see that the German question is not dropped from the international agenda. All our proposals for defence and disarmament must be made with our eye on this goal. The external political strategy of the Federal Republic must not, in its preoccupation with the immediate goal of Western cohesion, lose sight of the higher goal of German reunification.

The accomplishment of German reunification in one stroke is now completely improbable: its achievement as the result of a series of strokes, jointly conceived and negotiated, is equally improbable. We can only aim to take steps which might themselves give rise later on to further steps towards German unity, and to fight the erection of further new barriers.

One must see—as much today as ever it was in the past—one of these possible steps in the proposal to set up a Central European zone of arms limitation and of reciprocal control and inspection. It was for this reason that in the last chapter we gave detailed consideration to the problems and requirements of the creation of a zone of military "thinning out" in Central Europe, although in 1961 the attitude of the Federal Government under Dr Adenauer makes the prospects for such a proposal seem very slender indeed. Certain statements by United States Democrats speaking on foreign affairs give rise to the hope that Kennedy will be more accessible to such proposals than was his predecessor. If, however, things were to come to no more than a unilateral reduction of troops in Germany, the opportunity would pass by unexploited.

We must not lose sight of the fact that the setting up of a Central European zone of arms limitation would clearly be to the disadvantage of the Soviet Union, and that in view of the Russians' present estimate of the ratio of forces in Europe they can now scarcely be interested in reviving their proposals of 1957. Precisely for this reason it is in Germany's interest to permit no decisions in the course of NATO planning which would in practice rule out the achievement at some later date of such a zone in Central Europe. There would be a particular danger of this if, in the course of the readjustment of the NATO posture, the United States were to withdraw from Germany substantial proportions of its troops now there, without corresponding withdrawals of Soviet troops from the "D.D.R." If only for this reason it would be unwise for the numerical build-up of the Bundeswehr to reach such levels as might appear to permit the withdrawal of American divisions.

The Federal Republic cannot afford to participate in the worldwide disarmament debate with no more than the formula that it will fall in with any internationally negotiated agreement. It must contribute proposals to this debate of such a nature as to keep the German question alive and within the compass of political realism; it must also use the disarmament debate to influence events in the direction of Central European normalisation. Only if agreement could be reached on at least partial measures of arms limitation and control would there appear to be any possibility of creating an international climate in which a solution of Central European problems might still prove to be possible. In striving for this, and assuming the matter to have been carefully sounded out within the alliance—and in spite of Camp David—we need not fear the conduct of negotiations between East and West in the form of bilateral conversations between Washington and Moscow: for if the United States Administration does not have the necessary diplomatic talent and energy for bilateral negotiations with Moscow, this weakness will not be rectified by the participation in negotiations of the remaining Western powers.

Any negotiations assume that the new United States Administration brings to an end the period of Western weakness marked by

the Geneva Foreign Ministers' Conference of May 1959, Camp
David, the U 2 affair, and the Paris Summit Conference. Any
East-West negotiations must presuppose extensive Western
unanimity as regards the aims of the negotiations, and a maximum
of determination to uphold the jointly approved policy behind the
negotiations and the concessions that might be made. The West
was scarcely fit to enter upon negotiations in the state of disarray
accompanying Eisenhower's transfer of power to Kennedy.

A considerable degree of mutual trust and understanding
between Washington and Bonn is an indispensable prerequisite of
any reunification policy that is to hold out chances of success—but
it is not of itself alone an adequate prerequisite. The number and
scope of the prerequisites that must be met if Germany is to be
reunited grows from decade to decade, and even from year to year.
They are to be found to only a small extent within the ambit of
German policy-making; they are to be found to only a limited
extent within the ambit of Western policy-making as a whole. It is,
however, up to us, irrespective of our determined participation in
the creation of a meaningful European defence capability, to keep
alive the aspirations of those seventy million Germans inhabiting
this clearly defined region of Central Europe.

11

NATO in the Next Decade

WE have seen that the risk of an outbreak of hostilities does not lie specifically in the Soviet Union's strategic missile armament, but rather in two other factors: on the one hand in the very flexible nature of Soviet armament and strategy, which enables the Russians to contemplate a wide range of measures that could be carried out by a variety of different means towards a variety of different objectives; and on the other hand in the possibility of Soviet misinterpretation of the West's deterrent and defence strategy and armaments, and in Soviet miscalculation of Western reactions. Such miscalculations are more probable as a consequence of the fact that Western strategy is now more ambiguous and less credible than it was even three years ago.

Europe is Defensible

The chief task of NATO remains that of preventing the outbreak of a military conflict. Up to the present time it has been possible to achieve this goal. Despite all the doubts voiced in previous chapters regarding the ability of NATO's present armaments and strategy to meet present demands, there is no reason why NATO should not be able to carry out its task in the future. Of this we need have no fears. But this will only be possible if the defence structure and strategy of NATO poses risks that will be intolerable for the potential aggressor in *all* the conceivable circumstances in which military conflicts and wars might break out, and if these risks are felt by the enemy in every instance to be real ones. NATO's armament and strategy must therefore be predicated on three basic principles:

1. The military means, the threat of which is intended to deter the potential aggressor, and the strategic plans for their use, must

be identical with the military means and strategy that will actually be used in the event of hostilities. No inconsistency must be allowed to arise between the strategy aimed at deterrence and that directed towards actual defence. The potential aggressor must be left in no doubt that the strategy developed in peacetime for the purpose of threatening and so deterring him, will in fact be put into operation should the occasion arise.

2. For no other reason than to make them credible to the potential aggressor, the military forces posing the threat and the plans governing their use must, as far as possible, be shaped so as to rule out the inevitability of escalation to nuclear war, and so to expose all that constitutes European civilisation to the smallest possible risk of destruction.

3. The creation of a NATO defence structure and strategy in accordance with the above principles must be so calculated that its form and dimensions do not provoke the potential enemy to preventive aggression.

Almost every armaments policy has, at one and the same time, a potentially deterrent as well as a potentially provocative effect. In particular the very assertion that such and such a power must be deterred from attacking may the more provoke him the less he is actually thinking of aggression. An instructive example of this is afforded by Castro's allegations at the end of 1960 that the United States was preparing for aggression against Cuba, and by the Kremlin's deterrent propaganda against the United States designed to harmonise with the allegations. Despite the much-quoted maxim—much quoted by the military but, nevertheless, of doubtful validity—that attack is the best method of defence,[1] the West's armament must be so devised that its deterrent effect is maximal and its provocative effect minimal. NATO must therefore be concerned so to arrange its side of the military equation that the West will always be able to cause the enemy intolerable losses at all levels of possible warfare, and at the same time contrive to avoid giving the impression that its armament is suitable—nay, designed —to support a Western aggression. To preserve the military balance in Europe it is not necessary for the armaments maintained by both sides in Europe to be exactly equal in terms of overall war

---

[1] This catchphrase is more dashing than considered. For a contrary view cf. Clausewitz's thoughtful characterisation of defence as the "strongest form of warfare."

potential. It will be enough if, in the event of aggression from the East, the West can inflict on the attacker risks and losses that must seem intolerable to him irrespective of the possibility that he might be able to inflict greater losses on the West. If it were possible to establish and preserve a balance of this sort, the chances of peace in Europe would be maximised. The task of preserving peace in Europe thus becomes identical with that of defending Europe. Those (e.g. Franz Josef Strauss) who speak of the indirect defence of Europe are therefore not wide of the mark.

The chances of an irrational military decision cannot by any means be ruled out by measures of this sort. It is true that they can be reduced by mutual arms control measures and inspection; but they cannot be entirely removed. For this reason the strategies devised by the West in peacetime must be of such a nature that they can immediately be put to work in the event of hostilities resulting from irrational policy decisions.

Nuclear War must not be Inevitable

The military forces maintained for defence against acts of local aggression and the plans for their use must be of such a kind that successful defence is possible without resort to nuclear weapons of any kind, but exclusively through the use of conventional weapons —unless, that is, the enemy launches his attack to the accompaniment of nuclear weapons. The same applies in the case of regionally limited acts of aggression. The units of NATO's ground and air forces must be so equipped and trained that they can carry out such tasks without falling back on nuclear weapons.

Even in a non-nuclear conflict we must allow for the possibility that the scope of the battle will widen and ultimately involve the use of nuclear weapons. NATO must therefore also have the means, should the enemy carry out locally or regionally limited acts of aggression with tactical nuclear weapons, of defending its territory with the same weapons without, at the same time, having to call in the support of long-range nuclear weapons of mass destruction. In other words NATO must be in a position to defend its area, i.e. to inflict unbearable losses on the enemy, with the same weapons as he uses for his aggression—irrespective of the extent to which the attack is limited by locality or region, or by its objectives or the weapons used. What is more, NATO must be able to fight a general or total war in the defence of Europe in case the enemy's attack is made at that level, i.e. includes the use of strategic nuclear weapons. NATO must be able to inflict intolerable losses on the enemy at this at present supreme level of warfare also.

The overall structure of NATO must, furthermore, be so unassailable in its consistency both in political and military respects, and must seem to the enemy to be so firmly welded together, that he will not expect to be able to bring a single NATO member state to its knees by means of acts of blackmail. In order to make anything of this nature impossible, the military and political structure of NATO must also convince, by virtue of its unassailable consistency, the government of each single member country of the alliance.

Graduated Deterrence

It was stated in Chapter 6 that, at the present time, the one-sided nature of NATO's armament and strategy could ensure that a local war, no matter how limited, could logically lead on to nuclear war, and most probably would do so. We touched on a number of different ways in which a conflict might break out, and saw how necessary it is to weigh up in advance the varying degrees of probability attaching to each of these various cases, and the prospects of successful defence in each. We are assuming that it makes no sense to commit oneself to a strategy of "all or nothing." The West's conventional means of defence must be so strong that nuclear defence becomes only a last resort instead of a panacea. If every sort of conflict were to lead inevitably to general nuclear war, then it would be absurd for the number of troops in Western Europe to be kept at their present level. Instead, NATO needs a strategy of "flexible response" (Maxwell Taylor).

The strategies devised for the defence of Europe must make up a continuous system extending without gaps from cold war to total and general war. NATO must be ready to present the aggressor with intolerable risks at the lowest as at the highest level of possible warfare, and also at every conceivable intermediate level. We call this concept "graduated deterrence." It was first worked out by a number of British strategists, and was soon afterwards taken up in the United States: it made its appearance in the course of 1960 in official statements by Norstad, expressed in the form of requirements or of desirable goals. In Germany Strauss and Speidel have made statements suggesting that they might be thinking on the same lines.[2] The concept of graduated deterrence demands that NATO should bring to bear no more than the minimum of armed force required for defence on any given occasion. Or, in other words, NATO must be put in a position to deter and, if necessary, to repel all Soviet attacks limited enough not to merit recourse to massive nuclear retaliation and global war, with the same types of weapon that the enemy uses to carry out his aggression. Europe can only hope to avoid nuclear destruction in the event of war if strong, highly mobile, conventional forces are built up. Europe and its peoples can only hope for survival in war if they have the means for conventional defence: for only a defence capability of this kind will put an end to the situation which has existed up till now, whereby the defence of Europe in war leads inevitably and immediately to the destruction of Europe.

NATO must think again. The forces hitherto known as the "Shield" must be converted into the decisive deterrent factor in Europe. This process will have far-reaching consequences. Given our assumption that deterrent strategy and effective defence strategy are identical, the concept of graduated deterrence implies the removal of all nuclear weapons from the ground force units assigned to the task of conventional defence.[3] So as to rule out

[2] The meeting of the NATO Council which took place from 15 to 18 December 1960 in Paris (after this book went to press) gives grounds for thinking that the idea of graduated deterrence is beginning to penetrate the official mind. The communiqué issued after the meeting included these words: "There must be a proper balance in the forces of the alliance of nuclear and conventional strength to provide the required flexibility." Norstad had himself said shortly before to a conference of NATO parliamentarians: "Our first priority is . . . the build-up of the deterrent. . . . A second task is . . . to defend the territory of the NATO countries. I believe that this object can be achieved. . . . Thus I believe that our forces must have a substantial conventional capability. They must be able to operate where the military situation permits without using arms and weapons equipped with nuclear warheads. . . . The threshold at which nuclear weapons are introduced into the battle should be a high one. Further, the use of these weapons should be the result of a specific deliberate decision. . . ." In this speech distinct signs of the beginning of a far-reaching swing in strategic conception can for the first time be discerned.

[3] The so-called "Generals' Memorandum" of the Federal Ministry of Defence of August 1960 is remarkably vague on this point. In one breath it says (rightly): "The enemy's armament makes graduated deterrence indispensable"; a little later it goes on : "Those who want their country to be effectively defended cannot close their eyes to the necessity for the equipment of the 'Shield' forces with atomic weapons." In fact, graduated deterrence becomes almost impossible if the "Shield" forces deployed forward are already equipped with nuclear weapons.

unintentional and unforeseen developments, these units should not
have nuclear weapons of any sort at their disposal, just as the
armoured or grenadier battalions of World War II did not have
gas shells at their disposal. In particular these NATO units should
include no battlefield nuclear weapons in their equipment, and
"clean" nuclear weapons should be similarly excluded. Their
posture in peacetime as in war must be such as to permit them to
fight without the support of nuclear weapons of any sort. Their
operations must, however, be planned on the assumption that the
enemy might make use of nuclear weapons: they must be prepared
to meet this eventuality by continuing to fight with nuclear support
furnished by their own side. The decision to adopt a strategy of
graduated deterrence will require an extensive conversion of
NATO's armament and—more than all else—the raising of further
troops. This reorganisation will take some years and a considerable
financial outlay. It will not be popular at first. To the extent,
however, that the peoples of Europe become aware of the danger
of annihilation that threatens them in consequence of NATO's
present one-track nuclear concept, to this extent may one hope
that European public opinion will be determined to do justice to
the new imperatives now emerging with the strategy of graduated
deterrence.

But let us not delude ourselves: the strategy of graduated deterrence can never be effective to the same absolute degree as was the
concept of threatened nuclear strategic retaliation (i.e. annihilation
of the enemy) in the first half of the last decade. The parity in the
technological means of warfare achieved in the meantime by the
Soviet Union makes this latter concept impossible for the future.
The strategy of graduated deterrence lacks the vital premise of
Dullesian total deterrence, viz. the absolute invulnerability of the
strategic weapons and of the population of the country posing the
threat of retaliation. Instead, one can only hope to deter the Soviet
Union from using its nuclear mass destruction weapons by maintaining in being the Western nuclear strategic strike forces and the
threat of retaliation which they pose; one can only hope to deter
the Soviet Union from the use of tactical nuclear weapons by
holding our own at readiness; and one can only hope to deter them
from attacking Europe with conventional weapons by maintaining
adequate Western conventional strength. The strategy of graduated
deterrence holds out today "relatively the best chances . . . it will

serve us best if we do not place *too much* trust in it" (v. Weiz-säcker).

The Front is no Place for Nuclear Weapons

Until appropriate measures of disarmament are agreed NATO must, of course, continue to keep its nuclear weapons in a state of readiness. Irrespective of the difficulties, discussed in Chapter 6, about defining the limits between tactical and strategic nuclear weapons, the West must have such nuclear weapons at its disposal for the support as necessary of its conventional formations in battle. Secondly, it must have nuclear weapons for interdiction purposes. And thirdly it must have strategic nuclear weapons for strategic retaliation. These are all necessitated by the enemy's possession of similar weapons. NATO's nuclear weapons must, however, be so deployed and organised that they cannot be drawn into the battle against the wishes of the Supreme Political Commander, but only at his express command. The Supreme Political Commander must proceed on the assumption that the so-called tactical nuclear weapons are his "penultimate resort" (Liddell Hart), while the strategic nuclear weapons are his last resort.

Nuclear weapons have no business, therefore, either at the front with the field army or at the forward airfields of the air forces. As far as the ground forces are concerned, they must be removed, not only from the control of brigade and divisional commanders, but also from the control of corps and army commanders. They must be segregated, concentrated in special task forces equipped with nuclear weapons for tactical use, and incorporated in a branch of the armed forces (as it were, in a separate service) separated from the general organisation of the ground forces and directly subordinated to the Supreme Political Commander. Their command structure must conform to that of the field forces so that the individual nuclear task forces may, as required in the course of the battle, be subordinated to the various separate divisions, corps and armies.

The nuclear task forces will need high mobility: they must to some extent be given their own air transport, and they must be stationed well to the rear of the forward zones of the area to be defended. Those types of tactical weapon, from Davy Crockett to Honest John, which are at present allocated directly to NATO's

British and American divisions, must be included in the new nuclear force. The example of the Southern European Task Force (SETAF), now in Italy, provides some clues as to how the task forces might be organised.

It is clear that in their rearward concentration areas the nuclear task forces will be exposed to risk of attack by the enemy: for this reason any mass concentrations must be avoided in peacetime. It is desirable therefore that they should be dispersed over a wide area under peacetime conditions, since any movement of nuclear task forces once fighting had begun might be interpreted by the enemy as the beginning of nuclear war. For this very reason they must be fanned out behind the areas where they might have to be used. In general the distances between their assembly areas and those where they might have to go into action should not be too great.

Since the air forces do not fight a continuously interlocked battle with the enemy, it seems unnecessary to create within tactical air forces separate formations for purely conventional and for exclusively nuclear employment respectively. What should on no account be permitted, however, is that nuclear weapons of any sort should be deployed among the forward units of the tactical air forces. Nuclear weapons must be concentrated in rearward positions under separate command, so that they can be quickly moved up to the front-line formations at the command of the Supreme Political Commander. This applies also to the air defence forces.

A difficulty arises in the case of all the so-called dual-purpose weapons. In so far as their use with ordinary conventional warheads makes sense and is appropriate to the situation there is no objection to their forming part of the equipment of ground and air force units in the front line. Nuclear warheads for these weapons must not, however, be at the disposal of the units: they must, on the contrary, be held in the depots of the nuclear branch of the armed forces deployed in the rear, or alternatively in those of the nuclear units of the air forces. Weapons that are not genuinely dual purpose (i.e. those whose use only makes sense with nuclear warheads) must not be under the control of front-line formations: they would handicap these formations' ability to fight a purely conventional defence. This applies also to such guided weapons as Matador or Mace.

There should be no relaxation whatsoever in the application of the principle of reserving nuclear weapons exclusively for special nuclear units. The organisation, command channels, strategy and tactics of NATO and its commanders must be so ordered that exclusively conventional weapons are earmarked for the "first encounter," and nuclear weapons of any kind exclusively for the "second encounter." In so doing everyone must be guided by the principle that the "second encounter" would be ordered only if the enemy, for his part, went over to the use of tactical nuclear weapons. Without doubt preparations for and organisation of a "second encounter" will require more men, but there can be no serious objection on this score since the concept of graduated deterrence as a whole will require considerably more troops than NATO now has at its disposal.

Practical difficulties arise in the field of static air defences —particularly in the case of defence with surface-to-air missiles (A.A. rockets). The construction now envisaged of Hawk and Nike belts will take several years to complete. There would seem to be no question of establishing separate nuclear belts additional to the A.A. missile belts now under construction. It would similarly be irresponsible to reserve the Nike belts solely for conventional air defence since we must always reckon that the enemy air force might resort to the first use of nuclear weapons. We must therefore examine whether the fixed air defences, now designed to fire A.A. rockets and guided missiles, should not be organised in the same way as was recommended for front-line air formations, viz. that the weapons to be employed should be designed as dual-purpose (as is to some extent the case today), but that the nuclear warheads should be held exclusively by the special nuclear force under separate command and with its separate upward channels of communication. We must, however, note the objection that, at great heights, purely conventional A.A. missiles promise to be of only limited effectiveness. It is indisputable that A.A. missiles are considerably more effective in defence with nuclear warheads than they would be with purely conventional warheads (although this is not true of all dual-purpose weapons). If one wished to honour this objection and organise one's static air defences from the outset on the basis of the use of nuclear warheads, the following considerations might justify this course: firstly, A.A. missiles with nuclear warheads by no means constitute weapons of mass destruction; secondly, their nuclear fall-out is practically insignificant when compared with that of other nuclear weapons; and thirdly, their employment would be

confined to one's own territory. Nevertheless, an *a priori* commitment to use nuclear warheads for static air defence would invoke
the danger of nuclear escalation. Air attack on protected areas or
targets will be preceded by attempts to eliminate the static air
defences. If, however, the static air defences attack the enemy air
formations with nuclear weapons there is no reason why the enemy,
so attacked with nuclear weapons, should not reply in kind in his
attempts to neutralise the air defence positions: on the contrary,
he will feel himself bound to do so. And this would lead unavoid-
ably to the devastation of the civil population living in the area.
It is not difficult to foresee that the Supreme Political Commander
would be disinclined to accept this devastation of a part of the
population committed to his charge as an unavoidable concomitant
of otherwise purely conventional hostilities. In such a contingency
nuclear escalation would be likely, to say the least. For this reason
static air defences also should be restricted to conventional weapons
and the resulting diminution of their effectiveness accepted: they
should be prepared for nuclear defence in the sense of having dual-
purpose weapons available, but the nuclear weapons should not
be normally under the control of the air defence commander, but
should—like all other nuclear weapons—only be allocated to him
by special order of the Supreme Political Commander.

One Operational Commander for Nuclear Weapons

The general necessity therefore emerges for the segregation of
special units for nuclear warfare which, organised into a special
branch of the forces, should have their own special chain of
command, be exclusively under the Supreme Political Commander,
and receive orders to go into action only from him. If such an
organisation were to be adopted, the nationality of the troops
serving in the nuclear units would be a subsidiary matter. No doubt
there would be weighty arguments in favour of limiting them to
certain nationalities: these arguments were ventilated in Chapter 6
and, in relation to the specifically German aspects of the question in
Chapter 10. The question is now: how should the highest command
authority in the nuclear branch of the forces be organised? Should
it be integrated into the staff of the Supreme Allied Commander,
Europe (SACEUR), or into a separate command?

These questions become more pressing if we bear in mind that,
when we speak of NATO's nuclear formations, we shall be con-

cerned in future not only with formations intended solely for tactical employment, but also with the possibility that NATO might in future also have strategic nuclear weapons under its control. We have discussed the considerable disadvantages of an integrated NATO nuclear strike force earlier, but the point made by the French—that the American threat of strategic nuclear retaliation has tended to weaken NATO—could yet persuade the United States that its European partners in the alliance should create a European strategic nuclear force, and to offer either to help them in this or themselves participate in the project. We must hope that such a measure can prevent the evolution of separate independent national strategic nuclear forces. We must also hope that, if an integrated NATO strategic nuclear force is created, it will not lead NATO once again to thinking in terms of that monolithic rigidity that in recent years has so impaired the process of adapting its armament structure and its strategy to the changed world situation. A NATO strategic nuclear force must, at all events, only be regarded as the *ultima ratio*.

Should the coming years see the creation of a NATO strategic nuclear force, we might consider organising it in such a way as to embrace the units destined for strategic use and also the tactical nuclear force suggested earlier in this chapter. It should be under a newly created military command which would initially not be subordinate to SACEUR as regards orders to go into action.

The question nevertheless remains open whether the governments of the NATO powers could confer on a NATO Supreme Political Commander from the outset full powers for the operation of tactical and strategic forces, and of what nature these powers should be. Up till now NATO has had no "Supreme Political Commander." There is little prospect of the creation of such a post in the future. On the contrary, this function is vested in the fifteen-man NATO Council whose ability to make quick decisions would, in an emergency, most probably be grievously impaired.

The final say in the decision to use nuclear weapons cannot, however, be left to a military officer, nor could a military officer be expected to assume this responsibility. The suggestion that, instead, SACEUR be subordinated to a European political leader, representing all participating European governments, might give rise to the danger that the situation would be polarised between the European members on the one hand and the United States on the other. This, in turn, might give rise to the danger of the dissolution of the alliance. This danger would not be removed if we were to adopt Norstad's idea of creating an additional NATO body which —like the United Nations Security Council—would consist not of all the members of NATO but of only three or four states. Nor would such a move solve the problem of the form in which the remaining NATO states should be given the opportunity of stating their case, particularly if the question should arise of using nuclear weapons from bases on their sovereign territory.

The question of a Supreme Political Commander over nuclear weapons, and how he should be controlled, can obviously not be solved in a manner satisfactory to all sides. The most practicable solution would be to concentrate in the hands of one politically responsible figure the political powers and control over the "safety bulkhead" between conventional and nuclear defence that has got to be built into NATO's organisation. Until there is a Prime Minister of the United States of Europe this figure could only be the President of the United States. It would be, practically speaking, up to him to make the decision which, should the need for defence arise, would subordinate the commander of the NATO nuclear force to the NATO Supreme Commander (SACEUR) and direct him to execute the operational plans drawn up in peacetime. The question of whether the governments of European NATO states should have the right to veto any use of nuclear weapons from bases on their territory is one that must be carefully gone into. Other solutions are conceivable which would do more to meet the prestige requirements of European governments. In an emergency, however, they would be less effective. The greater the number of voices which are given a chance to speak when crucial NATO decisions are made, the greater will be the danger of our succumbing to strategic nuclear surprise actions.

The New Strategy of the New President[4]

The United States and its allies (fifteen of them in NATO, eight in SEATO, and twenty-one in the Organisation of American

---

[4] Since this book was written, President Kennedy has made various proposals for the future shape and size of the American armed forces, notably his Defense Message to Congress of 28 March 1961. The substance of the majority of these proposals was correctly foreshadowed by Helmut Schmidt in the following section. (Trans.)

N

States) possess in all about 200 divisions. None the less, the United States does not have at its disposal sufficient highly mobile units at constant readiness. In the summer of 1960 Nelson Rockefeller told his fellow governors of the United States that over the last fifteen years the relative military strength of the United States had steadily and drastically declined compared with that of the Soviet Union. He went on to say that this decline was apparent not only in the strategic retaliatory forces of the United States, but also in the tactical forces which were necessary for defence against limited local attacks.

This situation has since become public knowledge in the United States. Had Rockefeller succeeded Eisenhower in place of Kennedy, his summing up of the military situation and its requirements would not have differed to any marked extent from that which Kennedy will develop and put before the public during 1961. Neither would Rockefeller's fellow Republican, Nixon, have deviated to any significant degree from this line had he become President. Because of his association with the Eisenhower administration, however, he would have found it hard to put the new imperatives over to the American people. In the United States several hundreds of military and intellectual strategists are constantly exchanging ideas with one another; a large number of civilian research institutes (from those attached to the universities to the Rand Corporation), government departments and military staffs are in constant touch with each other, and the leading politicians of both parties participate in the strategic discussion to a degree inconceivable to us in Germany. A wide-ranging discussion unfolded in the United States after the shock of Sputnik I in 1957. This has now led, generally speaking, to a substantial measure of agreement. Some individuals still dissent, however, and there is also some special pleading which reflects the rivalries between the American armed services.

A clear-cut decision for or against an American first or second strike capability seems neither likely nor possible in the United States today. The final solution will probably reflect an attempt to combine both and will probably provide for the complete hardening, in as short a time as possible, of the second-strike forces. The way thither will lead initially via Polaris and, later, Minuteman ballistic missiles. The last-named weapon systems will receive top priority. Maximum effort will simultaneously be devoted to the development and production of warning and reconnaissance satellites and of anti-missile missiles.

The time of the "New Look" is gone forever. The United States will go over to the strategic concept of "flexible response." For this reason it will not be possible to give up the American overseas bases without serious thought to their importance for every sort of overseas limited war: military and politico-psychological necessities will have to be weighed against one another in every single case. The conventional forces of the United States Army and Marine Corps will be substantially reinforced. This will apply both to their numbers and to their weapons and equipment. The tactical air forces will be similarly augmented and modernised. These forces will be trained and armed in such a way that they will be able to fight limited wars through to the end with conventional weapons. Larger mobile reserves and stocks will be set up. Air and sea transport capacity will be increased. Anti-submarine naval forces will receive special priority. A reorganisation of the Pentagon will be undertaken at the same time in order to ensure a better concentration of forces and greater unity of political and strategic leadership.

Kennedy has left no one in any doubt of his conviction that NATO as a whole must be converted into a "vital and coherent military power," able "to deter every sort of attack." He will also ask his European allies to contribute to the defence of Europe on a larger scale than hitherto: he will try to put an end to the divisive rivalries of the Six and the Seven. It may be hoped that under his leadership the state of near anarchy prevailing in NATO during Eisenhower's last years will be terminated. His administration will be concerned to bring about more and firmer co-ordination within NATO. In so doing there is no doubt that he will make greater financial demands both on his own people and on his allies than have been made in recent years. We must not blind ourselves to the danger that the financial implications of this policy might lead to the partial withdrawal of American troops from Europe without corresponding Soviet troop withdrawals.

Kennedy will probably try to convince the NATO Council of the necessity of the concept of graduated deterrence, though possibly without referring to it by name. The United States will arm itself in such a way as to make it possible, in concert with its allies, to bring adequate force to bear, both as regards strategic nuclear and tactical nuclear warfare, and also in conventional wars initiated by the Soviet Union in all conceivable theatres. The United States will try to influence its allies to increase the number of operational divisions in Western Europe and also to maintain a larger number of reserve divisions capable of being thrown into battle within a few weeks. The United States itself will build up a strategic reserve of high mobility both for conventional and for nuclear war. This reserve will be designed for fighting side by side with European forces if necessary.

Kennedy will make renewed efforts to re-start disarmament talks between East and West, and will call in the help of comprehensive scientific analysis to help him. Nevertheless, he is fully conscious of the possibility of future "breakthroughs" in the field of military technology: he will make every effort to prevent the Soviet Union from making unilateral breakthroughs in the field of space travel. The danger of technological breakthrough exists not only as regards reconnaissance and warning satellites, and satellites for missile guidance or missile launching platforms, but also as regards vertical take-off fighters and bombers, nuclear-powered heavy bombers as missile launching platforms, and the whole field of electronic warfare. America is aware that the military balance can be upset by technological breakthrough.

We may assume that the new President is willing to give a firmer stamp to American leadership within the alliance than did his predecessor after the death of J. F. Dulles. This will by no means be restricted to the strategic or military spheres, but will extend in particular to those of political and economic co-operation. The internal, as also the external situation of the alliance is overripe for a new initiative. The prospects of success for a new initiative by Kennedy are none too bright in view of France's political situation, the endless Algerian war,[5] the obduracy of Bonn, and the increasing difficulties encountered by the United States in its own hemisphere. It might help Kennedy's efforts if there were to be a recrudescence of that immoderate political aggressiveness that led Khrushchev to bang his shoe on the table at the autumn session of the U.N. General Assembly in New York. In other respects, however, the aggressiveness of the Soviet leaders between 1958 and 1960 shows how dangerously their consciousness of their

[5] Without going into the matter in detail, may we say that these two things are beginning seriously to jeopardise the consistency and purpose of NATO.

power has increased. This danger will not disappear until the military and political re-equipment of NATO, and the reorientation of its armament, have been accomplished. It may well be that the world will be nearer to war in the first years of the new decade than in the last. If peace is to be preserved during this period, the West must leave no room for doubt as to its determination to defend freedom.

NATO Needs Troops

The number of combat-ready divisions in Central Europe at the end of 1960 can be said to be the equivalent in fighting power of at best 14 divisions. If, within a few years, the German Army is fully built up, armed and trained, the total fighting power of NATO in Central Europe will be of the order of 19 divisions—assuming, that is, that the forces of the other states are not in the meantime further depleted. While, therefore, we may reckon with an average fighting power of at the most 20 divisions for NATO in Central Europe during the early sixties, the alliance will be confronted, as it is today, by 20 war-ready Soviet divisions in the "D.D.R." which in the event of war could be increased to 40 divisions in less than two weeks, and could later be further increased to 80 divisions. The Polish, Czech and East German forces are not included in this. In an emergency under present conditions the ratio of military power after about 10 days would be about 3 : 1 in favour of the Eastern bloc, and would further and more substantially shift to the Soviet advantage from the eleventh day onwards. The reserve divisions at NATO's disposal today may be put at the equivalent of at the most 3 divisions.

A general military power ratio of 3 : 1 would permit the Soviet leaders to bring a substantially higher numerical superiority to bear at the focal point of any attack. In the long run Europe could not be defended by conventional means if this ratio were to persist. A higher degree of numerical inferiority would make the conventional defence of Europe completely illusory. Assuming the fighting of a purely conventional war, therefore, we must on no account fall short of a ratio of military power of 3 : 2 to the disadvantage of NATO if decisive enemy frontal breakthroughs are to be avoided. If at the end of the initial stage of hostilities the Soviet Union were to be left with 40 divisions on the Central European battlefield, NATO would need to have at least 25 war-ready divisions at its disposal. Since we must assume Satellite co-operation with the Soviet Union, the number of divisions required by NATO in Central Europe would therefore be more like 30. If this requirement, put forward year after year by NATO and W.E.U., were to be met, NATO would at all events be able to fight a purely conventional war for as long as any conflict has lasted so far without turning into general war.

In the event of a war lasting longer, NATO would furthermore clearly need to be able to bring up reserves. Every limited war fought since 1945 (Korea, Indo-China, Algeria) shows that such wars are unlikely to be settled quickly. In this situation it is assumed that the reserves will receive a good tactical training so as to remain capable of operations even under the conditions of, albeit temporary, air superiority which we must expect the enemy to have.

It is operationally unnecessary—assuming the continued main-tenance of the concentration of Soviet forces in the "D.D.R."—for more than 20 divisions to be maintained in peacetime on West German soil; indeed the danger of surprise, and logistical consider-ations counsel against it. What is, however, necessary is that NATO should be able to bring up the remaining formations and the reserves concentrated in the rear in the same period as it would take the Soviets to bring up their formations stationed in the Western U.S.S.R. and also their reserves.

Liddell Hart and others (among them, earlier on, the German Social Democrats) have suggested, in place of the 30 divisions here considered necessary, the creation of a small number only of armoured divisions with an unrestricted capacity for cross-country movement, plus a small number of highly mobile light infantry divisions: they further suggested closing the gaps with a territorial-type militia, while the regular units just referred to should consist of professional soldiers serving for fairly long periods.[6] Both concepts have their advantages and their disadvantages: we cannot go into these in detail in these pages, since to do so would require a capacity for making detailed judgments on operational and tactical matters. The territorial concept has, however, the inestim-

---

[6] It is not necessary to explain that the Social Democratic Party was true to the logic of NATO's general strategy in the fifties when it wished (as it then did) to limit Germany's contribution to relatively small regular units and a territorial (militia) system manned in the first instance on a voluntary basis.

able political advantage of being minimally provocative. In neither case could NATO get by without retaining universal military service in the member states. The stumbling-block at the moment is that the European countries have at their disposal neither 30 divisions nor their equivalent in small, highly mobile formations of long-service professionals plus a territorial militia to fill the gaps.

It is hard to see why the nations of Europe and the NATO states should not make the sacrifice of raising larger forces if this were to give their peoples a better chance of survival in an emergency. The total population of the United States is at the moment 180 million as opposed to the 210 million of the Soviet Union. Together the populations of the NATO countries number 450 million as against the 300 million of the Warsaw Pact countries. The United Kingdom, France, Germany, Belgium and Holland have a total population of 160 million, yet at the moment their contribution to NATO comprises less than a dozen divisions. Relative to the size of its population, the Soviet Union has ten times the number of troops of the NATO countries just named.

Efforts should be made to place at NATO's disposal 6 American, 4 British and at least 4 French war-ready divisions in addition to the 12 Bundeswehr divisions which will materialise before long. On German territory only the German divisions and the bulk of the British and American formations will be required. All others, and especially the French, Belgian and Dutch formations, could withdraw further back and remain drawn up on their own national territory. And in addition it would still be necessary to create the separate nuclear formations discussed above.

To maintain an American division in Europe costs annually something short of £100 million: to maintain a German, British or French division might cost as little as one-third of this sum. To object on fiscal grounds, therefore, is as unconvincing as to maintain that the available reservoir of manpower is inadequate.

The continuation of the Algerian war would, on the other hand, be a decisive obstacle. If this superfluous and senseless war could be ended, many of Europe's worries would vanish.

The number alone of NATO divisions is not, however, the crucial factor: they must above all be in a position, as regards equipment with vehicles and weapons, and also training, to stand up to the outstandingly well-equipped and well-trained Soviet divisions in East Germany. In view of the special suitability of the

North German plain for armoured breakthroughs, NATO must above all have a capability for rapid movement on and off roads. The number, fire power, mobility and radius of action of NATO's tanks is more important than their armour and their weight. The equipment of NATO's formations as a whole must be adapted to the purpose of conducting a mobile defence. Great emphasis must be placed on a full capability for cross-country movement and the equipment of all formations, on an adequate scale, with modern and effective anti-tank weapons. We must look again into the aircraft and weapons complement of those units of the tactical air forces earmarked for ground support: the existing number of such formations will probably need increasing at the expense of those at present earmarked for nuclear interdiction.

The conventional ground forces require, in addition, certain specialised "fire-brigade" units with air transport constantly at their disposal, whose mission will be to intervene rapidly in local conflicts or in local outbreaks of violence. For psychological reasons it is desirable that the "fire-brigade" should be an integrated one; but it should not be confused with the integrated strategic nuclear force demanded by Norstad and Bowie.

The tasks outlined above have been neglected for years in the name of the strategy of nuclear retaliation, which has been favoured principally by the air force. It therefore seems plausible that when the post of Supreme Allied Commander Europe next falls vacant, the nomination should go once again to a General of the Army rather than to an Air Force General as at present: this would not only underline the importance of the "first encounter," but, most of all, would signify that the expansion and modernisation of the conventional ground forces had become a guiding principle at the command level.

Integration and Division of Labour

The governments of NATO member states who demand the same weapons for their countries "as the enemy has," do no service whatsoever to the effectiveness of the alliance. This was argued in detail earlier when we discussed national nuclear strategic forces. What is much more important is that NATO as a whole should be put in the position where it can create an equilibrium at all levels of possible warfare. In addition, a far-reaching division of labour is necessary within NATO not only for political and strategic reasons, but also for those of financial and economic policy. How the tasks are divided must be decided in the light of political and military interests. The smaller and medium powers must not try to set themselves up as great powers. A handful of Polaris missiles allocated to the German Bundeswehr would benefit NATO as little as the single aircraft carrier of the Netherlands Navy. Neither may the small powers take on tasks appropriate to the major powers, nor all fifteen members of NATO perform the same tasks. Those involving nuclear weapons must fall on the shoulders of the United States, while the particular task of the European member nations must be to bring NATO's conventional armament up to a really modern standard and to establish a reasonable numerical balance in face of the strong Soviet armoured and infantry forces. This would end NATO's dependence on paper soldiers which either do not exist or are not fit for combat. It is equally impermissible for the smaller member nations to indulge their desire to assert themselves by embarking on the development and production of prestige weapons and thus prejudice the availability to NATO of forces of the sort that are really needed. NATO's defensive power would not be advanced if all member states wished to participate in the setting up of the separate tactical nuclear branch of the forces.

The re-establishment of NATO's deterrent capability and, with it, of a genuine defence capability on the part of Europe, is only possible through the agency of a meaningful division of labour on the one hand, and of a far-reaching integration of military planning and direction on the other: the latter is a priority requirement. The armament, training and size of the forces of the individual member states must accord with NATO's operational imperatives and the capabilities of the member states. Above all it will be necessary to achieve a high degree of practical integration in the following three fields: air defence; weapons development and production; and logistics. The imperative need for closer *political* co-operation and co-ordination between the European NATO powers does not need further elaboration here.

European air defence is in a wretched state. The aircraft, equipment, procedures and tactics of the two tactical air forces differ among themselves. In particular there is a lack of air defence in depth, since French air space has not been up till now at NATO's disposal. But, even with complete integration of Western

European air defence, the tasks ahead would still be most formidable because of the shortness of the warning period. Even if effective anti-missile missiles were available, defence against enemy missiles would scarcely appear possible on account of the limited warning available: even against light and medium bombers the warning would be short enough in all conscience. In order to be effective, therefore, NATO's air defence must be predicated on offensive action against the enemy's air forces. The defensive forces available for air defence missions consist of interceptor fighters, static surface-to-air missiles, and the so-called anti-aircraft defences of the combined forces. Interceptor fighters and anti-aircraft missiles must be welded into one system under unified tactical command. The present multiplicity of systems and procedures is intolerable and should be ended as soon as possible. The present practice of producing interceptor fighters for European air defence simultaneously in six different countries seems pointless as much for economic reasons as for those of military technology. Greater efforts should be devoted to the development of vertical take-off fighters. It may be in the interest of everybody if, in working towards suitable forms of air defence, we based our efforts to a greater extent than hitherto on British experience and British production in the field of fighter aircraft. In the field of anti-aircraft missiles the present dependence on American development and production seems à propos; but we must examine whether our dependence on liquid-fuelled missiles should be abandoned forthwith. There is at present no means of combating very low-flying aircraft: in this field there is a crying need for the development of effective modern conventional weapons.

The development and production of a standard tank for use by European NATO countries is an equally urgent need. Little has as yet been seen of such a weapon though there has been talk of it for years. It should weigh relatively little, should be shallow in profile, should have high mobility and speed, and should have a wide radius of action. It should be able to use diesel fuel (i.e. have a multi-fuel engine). It might be expedient to rely to a greater extent on German experience in this field. Great attention should be paid, furthermore, to the development of multi-fuel motors for all other military vehicles also. At the same time we must call a halt to the unbelievable multiplicity of types of motor vehicle in service. This applies to armoured personnel carriers also: the German A.P.C. is, incidentally, a misfire and constitutes a serious weakness in the German formations.

It is equally important to develop and produce modern, light-weight, tank-busting weapons in the upper range bracket, and with a crew of one, or at the most two men: the bazooka of World War II, still to be seen in service, should be packed off to the museum.

The modernisation of the field artillery is also in need of priority effort. There is a need for the large-scale introduction of light, non-recoil, multi-purpose weapons. We should in particular examine whether the large-scale introduction of multiple rocket launchers for massed field use, on the Soviet model, might not be desirable.

Finally, the equipment of the army air force needs urgent examination and standardisation. The present aircraft of the German ground forces are good for no other purpose than for transporting quite small numbers of hospital cases, couriers or generals.

The standardisation of the equipment of the Western European ground forces and NATO's tactical air forces in Europe cannot be achieved within a few months, and probably not even within the space of a few years. Nevertheless, the hitherto prevailing trend towards making the equipment of the troops more varied and more chequered from year to year must resolutely be reversed. There are still three separate calibres for rifles and machine guns, and as many as five separate calibres for tank guns. Working with the present variety of weapons, vehicles and equipments is, for the operational staffs concerned, like having to piece a jig-saw puzzle together. Standardisation of all aspects of logistic support is impossible under present-day conditions. Up till now it would only have been possible to commit formations to battle in an emergency if their umbilical cords to their national supply and logistic organisations could have been prevented from crossing and generally fouling one another. Only the most far-reaching integration of the planning, development and production of the new weapons that are to come can succeed in future in putting an end to this shambles.

It is true that the necessity for technical integration on the weapons side has long been recognised and desired by many military officers, but they have not been able to agree either on a unified approach, or on how to push it through. Many varied national interests—some real and some imaginary—are at work here. The arms industries have acquired colossal power behind the scenes. Without the European governments waking up to it, the European arms industry has once again developed into a sinister complex of forces. This jungle can only be cleared, and the silent, hidden hand of the arms lobbies—whose activities resemble those of a secret shadow cabinet—can only be brought out into the light if the governments concerned decide, within their own cabinets, to make a single minister responsible for the whole field of arms procurement, and give him the necessary powers. Today, in the various different countries of the alliance, the activities of single service commanders, of defence ministers and ministers responsible for single services, of ministers in charge of financial and economic departments, and of the permanent heads of all these departments —to say nothing of the representatives of the private and semi-nationalised arms industries—will all be found to overlap. NATO needs a joint organisation at the political policy-making level to help it sort out this confusion. At its head there should be a political appointee in the shape of a Chief of Armaments Planning who, dealing jointly with whoever was at the time the single responsible negotiator of the participating countries, would bring about the necessary co-ordination. The NATO Council must face up to taking the final decisions itself in every case where co-ordination by negotiation fails to deliver the goods.

Only as modernisation proceeds will it be possible to standardise, and thereby build up, a unified system of logistic support if the countries concerned agree to unified decision-making and to simultaneous sharing of tasks in the fields of the development, standardisation and production of weapons, vehicles and equipments. It has been said that, in the event of war, European NATO would need civil and military stores to the tune of at least 250,000 tons daily. This would have to be brought across the Atlantic in convoys. Apart from certain standard items of fuel, ammunition and mass consumption foodstuffs, it is difficult to see what specific items in the way of spares, reinforcements and reserves would be brought over: it is similarly difficult to see which units would get the benefit of these supplies and which would not. This is an indefensible situation and one that must undermine the general confidence in NATO's ability to defend itself. One must agree in principle with the many attempts of the German Defence Minister to rectify this situation in the NATO Council: the same goes for his applications to the allied governments for assistance towards the establishment of stores depots and supply bases for the German armed forces. Because of the likelihood that West German territory would, in the event of a general war in Europe, rapidly turn into a battlefield, it is logical to instal such depots and bases to some extent west of the German frontiers—especially in view of the requirement for all NATO forces to be stored on such a basis that they could hold out for two or three months without supplies from overseas. NATO needs integration of its logistic supply installations. Although supply matters rejoice in the NATO title of "logistics," it is the one field of joint defence planning where logic is least apparent. This problem also can be solved only at a high political level.

In several fields NATO is in need of stronger military co-ordination: we cannot in these pages suggest solutions for every problem, however briefly. Let us, however, conclude our survey by drawing attention to the need for better co-operation between the intelligence and secret services of the NATO powers. It is, perhaps, inevitable that a certain amount of mutual observation should go on inside NATO: but one can at least ask that information should be exchanged on the actions and intentions of the potential common enemy.

What, however, is wanted *least* of all is without any doubt the working out of a common "counter-ideology." This is something at which the repeated attempts—mainly within certain German circles—to organise an integrated "psychological defence" are presumably aimed. Let us repeat: the West needs no common ideology for fighting Communism. It needs no ideology at all. What we need is to be conscious of commonly affirmed, socio-ethical basic values, to make headway towards the realisation of individual freedom and social democracy, and to identify our peoples consciously with this process. To create such a consciousness would indeed be true psychological defence. If the NATO allies could inculcate this consciousness in their peoples during the coming decade there would be no need to doubt Europe's ability to look to its defence.

12

Stability is Possible

NOT only has yesterday's so-called "balance of terror" given way to a balance with little stability about it, but the balance of military forces throughout the world has become an altogether tricky business. New forces affecting the balance of power are constantly making their appearance—the rise of China as a first-class military power, the economic growth of the principal powers concerned, new developments in the field of military technology, and new strategic insights. The balance of power never stands still. All powers concerned have, therefore, a vital interest in creating the counterbalances relevant at any given time. The West cannot attempt to maintain the so-called military *status quo* and no more. It must, on the contrary, make sustained efforts in the political, military and economic spheres aimed at the constant renewal of the balance at all levels if it is to be in a position to negotiate on all the old subjects of dispute (e.g. German reunification, Berlin, disarmament and control) and on the new disputes that might arise at any time in Africa, South-East Asia, the Middle East or other parts of the world. We are persuaded that the West has, in sufficient degree, the necessary moral, spiritual, political and material resources.

Back to the Beginning

This book began by quoting the opinion widely heard in Germany that, should war break out in Europe, Germany's physical devastation would inevitably follow; that it would, moreover, be absurd to make special preparations for a possible future war on the basis of hypothetical expectations or forecasts, for, in the event of war, these would inevitably be falsified. There is considerable justification for both statements. There would certainly be very little left of Germany after a war in Europe—particularly in view of NATO's present strategy. A future war would certainly turn out quite differently from what we imagine, attuned as we are to the experiences of past wars. Nevertheless, the struggle with Communism is something from which we cannot turn aside. A constantly re-stabilised balance of effective military strength will be necessary in Europe so as to prevent the struggle from assuming the shape of war. We must try in peacetime to tailor our forces and to measure them against those of the other powers in such a way as to ensure that war does not come about.

Correct solutions to this problem cannot be reached by intuition: they require hard work. To have any hope of reaching an optimum solution we must base our ideas on comprehensive analysis of the problems and impartial probing of their every aspect. A British *rapporteur* of the Parliamentary Assembly of Western European Union stated at the conclusion of a report submitted to this Assembly: "It is easy to define the problems; but almost impossible to be certain about the answers." And Liddell Hart has this to say: "There is no panacea for peace that can be written out in a formula like a doctor's prescription. But one can set down a series of practical points. . . . Study war, and learn from its history. Keep strong, if possible. In any case, keep cool. Have unlimited patience. Never corner an opponent, and always assist him to save his face. Put yourself in his shoes—so as to see things through his eyes. Avoid self-righteousness—nothing is so self-blinding. Cure yourself of two commonly fatal delusions—the idea of victory and the idea that war cannot be limited."[1]

No one will doubt that very many different concatenations of events and processes are possible that could lead to the unleashing of a military conflict in Europe. So long as Soviet forces remain deployed in the "D.D.R." and in Poland they could attack almost any country of Europe with conventional weapons and tactical atomic weapons. They are in a position, furthermore, to launch a strategic nuclear attack on any country of the globe. There is no single country that can deter the Soviet Union from all conceivable aggressive acts. The threat of American nuclear retaliation will in future be only of limited strategic significance: it is being replaced by the growing necessity for a joint conventional defence capability. The strategic nuclear armament of a major power is becoming, as it were, an umbrella under whose protection against strategic nuclear retaliation every other form of aggression and of warfare

[1] Liddell Hart, *Deterrent or Defence*, p. 247.

is once again becoming possible. If, therefore, we are to avoid confusion in our ideas, we must abandon the old concept of "the Sword and the Shield." The existence of the nuclear bomb has not so far made war impossible: Korea, Vietnam, Suez and Hungary testify to the contrary. Nor has the bomb helped to bring about a disarmament agreement. The differences between Moscow and Peking cast threatening shadows across the present state of "truce" between the major powers. The danger that the Soviet Union might be drawn by China into a war she does not want can no longer be dismissed out of hand.

The drawing up of realistic deterrent and defence strategies remains the unaltered task of governments, as does the drawing up of plans for achieving arms limitation and control. "The conduct of grand strategy rests with statesmen—though soldiers ought to understand it, as servants of government. While it is primarily political . . . it requires on the part of the political leaders an understanding of war, and particularly of how wars come about."[2]

Not all political leaders within the Western alliance have yet shown us that they understand the manifold dangers of war implicit in the old NATO strategy and armament. Many of them have a wrong idea of NATO's present-day deterrent effectiveness and general defence capabilities today. Many of them—contrary to Clausewitz's stipulation—"promise themselves a wrong effect from certain military means and measures, an effect opposed to their nature."[3] We hope that these political leaders and their public behind them will not misunderstand the dangers arising from miscalculation of the military situation. It is our hope that the reader of this book also will grasp the horrifying nature of the dangers: at the same time we hope that he will not blind himself to the awesome problems involved, but will be prepared to face up to their practical implications.

Conclusions

Strategic and military policy conceptions are—like policy in general—determined by moral and political principles on the one hand, and by the real facts of the situation on the other. The application of unchanging principles to changing circumstances necessarily gives rise to fresh strategic and political conceptions.

[2] Liddell Hart, *op. cit.*, p. 252.
[3] See the quotation from Clausewitz at the front of this volume.

The situation confronting the West in the sphere of defence is different from that of 1954: in the sixties it will differ fundamentally from that of the fifties. We must make up our minds as to the practical implications. We must have the courage to discuss our problems publicly before we do so. As a basis for this discussion we need better information than hitherto and to be told the true facts about the situation today. The politicians making the decisions do not need to be ex-captains or ex-generals—they do not even need ever to have been in the Services. But they must be capable of hard work, power of decision and honesty.

In this book we have only been able to touch on many opinions currently held: it has not been possible to do justice to important conclusions drawn notably by British and American authors of works of strategic analysis.[4] Let us now, though conscious of their imperfections, set down a few brief conclusions which the writer believes to be important for the strategic decisions which the West must make before long.[5]

1. Deterrence is a traditional factor in defensive strategy. Deterrence is not identical with retaliation; it means generally threatening a potential aggressor with an intolerable risk. The principle of deterrence can fail if the aggressor holds that the threatened risk is acceptable, whether by error or by correct appraisal; or when the aggressor is not convinced that the opponent has the will or the capability to carry out his threat; or when no other course of action remains open to the aggressor; or when the aggressor does not make his decision as the result of a rational evaluation of the situation. The principle of deterrence can also fail if the defender is mistaken about the degree to which the threatened risk is unbearable to the aggressor. Protection of the allied nations of Europe from the outbreak of a war can be achieved if a potential attacker is deterred by the creation of risks which would in his judgment outweigh the benefits to be gained by his attack.

2. In the long run, the threat of weapons is effective only if there is no doubt on either side that they will in fact be used for defence if necessary. Therefore military strategies drawn up in

[4] It would be a good thing if some responsible publisher would make the most important American books available in German, so that the German reader may be better informed.

[5] The translation of Conclusions 1-20, made by the author, first appeared in *Survival*, III, No. 4 (Jul.-Aug. 1916). (Trans.)

O

peacetime for their deterrent effect, and threatened as such, must be completely congruent with strategies to be used in an actual defence operation. Any gap between the damage which is merely threatened, and that which is actually to be carried out, can induce a potential aggressor to act.

3. The deterring factor which until now has been the most important, the threat of massive retaliation by the U.S. Strategic Air Command, inevitably loses significance with the approach of a stable nuclear balance between the world powers. The threat of thermo-nuclear destruction against a world power of strategic nuclear capacity is not an effective deterrent against any aggression except a total one, because of the risk to the defender's very existence which is bound up with realisation of the threat. The actual use of thermo-nuclear retaliation in reply to limited or even non-nuclear aggression proves itself to be irresponsible; the threat of it therefore loses credibility and leads to self-deception by the defender as to his own security against such aggression. Retaliatory nuclear destruction with strategic weapons can in the future be inflicted on another nuclear power with strategic capacity only when the latter commits aggression with such weapons. Only against a power with such intentions can the threat of nuclear retaliation have lasting credibility and deterrent effect. Therefore the West needs a strategic nuclear force which is largely immune to damage (that is, hard), solely to deter aggression of this type. The era of unlimited effectiveness is rapidly approaching its end as far as the nuclear retaliation threat in other cases is concerned. As the time draws nearer when the Western strategic force will be confined to the above-mentioned single purpose, the probability of a total nuclear war between East and West decreases; at the same time, however, the deterrent effect which was previously gained by the threat of nuclear destruction against smaller-scale aggression will be reduced.

4. Continued maintenance of the *general* conception of strategic nuclear retaliation is foolish. Anyone who fails to understand that the threat of nuclear destruction is a deterrent against certain definite forms of aggression only, lays Europe open to subjection or destruction. The theory of the inevitability of nuclear defence is fatally wrong.

5. It is highly probable that a conflict could increase and accelerate in intensity, ending in the use of the most powerful weapons

CONCLUSIONS 211

and the related risk of the defender's own thermo-nuclear destruction. Therefore the threat to use limited, or tactical, nuclear weapons against a nuclear-armed world power is no longer entirely credible in so far as it is meant to deter the latter from committing non-nuclear, or conventional, aggression. Defence with limited use of nuclear weapons will in the end serve as a serious threat only against aggression in which a similar use of weapons is intended. Solely for deterring aggression of this type, NATO therefore needs in Europe an adequate number of tactical nuclear weapons.

6. Defence against a non-nuclear aggression in Europe with the aid of tactical nuclear weapons, even in the unlikely event of both sides keeping within bounds and avoiding the upward acceleration of weapons, would most probably mean the extensive destruction of Europe and, at all events, of Germany.

7. In the interest of maintaining the substance of Europe and particularly of Germany, NATO must therefore have troops and weapons on a scale ample to make non-nuclear aggression appear hopeless, and sufficient in an emergency to force one of two courses on the aggressor—to halt or to extend the conflict.

8. Conventional defence of Europe against non-nuclear aggression, and therefore a conventional deterrent, is possible. Setting up the necessary deterrent and defence structure of NATO requires penetrating analysis by participating governments, by NATO and by the military staffs of both; it requires political decisions with their corresponding financial and legislative consequences as well as corresponding directives to military staffs. The change-over to the necessary defence structure will take several years, and this period will be accompanied by risks in foreign policy. But if because of these risks the change is not made, we can be certain that towards the end of the sixties Europe will not be able to defend itself against non-nuclear aggression at all. So those who think that it is not possible or not worth while to limit military conflicts to conventional weapons must not be allowed to exercise any influence on the strategy of NATO.

9. In the present circumstances, to defend Europe in a conflict with conventional weapons, NATO needs:

(*a*) some 30 divisions with exclusively conventional weapons for the central European sector;

(*b*) small, highly manœuvrable conventional action groups (or "fire brigade");

(c) preparation for larger reserves;

(d) modernised arms and equipment of considerably better quality;

(e) joint planning of development, production, supply and logistics;

(f) integration of air defence.

10. Conventional forces which are intended to defend Europe against non-nuclear aggression or as a deterrent against such aggression must in future be kept strictly apart from nuclear forces intended to combat or deter nuclear aggression. Any possibility of a conventional conflict turning into a nuclear one only because of NATO's structure and strategy must be carefully excluded by means of appropriate provisions in political and military planning.

11. The overall defence structure of the West must in future be adequate to present an intolerable risk to a potential aggressor in all types of conflict. Conventional forces on land, on sea and in the air make the first encounter; they must be capable of operating without nuclear support. A special force armed with tactical nuclear weapons, the "second encounter," is needed for defence with limited nuclear firepower, and it must be capable of working together operationally with "first encounter" units if nuclear defence is needed.

12. Far-reaching division of labour is necessary between the European members of NATO for the sake of higher efficiency and to shorten the period of transition. The task of perfecting and maintaining an effective strategic nuclear force should be left to the United States. The task of releasing troops armed with tactical nuclear weapons from the existing "Shield" forces and their formation into a separately organised tactical nuclear force should be entrusted to those states which have already made considerable investments in this field and have created such units.

13. The creation of new independent nuclear (tactical as well as strategical) forces in the control of individual NATO countries would endanger the consistency and the cohesion of the alliance. The distribution of control over nuclear weapons among additional governments increases the probability of a nuclear catastrophe with mathematical certainty. In present-day conditions, transferring control over nuclear weapons to the German Government would contribute considerably to fears which already exist. NATO must make every conceivable effort to oppose the spreading process. If

contrary views on the part of individual member states cannot be changed in any other way, joint and integrated participation by other member states in strategic and tactical nuclear forces would appear to be the lesser evil. And yet NATO does not by any means need extra nuclear weapons to defend Europe—it needs more soldiers, tanks and conventional weapons in general.

14. Any strategic nuclear forces, as well as a special tactical nuclear force of NATO, would require special political leadership and control. So far there are no convincing suggestions for solving this problem; it is, however, a problem of extreme urgency and greatest significance, that must be analysed much more thoroughly than has been done in Europe until now, so that the NATO Council can come to a well-founded political decision. It might be appropriate if the political leadership and control of both were placed under the command of the American President and—in an emergency—of a joint command subordinate to him.

15. The supreme aim of all efforts made by NATO and its members in the military sphere must be the achievement of a stable balance of power. Arms control and limitation as well as inspection are suitable means of achieving greater stability. Agreed limitation of arms presumes an approach towards balance at all levels of weapons and troops on both sides. So long as NATO has to rely largely on nuclear weapons, while the Soviet-led military bloc has great numerical superiority in conventional forces, it is not very probable that far-reaching agreements will be achieved.

16. However, there is intense interest in both world powers and all over the rest of the world in a speedy and final ban on nuclear tests. Such an agreement could prevent the spread of nuclear weapons to other governments. An agreed halt to tests does not presume a general balance at all levels. It is therefore more pressing than other disarmament problems. If it is not brought about, with the participation of all countries concerned, a considerable deterioration in the strategic nuclear situation of the world will probably set in within a few years; such a deterioration could force new and unwanted decisions on NATO and its member states.

17. In the western world the problems of armament limitation and control, and inspection as a safeguard against surprise attack, have so far been scientifically investigated less than have the problems of deterrence and defence; results of analyses which have so far been made on disarmament and arms control have been kept

more secret than those on defence. But deterrence and defence on the one hand and disarmament and control on the other are only different aspects of the same complex set of questions; the two sides of the coin. If better results are to be obtained, much more comprehensive information and greater use of scientific research methods are indispensable. The Federal Republic has also to contribute to this.

18. The Federal Republic has in particular an urgent interest in careful examination of any such possibility of limited regional disarmament, control or inspection, which would offer a prospect of easing the political situation in central Europe without endangering the military balance of forces and its stabilizing.

19. In the present state of the world and of Europe, there is hardly anybody who depends more on NATO's protection than Berlin and with it the Federal Republic of Germany. For this reason Germany should be the last to pursue political or military intentions which could impair the power to deter and defend of the alliance; on the contrary, she must oppose such intentions. In this connexion Germany has to realise that many of her allies still do not place full or finally established confidence in her, and that many regard legitimate German claims arising from the partition of the country as a threat to peace. So the Federal Republic must neither give the impression that she will in her defence preparations go farther than the NATO Council's decisions, nor must she give rise to any suspicion that she is toying with the thought of a policy that would make her independent of NATO. Political forces in the Federal Republic must not endanger confidence in the country's loyalty to NATO either by setting exaggerated armament aims or by demanding a reduction in Germany's commitments to the alliance. The size, equipment and training of the West German armed forces must fit the needs of NATO.

20. Closing of the missile gap by the United States and the reform of NATO's defence structure which has been demanded above will take two or three years. It is probable that the Soviet leaders will exploit this period with new foreign policy offensives. The greatest possible unanimity is therefore to be desired in NATO, and enough solidarity to ensure a national existence is to be demanded from all political forces within the Federal Republic.

Some readers may wonder to what extent these propositions are reasonable and represent the full answer. They may regard my demand for a shift of emphasis to conventional weapons as the reaction typical of a soldier whose ideas are still monopolised by the conceptions of past wars. But even these readers must share at least *one* of the writer's convictions, viz. that the shrewdest possible re-examination of our strategic situation is a matter of supreme urgency. At a later date no one will forgive delays and errors committed through thoughtlessness and political indolence, or through lack of candour and deficient powers of decision. In a democracy the statesman cannot shuffle the responsibility off on to the shoulders of the military.

Unanimity and solidarity in implementing the agreed measures of defence against Soviet threats depends on a minimum of agreement on the part of the political forces in the Federal Republic as to the imperatives of German foreign policy, and vice versa. Reunification policy and readiness for defence are similarly interdependent.

The Decisive Battle will not be a Military One

If a stable military equilibrium can be maintained in Europe the real danger from the East will not in future lie in the military threat, nor will it lie in scientific, technical or economic competition for higher production levels and higher standards of living: it must rather be sought in the competition for influence over the under-developed countries. The crucial danger will, however, be the East's spiritual and intellectual challenge to the West. If we pretend that it is enough just to preserve the military balance, or to do no more than maintain our lead in productivity—if we pretend that we can rely for our defence on the ideology of a so-called "psychological defence," we will one day suffer a rude awakening. Of course the West needs soldiers. Of course the West needs a flourishing, high-performance economy. Of course it must protect itself against Communist ideological infiltration. But what is just as clear is that we must have a progressive increase of social justice in our society. Above all else, however, what we need is a profound and unassailable consciousness of the moral superiority of spiritual and intellectual freedom in a democratically ordered society. The European nations must conquer their frustration at no longer being the active hub of world affairs by extending their moral, spiritual and intellectual horizons. It is in this field that Europe's struggle with Communism will have to be decided—not in that of missiles and nuclear weapons. "Statesmen . . . can work only with what they have. Of this, the armies and weapons are only the smaller part."[6]

The challenge of the new decade is before us: it is not to be evaded. We need have no fear of Communism. We have everything necessary to combat it. Nevertheless, Germany divided is once again confronted by a test of its probity. Those who recognise this will not allow us free Germans to get lost in quarrels over secondary issues which dissipate our strength and will to prove ourselves. The problem of our existence as a nation demands that we have the will to act together.

[6] G. F. Kennan, *Russia, the Atom, and the West*, p. 102.

APPENDIX

Explanation of Technical Terms and Abbreviations

The terms explained below relate in general to ideas that have been taken up by the daily press and specialist journals. The need for striking a compromise between brevity and clarity has entailed some loss of accuracy and detail. These explanations are therefore intended less for the highly specialised professional than for the reader who has some interest in the subject but no special knowledge of it: they are not intended to replace a military dictionary.

Shortage of space has prevented the incorporation of many—unfortunately too detailed—suggestions from specialists. Only under the heading "Nuclear Weapons"—on account of its great importance—have more of these suggestions been utilised than elsewhere, and only here have we given a detailed description.

The sizes, weights and performance data quoted in the explanations of certain technical terms are often approximate. The dates quoted are in many cases subject to qualification owing to the obsolescence of the weapon, etc., in question, to the introduction of new types, to operational considerations, and to other causes. This is, however, true also of many internationally recognised works of reference.

ABC weapons=Atomic, biological and chemical weapons.

AFCENT=Allied Forces Central Europe; NATO Command with H.Q. at Fontainebleau; Command area extends from Germany's southern frontier to the Elbe.

AFNORTH=Allied Forces Northern Europe; NATO Command with H.Q. in Kolsaas (Norway); Command area extends from the Elbe to North Cape.

AFSOUTH=Allied Forces Southern Europe; NATO Command with H.Q. in Naples; Command area from Italy to Turkey.

Aircraft carrier=Type of warship available only to NATO states. A total of about 30 are available with speeds of between 30 and 35 knots, displacement tonnages between 30,000 and 80,000 tons, aircraft complements of up to 100 and more, crews of up to 4,000 men. Nuclear-propelled carriers (*Enterprise*, displacement about 100,000 tons) now under construction in the U.S.A., cost= about 400 million dollars.

A.L.B.M.=Air-Launched Ballistic Missile, i.e. air-to-surface missile launched from aircraft.

All-out nuclear war=Total nuclear war.

All-weather fighter=Fighter equipped with electronic navigational and tactical instruments enabling it to fulfil its mission independent of weather and visibility.

ANZUS Pact=Members: Australia, New Zealand, U.S.A. (1951).

A.T.A.F. 2 and 4=Allied Tactical Air Force; NATO air forces deployed in Central Europe: H.Q. München Gladbach (2nd A.T.A.F.) and Ramstein/Pfalz (4th A.T.A.F.).

Atlas=American I.C.B.M., liquid-fuel rocket motor, range about 6,000 miles; nine(?) missiles were operational as at September 1960, and about a dozen(?) bases were under construction to accommodate several missiles each.

B 36 (Convair)=American strategic bomber aircraft, now obsolete.

B 47 (Boeing)=American strategic bomber aircraft, 6 jet engines, speed about 600 m.p.h., range about 3,250 miles: over 1,200 B 47s were available in 1960; standard equipment of S.A.C. today.

B 52 (Boeing)=American strategic bomber aircraft, 8 jet engines, speed over 650 m.p.h., range 6,000 miles: in 1960 a total of 500 B 52s were available to S.A.C.

B 58 ("Hustler," Convair)=American strategic bomber aircraft, in course of being delivered to units in 1960, intended as replacement for B 47, supersonic speed (about Mach 2).

Badger=Soviet strategic bomber aircraft (Tu 16), 2 jet engines, speed about 600 m.p.h., range about 3,500 miles: about 1,000 Badgers available in 1960.

Ballistic missile=Missile which cannot be influenced after its start (or after short initial flight): thereafter follows ballistic trajectory.

Bazooka=U.S. recoilless anti-tank weapon for use at short ranges; uses conventional warhead.

B.C.=Bomber Command, the British strategic air force (also called "V force").

Bear=Soviet strategic bomber aircraft (Tu 20), 4 turbo-prop jet engines, speed 550 m.p.h., range 7,000 miles: fewer than 100 Bears were available in 1960, some of them in use as tanker aircraft.

Bison=Soviet strategic bomber aircraft (Ilyushin-Myasishchev), 4 jet engines, speed 600 m.p.h., range 6,050 miles: 100 available in 1960.

Bloodhound=British anti-aircraft missile (surface-to-air ballistic missile), operated by R.A.F.

Blowlamp=Soviet tactical bomber aircraft, 2 jet engines, supersonic speed, low-altitude range 360 miles: together with the older types Backfin and Beagle (Il 28) about 4,000 available in 1960.

Blue Steel=British air-to-surface missile ("stand-off bomb"), range said to be about 370 miles: not yet operational(?)

Blue Streak=I.R.B.M./I.C.B.M., development abandoned by U.K. after expenditure of about £70 million, range about 2,800 miles.

Blue Water=British surface-to-surface ballistic missile: intended to replace Corporal.

Bomarc=American unmanned interceptor, air breathing, supersonic capability, range said to be over 370 miles: intended to be deployed for air defence purposes in north U.S.A. and Canada.

Canberra=British tactical bomber aircraft.

CENTAG=Central Army Group, NATO designation for the more southerly of the two army groups stationed in Germany; H.Q. Heidelberg.

CENTO=Central Pact Organisation (1955), members: U.K., Iran, Pakistan, Turkey; former designation "Baghdad Pact" abandoned after defection of Iraq.

Chain reaction=Process in nuclear physics giving rise to self-propagating factors which make it possible for the reaction to be renewed and continued.

Channel Command=NATO command area equal in status to SACEUR and SACLANT; embraces the southern North Sea, the Channel and the latter's western approaches.

Clean bomb=Nuclear bomb with relatively little radioactive fall-out.

Close ground support=NATO designation for battlefield support of the fighting forces by tactical air forces.

Coleopter=Annular-wing aircraft for vertical take-off.

COMECON=Council for Mutual Economic Assistance (1949); organisation comprises Albania, Bulgaria, Czechoslovakia, "D.D.R.," Hungary, Poland, Rumania and U.S.S.R.

Comlandschleswig=Commander of the NATO Ground Forces in Schleswig-Holstein; post combined with Commander of Wehrkreis 1.

Conventional weapons=All non-atomic, non-bacteriological and non-chemical weapons, missiles with T.N.T. warheads are regarded as conventional weapons; the Americans sometimes use the expression "conventional" for low-yield nuclear weapons (e.g. Davy Crockett), but this is misleading.

Corporal=American surface-to-surface tactical missile, range 75 miles, nuclear warhead 15-20 KT and over; operated by U.S. Army and delivered to allies.

Count-down=Interval of time between the giving of the order and the firing of a missile.

Counter-air=NATO concept for the initial operation of general war whereby aircraft and missiles are despatched to eliminate the enemy air force and, primarily, his airfields.

Counter-force strategy=Nuclear strategy aimed at the destruction of enemy strategic air and missile forces on the ground.

Davy Crockett=American tactical nuclear weapon (various versions, including anti-tank) for use by the ground forces, yield 2 KT and below, crew 1-2 men; not yet deployed in Europe.

Deterrence:
    active=Threat of own strategic nuclear first strike in the event of enemy aggression: active deterrence is the strategy underlying the original concept of "massive retaliation."
    minimum=Maintenance at readiness of strategic nuclear retaliatory forces required for carrying out passive deterrence.
    negative=A form of own armament and strategy designed to persuade the enemy that one cannot resort to first strike, so that the enemy is, for his part, removed from the temptation to strike first: this notion has little to do with deterrence in the strict sense.
    passive=Threat of own strategic nuclear second strike in the event of enemy strategic nuclear aggression against one's own country.

Deterrent=Anglo-U.S. expression for a nuclear retaliatory force.

DEW-line=Distant Early Warning radar chain in northern Canada and Greenland.

Dual-purpose weapons=Weapons capable of being used with both conventional and nuclear warheads, e.g. Nike, Honest John, the majority of modern fighter bombers.

Earth satellite=Missile put in orbit round the earth by means of a multi-stage rocket.

E.D.C.=Project for a highly integrated European Defence Community, collapsed in 1954; precursor of the Paris Treaties of 1955 which led, among other things, to the admission of the German Federal Republic to NATO and W.E.U.

E.E.C.=European Economic Community; European Common Market, 1957. Members: Belgium, France, German Federal Republic, Italy, Luxembourg, Netherlands.

E.F.T.A.=European Free Trade Area, established in opposition to European Common Market in 1959. Members: Austria, Denmark, Norway, Portugal, Sweden, Switzerland, United Kingdom.

Escalation=Uncontrolled, mutual commitment to the battle of weapons with growing destructive effect (in Germany called "nuclear spiral").

F 84=American fighter-bomber of older type (various versions); delivered to various countries, particularly to the German Air Force.

F 86 ("Sabre")=American interceptor fighter (various versions), older type; delivered to various countries, particularly to the German Air Force.

F 100 ("Super Sabre")=American (or Canadian) interceptor fighter or fighter-bomber, speed up to sonic; also delivered to allies.

F 104 ("Starfighter")=American interceptor fighter (various versions), supersonic speed possible: F 104 G is being delivered to the Federal Republic and is being built there under licence as in other European countries; is to become standard equipment of the German Air Force as multi-purpose aircraft.

Fall-out=Radioactive precipitation from the atmosphere after nuclear explosions.

Fiat G 91: *see* G 91.

Fire-brigade=Term for a highly mobile (air-transported) NATO force such as has been demanded in several quarters; force should be capable of being deployed immediately on the spot in the event of local aggression: should not be confused with various projects for setting up a NATO strategic nuclear force.

Firestreak=British air-to-air missile.

Force de frappe nationale=Projected independent French strategic nuclear force; should be built up by 1965 in the form of 50 light bombers (type Mirage IV) plus nuclear bombs.

Forestalling blow=Soviet, and recently also American, term for pre-emptive strike (*q.v.*).

Fusion: *see* Nuclear weapons.

G 91 = Italian fighter bomber primarily intended for battlefield support of ground forces; is being delivered to various European members of NATO or, alternatively, is being built by them under licence (particularly in the Federal Republic); future standard aircraft for the NATO tactical air forces in Europe destined for the ground support role.

Golem = Soviet liquid-fuel missile, some also with solid propellant(?), designed to be fired from surfaced submarines (and possibly of late from some submerged submarines also); ranges 325-1,100 nautical miles according to type; possibly fitted with nuclear warhead.

Guided missile = Missile whose flight can still be influenced even after launching.

Hard bases = Missile or aircraft bases which, on account of being built underground, their armed protection, camouflage or mobility, can withstand a nuclear strike (notably a strategic nuclear first strike) and thereafter remain operational.

Hawk = American anti-aircraft missile, particularly against low-flying aircraft; range 15 miles, conventional warhead; being delivered to Federal Republic; intention is that it should in future be built in Europe under licence.

H-bomb = Hydrogen bomb, also called fusion or thermo-nuclear bomb; yield normally measured in megatons (MT) of explosive power (T.N.T. equivalent).

Honest John = American tactical missile; range 12 miles; dual-purpose weapon, nuclear warhead up to 5 KT or conventional high-explosive warhead; part of the standard equipment of U.S. Army troops; also delivered to allies.

Hound Dog = American air-to-surface missile (stand-off bomb), carried by B 52 aircraft; range 350 miles.

Hunter = British fighter aircraft.

I.C.B.M. = Intercontinental Ballistic Missile; approximate ranges 2,500-7,500 miles and above; almost invariably carries thermo-nuclear warhead.

Infrastructure = NATO term, mostly for fixed installations and such military support items as barracks, ports, airfields, roads, railways, pipelines, etc.

Interdiction = NATO term for aircraft and missile attacks designed to destroy or cripple the enemy communications system over which his supplies, and troop reinforcements in particular, would be moved.

I.R.B.M. = Intermediate Range Ballistic Missile with ranges of up to about 1,750 miles; nearly always intended to carry nuclear (and sometimes thermo-nuclear) warheads.

Javelin = British all-weather fighter.

Jet engine; more accurately, turbo-jet = Propulsion unit of modern aircraft with speeds of high subsonic and upwards. Forward thrust derives from the expulsion against the direction of flight of decompressed gases ignited in combustion chambers. Performance, which is measured in pounds, improves as air intake mounts, i.e. as speed increases (among other causes). If the engine also drives an airscrew (over a reduction gear at the forward end of the engine) it is called a prop-jet. This is a combination of jet and traditional piston engine and performance is measured in equivalent shaft h.p.

Joseph Stalin III = Old type Soviet heavy tank, 57 tons, carries 122 mm. gun.

Jupiter = American I.R.B.M., liquid-fuelled, range 1,250 miles; two bases in Italy and one in Turkey either under construction or in preparation (each base with 15 missiles) under the command of SACEUR.

KC 97 = Old type of American tanker aircraft.

KC 135 = American tanker aircraft; about 300(?) in existence in 1960, operate under command of S.A.C. (civil version: Boeing 707).

Kiloton (KT) = Unit of measurement of explosive power of nuclear weapons, corresponds to 1,000 tons of T.N.T. (Hiroshima bomb 20 KT).

Komet = Soviet solid-fuel missile fired from surfaced submarines and other surface ships: various versions range from 100 miles up to (?): possibly carries nuclear warhead.

Liquid-fuel missile = Rocket with liquid propellant: *see also* Solid-fuel missile.

Little John = American tactical missile for ground force units, intended to replace Honest John shortly(?)

Logistics = NATO term for supply.

M 47 (General Patton) = American medium tank, weight 44 tons, carries 90 mm. gun, also delivered to allies; now considered obsolete but still to be found extensively in operational service (also in the Bundeswehr).

M 48 ("Patton") = American medium tank, weight 45 tons, 90 mm. gun, development of M 47, also in use by Bundeswehr.

M 60=American medium tank, not yet available in quantity.

Mace=American surface-to-surface guided missile, air-breathing, range over 700 miles; in use by U.S. Air Force in Europe, replacement for Matador; dual-purpose weapon(?)

Mach=Unit of measurement of speed of aircraft and missiles, Mach 1=speed of sound=1,090 ft. per sec. or about 745 m.p.h.

Matador=American surface-to-surface guided missile, air-breathing, range 300-500 miles; in use by U.S. Air Force in Europe; also being delivered to German Federal Republic; dual-purpose weapon(?)

MC 70=Abbreviation for the NATO document (of the Military Committee) which prepared the ground for the NATO resolutions taken in Copenhagen in early 1958 and defined the military goals for NATO and its member states for the following three years.

Means of delivery=Vehicle designed to bring a nuclear warhead to bear on its target.

Megaton (MT)=Unit of measurement for the explosive power of thermo-nuclear weapons; equal to one million tons of T.N.T. (American H-bomb tested at Bikini=20 MT).

MIG 15, MIG 17=Soviet fighter aircraft, about sonic speed.

MIG 19, MIG 21=Soviet fighter aircraft, supersonic speed.

Minuteman=American I.C.B.M., range about 6,000 miles, solid-fuelled; not yet operational.

Mirage=French fighter aircraft, several versions (and as light bomber); also delivered to other states; Mirage IV intended to be future carrier of French nuclear bomb.

Missile=Unmanned vehicle whose trajectory after launching either can be influenced (guided missile) or cannot be influenced (ballistic missile); propulsion unit is either an air-breathing jet engine, an oxidant (solid- or liquid-fuel rocket), or a combination of both. Distinction is made between surface-to-surface, surface-to-air (anti-aircraft), air-to-air, and air-to-ground (stand-off bomb) missiles. These terms do not apply to conventional artillery projectiles or unguided free-fall bombs.

Missile gap=The U.S.S.R.'s lead over the United States in numbers of operational I.C.B.Ms.

NATO=North Atlantic Treaty Organisation (Treaty 1949). Members: Belgium, Canada, Denmark, France, German Federal Republic, Greece, Iceland, Italy, Luxembourg, Netherlands, Portugal, Turkey, United Kingdom, United States.

Nike-Ajax=American anti-aircraft missile (liquid-fuelled) rocket, range 25 miles, conventional warhead; standard equipment of anti-aircraft troops of U.S. Army; also being delivered to European allies, including German Federal Republic.

Nike-Hercules=American anti-aircraft missile (solid-fuelled rocket), range 75 miles, replacing Nike-Ajax, nuclear or conventional warhead.

Nike-Zeus=American anti-ballistic-missile missile still under development.

NORTHAG=Northern Army Group, NATO term for the more northerly of the two army groups stationed in Germany; H.Q. in München Gladbach.

Nuclear weapons=Weapons the effect of which depends on processes involving the transformation of the atomic nucleus. In the so-called atom bomb atomic nuclei of the uranium isotope U 235 (Hiroshima type) or of the artificial element plutonium Pu 239 (Nagasaki type) are subjected to fission, a process which is accompanied by the release of enormous quantities of energy. In the so-called hydrogen bomb (H-bomb) helium is produced by fusion of the atomic nuclei of the heavy water isotopes deuterium and tritium. The most important requirement in nuclear fusion is an extremely high temperature of several million degrees. A hydrogen bomb is for this reason "ignited" by an atomic bomb, since only this can provide the energy necessary for fusion of the nucleus. For this reason H-bombs are also called thermo-nuclear bombs. The term "nuclear weapons" is used as a comprehensive expression for both fission and fusion weapons. Nuclear weapons have a threefold effect: pressure waves, heat effect and radiation, and both local (direct) and global fall-out; the latter is also called tropospherical and stratospherical fall-out and its effects are long-term.

Whereas the heaviest aircraft bomb of World War II contained 6 tons of T.N.T. and produced absolute destruction over an area of 300-350 sq. yards, a fission bomb of the Hiroshima type of 20 KT, detonated at a height of 2,000 ft. (so-called air burst) will produce absolute destruction over an area of nearly 12 sq. miles and radiation damage over a much wider area. (According to some sources it is equal in effect to that of the explosion of three thousand 1,000 lb. conventional bombs or, against troops, to that of an artillery barrage of one hundred thousand 105 mm. shells fired from six thousand barrels within four minutes.) One fusion bomb of 10 MT will produce a range of damage equal to the effect of four hundred Hiroshima-type bombs.

According to F. Mulley (W.E.U. document 169 of 30 Apr. 1960) the following effects can be obtained under "optimal" conditions (the table gives distances from ground zero in yards):

1. *Effect on unprotected men and women:*

(a) Burns:	Yield			
	5 KT	10 KT	20 KT	40 KT
1st degree (reddening) . .	2,500	3,000	4,400	6,100
2nd degree (blistering) . .	1,600	2,200	3,000	4,400
3rd degree (charring). . .	1,200	2,000	2,400	3,300
(b) Radiation injuries:				
200 Röntgen (50 per cent. of persons affected after 1st day, but no immediate losses) . .	1,300	1,400	1,530	1,750
500 Röntgen (immediate loss of 50 per cent. of persons and subsequent death of most others) .	1,100	1,200	1,350	1,500
1,000 Röntgen (total loss of all persons within one hour) .	980	1,100	1,200	1,350

2. *Losses among troops subjected to tactical nuclear weapon attack:*

	Yield			
	5 KT	10 KT	20 KT	40 KT
Personnel unprotected in open air: immediate loss . .	760	870	1,040	—
Loss within four hours . .	1,100	1,200	1,400	—
Personnel in trenches and dugouts: immediate loss . .	550	600	760	—
Loss within four hours . .	870	980	1,100	—
Damage to tanks within one hour	330	380	550	—
Damage to vehicles within one hour	550	770	980	—

3. *Suction and blast effect on buildings:*

	Yield			
	5 KT	10 KT	20 KT	40 KT
Heavy damage to houses . .	1,600	2,000	2,500	3,280
Complete destruction of reinforced concrete structures or 1½ ft. brick walls	680	870	1,100	1,300
Total destruction . . .	280	310	380	600

Mulley assumes that most capital cities of the world could be destroyed by one H-bomb of 10 MT yield. Twenty to thirty well-placed H-bombs, or six thousand atom bombs, would suffice to destroy a country of average size (forty to fifty million inhabitants, two hundred to two hundred and fifty thousand sq. miles). According to G. Burckhardt ("The Transformation of the World by Nuclear Weapons" in *Frankfurter Hefte*, Nos. 9 and 10, 1959—an evaluation of a report by the Federal Civil Defense Administration on the hypothetical dropping of a bomb on St Louis with 1·9 million inhabitants—German in *Ziviler Luftschutz* (Civil Defence) XXII, 1958, p. 28) the dropping of one 20 MT H-bomb on Berlin would have the following effects: considerable damage to buildings in almost all Berlin; most cellars unsuitable for civil defence purposes; very severe direct radiation injuries to survivors; 10 per cent. only of total population would survive first week if no strict civil defence measures taken; in the worst case unprotected men and women would receive a 50 per cent. lethal radiation dose in a circle of about 50 miles radius; protection would be afforded by "optimal" shelter type (able to withstand pressures of up to about 2 tons per sq. ft., cost about £100 per person in Germany) in case of ground burst —with "over-destruction" at ground zero—presumably effective only at distances of 3 miles and more from ground zero (i.e. in that part of Berlin enclosed by the S-Bahn (electric railway) in which 40 per cent. of the total population is to be found during daylight hours); unassessable biological injury—particularly global, long-term radiation from long-lived fission products (notably strontium 90 and caesium 137 with half lives of 28 and 30 years respectively).

Pentagon=Term for the American Department of Defense in Washington (strictly only the building).

Pershing=American surface-to-surface missile (solid-fuel rocket), range 550 miles; intended to replace Redstone.

Piecemeal tactics="Salami tactics."

Polaris=American I.R.B.M. (solid-fuelled), various versions, nuclear warhead up to 1 MT; can be fired from mobile launchers and in particular from submerged submarines; Polaris submarine carries 16 missiles; two such submarines operational in 1960 and four more launched: range of missile 1,280 to 1,500 miles.

Radioactivity=Property of certain atomic nuclei, enabling them to undergo transformation while emitting radiation (Alpha, Beta and Gamma rays), i.e. to pass from an unstable to a stable state.

Ram jet=A simple cylindrical combustion chamber exposed on both sides, without compressor, in which air is compressed by the forward movement of the vehicle: can therefore only be ignited in flight.

RB 47 = American long-range reconnaissance aircraft; familiar from the aircraft of this type shot down by the Soviet Union in the Barents Sea area in 1960.

Redeye = American anti-aircraft missile under development.

Redstone = American surface-to-surface missile (liquid-fuel) in use by U.S. Army, range 200 miles.

Rio Pact = Treaty of mutual assistance between the following American states: Argentina, Bolivia, Brazil, Chile, Colombia, Costa Rica, Cuba(?), Dominican Republic, Ecuador, El Salvador, Guatemala, Haiti, Honduras, Mexico, Nicaragua, Panama, Paraguay, Peru, United States, Uruguay, Venezuela: signed 1947.

Rocket = Unmanned guided or unguided missile with its own oxygen-giving propellant, i.e. independent of atmospheric oxygen.

Röntgen = Unit of measurement for radioactivity, e.g. for the amount of radiation taken up by the human body; 25-50 r. = safety limit; 100 r. and above dangerous.

S.A.C. = Strategic Air Command of United States.

SACEUR = Supreme Allied Commander Europe, responsible for the defence of Europe and the Mediterranean (Scandinavia to Turkey), H.Q. Rocquencourt/Paris.

SACLANT = Supreme Allied Commander Atlantic (NATO) responsible for the defence of the Atlantic area (North Pole to Tropic of Cancer, Atlantic coast of U.S.A. to the coasts of Europe, less Mediterranean and Channel), H.Q. Norfolk, Va., U.S.A.

SEATO = South-East Asia Treaty Organisation (1954). Members: Australia, France, New Zealand, Pakistan, Philippines, Thailand, United Kingdom, U.S.A.; protected states (non-members)— Cambodia, Laos, South Vietnam.

Sergeant = American surface-to-surface ballistic missile, range 75 miles, intended to replace Corporal.

SETAF = Southern European Task Force, special American unit in Upper Italy, equipped solely with nuclear ballistic missiles.

SHAPE = Supreme Headquarters Allied Powers Europe; see SACEUR.

Shield Forces = Expression for NATO ground and air defence forces in Europe; in theory they are intended to hold up the enemy until the offensive (Sword) forces of NATO have successfully delivered their counterattack; the Shield concept prevailing hitherto is the subject of controversy.

Sidewinder = American air-to-air ballistic missile.

Sky Bolt=American air-to-surface ballistic missile ("stand-off bomb"), I.R.B.M.; not yet operational.

Snark=American intercontinental guided missile, air-breathing, subsonic range 5,500 miles, a small number operational in 1960.

Solid-fuel rocket=Rocket with solid propellant, requires only short count-down and can therefore, given timely warning, be fired before enemy rockets strike its launcher; in this it differs from liquid-fuel missiles; it is, furthermore, much better suited for operation from mobile bases.

Sound, speed of=At sea-level about 745 m.p.h., dependent on the density, height and composition of the atmosphere; the unit Mach (after the Austrian physicist) is used for measuring very high aircraft speeds; Mach 1·5 is, for example, one and a half times the speed of sound.

Space Programme=(a) Military: attack satellite (e.g. Dyna Soar), defensive satellite (e.g. Spad), reconnaissance satellite (e.g. Samos), early warning satellite (e.g. Midas); (b) Military and civil: communications satellite (e.g. Echo), navigation satellite (e.g. Transit), research satellite (for manned space flight, e.g. Discoverer, Sputnik), weather satellite (e.g. Tiros); (c) Civil: planetary research (e.g. Mariner), lunar research (e.g. Lunik), research and survey satellite (e.g. Explorer, Vanguard, Sputnik, Lunik).

S.S. 10, S.S. 11=French tactical, anti-tank ballistic missiles, being delivered to allies.

Standing Group=Permanent representatives of the NATO Military Committee (consisting of the Chiefs of Staff of the Armed Forces of all member states) and therefore the highest military executive organ of NATO: consists of representatives of the Chiefs of Staff of France, Britain and the United States; meets in Washington.

Stand-off bomb=Glide bombs and missiles (air-to-surface guided missile) which permit bomber aircraft to attack at some distance from the target.

Starfighter: see F 104.

S.T.O.L.=Aircraft constructed for short take-off and landing.

STRAC=Strategic Army Corps, mobile army corps held at readiness in the United States for sending into action in overseas theatres.

Strike:
    first=Strategic nuclear surprise attack.
    pre-emptive=Forestalling strategic nuclear attack on the enemy's strategic nuclear forces (counter-force strike) to prevent the latter from carrying out an intended surprise attack (first strike).

second=Strategic nuclear retaliatory or counterblow after absorption of enemy first strike, directed primarily at enemy population and industrial centres.

Super Sabre: *see* F 100.

Sword: *see* Shield.

T 1=Soviet surface-to-surface ballistic missile, range 400 or more miles, developed from the German V 2; intended for use in support of ground forces; standard equipment.

T 2=Soviet I.R.B.M., range over 1,250 miles.

T 3=Soviet I.C.B.M., several versions, range over 7,500 miles.

T 4=Soviet I.R.B.M., range 1,000 miles.

T 5, T 7=Soviet tactical surface-to-surface ballistic missiles (various patterns), range 15-95 miles; for support of the ground forces in combat.

T 6, T 8=Soviet anti-aircraft ballistic missiles, performance comparable to Nike-Ajax.

T 10=Soviet heavy tank, weight 54 tons, 122 mm. gun, later development of Joseph Stalin III.

T 34=Former Soviet standard tank, weight 30 tons, 762 mm. gun, still in use.

T 54=Soviet standard tank, weight 36 tons, 100 mm. gun, Diesel engine.

Thermo-nuclear weapons: *see* Nuclear weapons.

Thor=American I.R.B.M., liquid-fuel, range 1,500 miles, four bases in the United Kingdom (each with 15 missiles), under joint British and American control.

Thunderbird=British anti-aircraft ballistic missile (surface-to-air, ground forces).

Titan=American I.C.B.M., liquid-fuel, range 5,500 miles, in 1960 was not yet operational.

T.N.T.=Trinitrotoluene, conventional explosive (successor to gunpowder), discovered by Nobel (founder of Nobel prize); yardstick for indicating yield of nuclear explosions.

Tu 104, Tu 114=Soviet transport aircraft.

Turbo-prop: *see* Jet engine.

Two-key theory=Term for the principle agreed between Britain and the United States concerning the stationing and operational employment of the Thor I.R.B.M. The principle lays down that this missile may not be launched without the agreement of both sides.

U 2 = American high-level reconnaissance aircraft; famous through the forced landing (shooting down?) of an aircraft of this type in the Soviet Union in the spring of 1960.

Uranium = Chemical element with the highest atomic weight occurring in nature (238). Natural uranium contains only up to 0·7 per cent. of the uranium isotope U 235 (same number, different mass); this and the transuranic elements (e.g. plutonium) resulting from nuclear reaction processes form the basic material for the liberation of nuclear energy for both civil and military processes.

V-force = Expression for the Valiant Victor, and Vulcan aircraft of the British Bomber Command.

Valiant = British strategic bomber aircraft (some also used as tankers), range about 3,725 miles, speed about 680 m.p.h.

Valkyrie = So far the heaviest American strategic bomber aircraft (projected), all-up weight 270 tons, payload 13 tons, operational ceiling 80,000 ft., 6 jet engines, speed Mach 3, range 6,800 miles.

Victor = British strategic bomber aircraft, performance similar to that of Valiant.

V.T.O.L. = Aircraft designed for vertical take-off and landing.

Vulcan = British strategic bomber aircraft; performance similar to that of Valiant.

Warsaw Pact = Communist mutual assistance treaty (1955). Members: Albania, Bulgaria, Czechoslovakia, "D.D.R.," Hungary, Poland, Rumania, U.S.S.R.

W.E.U. = Western European Union (treaty now in force dates from 1954). Members: Belgium, France, German Federal Republic, Italy, Luxembourg, Netherlands, United Kingdom.

X 15 = Manned, high-speed research missile (for space flight) of the U.S. Navy, U.S. Air Force and the National Aeronautics and Space Administration. The results of the X 15 tests serve to pave the way for the manned, hypersonic long-range glide vehicle (attack and reconnaissance) project "Dyna Soar" (Dynamic Soaring); Dyna Soar, which derives from an idea of the German, Professor Sänger, is intended to have ranges of over 12,500 miles and a speed approaching that of a satellite; X 15, for which an operational ceiling of 25 miles and speeds of Mach 6-7 are projected, has so far attained a speed of Mach 5; the possibility must be allowed for that the U.S.S.R., also basing themselves on Sänger's project for a 12,500 mile rocket bomber aircraft, will have a lead over the United States in the development of this type of missile also.

BIBLIOGRAPHY

In this bibliography, which has been revised for the English edition, we have attempted only to list a usable cross-section of the sources that have appeared since 1955 and are devoted to the strategic aspect. A few older books are included where the author's importance, or the weight of his views or his prescience, were felt to deserve attention. Literature on the Communist countries—of either Communist or Western origin—is only sparsely represented. The publications of the Moscow publishing house International Books provide recent examples of Russian scientific—particularly technical—bibliographies.

Some of the entries are quoted at second-hand. Only a qualified assurance of their accuracy can be given. The bibliographical details of these entries are not always complete.

Certain works are listed of authors whose contributions, or who themselves are not above controversy. This has been done to enliven the discussion and will scarcely irritate specialist readers.

Pamphlets have been included under Literature.

If only one date is given for more than one place of publication, this date is applicable to all.

The place of publication of periodicals is given in most cases, both as an indication of the country of origin and as a help in tracing them in libraries.

The journal *Foreign Affairs* was of great assistance in the compilation of this bibliography, which was closed in November 1961.

Abbreviations of Titles of Periodicals and Organisations

A.F. =   *Air Force*, Washington.

A.P. =   *Aussenpolitik*, Stuttgart.

A.S.M.Z. =   *Allgemeine schweizerische Militärzeitschrift*, Frauenfeld.

Bu.A.S. =   *Bulletin of the Atomic Scientists*, Chicago.

Bu.P.I. =   *Bulletin des Presse— und Informationsamtes der Bundes-regierung*, Bonn.

C.I.S. =   Center of International Studies.

C.R. =   *Les Cahiers de la République*, Paris.

Dae. =   *Daedalus*. Journal of the American Arts and Sciences. Middletown, Conn.

E.A. =   *Europa-Archiv.*, Frankfurt am Main.

Enc. =   *Encounter*, London.

E.S.G. =   *Revista de la Escuela Superior de Guerra*, Argentina.

F.A. =   *Foreign Affairs*, New York.

I.A. =   *International Affairs*, Moscow.

Intav. =   *Interavia*, Geneva.

I.S.S. =   Institute for Strategic Studies.

List. =   *The Listener*, London.

M.R. =   *Military Review*, Fort Leavenworth, Kans.

N.Y.T. =   *The New York Times*.

R.D.N. =   *Revue de Défence Nationale*, Paris.

R.M.d.I. =   *Revue Militaire d'Information*, Paris.

R.M.G. =   *Revue Militaire Générale*, Paris.

S.A.I.S. =   School of Advanced International Studies (Johns Hopkins University), Washington.

Surv. =   *Survival* (Periodical of I.S.S.), London.

W.C.F.P.R. =Washington Center of Foreign Policy Research.

W.E.U. =   Western European Union.

W.K. =   *Wehrkunde*, Munich.

W.P. =   *World Politics*, Burlington, Vt.

W.W.Rd. =   *Wehrwissenschaftliche Rundschau*, Darmstadt.

Y.R. =   *The Yale Review*, New Haven, Conn.

Literature

ACHESON, D. *Power and Diplomacy*. Cambridge, Mass. and London 1958.

ADAM, R., and C. JUDD. *Assault at Arms*. United Nations Association of Great Britain and Northern Ireland. London 1960.

ALEXANDER, P. *Atomic Radiation and Life*. Harmondsworth 1957.

ALLEN, R. L. *Soviet Economic Warfare*. New York 1960.

AMSTER, W. *A Theory for the Design of a Deterrent Air Weapon System*. Convair Report OR-P-29. San Diego, Cal. 1955.

ANGEL, N. *Defence and the English-Speaking Role*. London 1958.

APPADORAI, A. *The Use of Force in International Relations*. Bombay 1958.

ARMINE, M. *The Great Decision. The Secret History of the Atomic Bomb*. New York 1959.

ARON, R. *On War: Atomic Weapons and Global Diplomacy*. London 1958.

ARONÉANU, E. *La Définition de l'aggression*. Paris 1958.

ARROW, K. J., S. KARLIN, and H. SCARF. *Studies in the Mathematical Theory of Inventory and Production*. Stanford, Cal. and London 1958.

BALDWIN, H. W. *The Great Arms Race; A Comparison of U.S. and Soviet Power today.* New York and London 1958.

BALL, M. M. *NATO and the European Union Movement.* London Inst. of World Affairs. London and New York 1959.

BEER, J. *Der nahe Osten.* Munich 1960.

BERGSTRAESSER, A. (ed.). *Das atlantische Bündnis.* Freiburg 1960.

BERLINER, J. S. *Soviet Economic Aid: The New Aid and Trade Policy in Under-Developed Countries.* New York and London 1958.

BIÖRKLUND, E. *International Atomic Policy during a Decade, 1945-1955.* London and New York 1956.

BLACKETT, P. M. S. *Atomic Weapons and East-West Relations.* Cambridge 1956.

BOCHÉNSKI, J., and G. NIEMAYER (eds.). *Handbuch des Weltkommunismus.* With comprehensive western and eastern bibliography. Freiburg and Munich 1958.

BOLTÉ, C. G. *The Price of Peace: A Plan for Disarmament.* Boston, Mass. 1956.

BONNET, G. *Les Guerres insurrectionelles et révolutionnaires.* Paris 1958.

BOUSCAREN, A. T. *A Guide to Anti-Communist Action.* Chicago 1958.

BOWLE, J. *Adapt or Perish: The Dilemma of Nuclear Politics.* London 1959.

BRIMMEL, J. H. *Communism in South East Asia: A Political Analysis.* Royal Institute of International Affairs, London 1959.

BRODIE, B. *A Guide to Naval Strategy,* Princeton 1958; London 1959.
—— *Strategy in the Missile Age.* Princeton and London 1959.

BRZEZINSKI, Z. K. *The Soviet Bloc: Unity and Conflict.* Cambridge, Mass. and London 1960.

BUCHAN, A. *NATO in the 1960's.* London and New York 1960.

BULL, H. *The Control of the Arms Race: Disarmament and Arms Control in the Missile Age.* I.S.S. London 1961.

BURGESS, E. *Guided Weapons.* London and New York 1957.

BUZZARD, A. W., and others. *On Limiting Atomic War.* Royal Institute of International Affairs, London 1956.

CENTRE D'ETUDES DE POLITIQUE ÉTRANGÈRE. Comité d'etudes des relations franco-allemandes. *Die Entwicklung der Waffentechnik seit 1945, ihre Auswirkungen auf die Strategie und die Fragen des Abrüstung.* Paris 1958. Also in French.

CHOH MIN LI. *Economic Development of Communist China.* Berkeley, Cal. 1959.

CLAUSEWITZ, K. VON. *Vom Kriege.* 16th edn. Bonn 1952; Eng. trans. *On War,* trans. O. Jolles. New York 1943.

COLLART, Y. *Disarmament: A Study Guide and Bibliography on the Efforts of the United Nations.* The Hague 1958.

CORNELL, M. *Russia and the Western Powers in the Post-War World.* London 1960.

CRAHAY. *Art de la guerre moderne.* Brussels 1958.

CROWLEY, D. W. "The Problem of Nuclear Weapons," in *The Background to Current Affairs.* London 1959.

DALLIN, D. J. *Soviet Espionage.* New Haven, Conn. and London 1956.

DAUGHERTY, W. E., M. JANOWITZ, and others. *A Psychological Warfare Casebook.* Baltimore and London 1958.

DEAN, G. *Report on the Atom.* New York 1957.

DELMAS, C. *La Guerre révolutionnaire.* Paris 1959.

DEUTSCHER, I. *The Great Contest, Russia and the West.* London 1960.

DINERSTEIN, H. S. *War and the Soviet Union.* New York and London 1959.

DODD, T. J. *If Co-existence Fails.* Washington 1960.

DOUHET, G. *Command in the Air.* New York 1942; London 1943.

DRÄGER, H., H. HEYE, and F. SACKMANN. *Problem der Verteidigung der Bundesrepublik, unter Berücksichtg. wirtschaftl. und techn. Belange.* Berlin and Frankfurt am Main 1959.

DZELEPY, E.-N. *Désatomiser l'Europe?* Brussels 1958.

ECCLES, H. E. *Logistics in the National Defense.* Harrisburg, Pa. 1959.

ELBERS, G. W., and P. DUNCAN (eds.). *The Scientific Revolution: Challenge and Promise.* Washington 1959.

ELIOT, G. F. *Victory without War 1958-1961.* Anapolis, Md. 1958.

EMME, E. M. (ed.). *The Impact of Air Power: National Security and World Politics.* Princeton 1959.

ENGEL, F. W. (ed.). *Handbuch der NATO.* Frankfurt am Main. Looseleaf edn. Supplements issued as and when necessary.

EUROPA-UNION. *Europäische Sicherheit: Grundgedanken, Probleme und Tatsachen in milit. und polit. Sicht.* Bonn 1958.

FELSZTYN, T. *Rakiety i podroze miedzyplanetarne.* London 1959.

FIEDLER, H. *Der sowjetische Neutralitätsbegriff in Theorie und Praxis. Beitrag zum Problem des Disengagement.* Cologne 1959.

FINLETTER, T. K. *Power and Policy: U.S. Foreign Policy and Military Power in the Hydrogen Age.* New York 1954.

FISCHER, R. *Von Lenin zu Mao.* Düsseldorf 1956.

FOWLER, J. M. (ed.). *A Study of Superbombs, strontium 90 and Fall-out Survival.* New York 1960.

FURNISS, E. S., jr. (ed.). *American Military Policy: Strategic Aspects of World Military Geography.* New York 1957.

GALLOIS, P. "L'Europe et la défense de l'occident," in *L'Europe au Défi*, Paris 1959.

—— *Stratégie de l'âge nucléaire.* Paris 1960.

GANTZ, K. F. (ed.). *U.S.A.F. Report on the Ballistic Missile; its Technology, Logistics and Strategy.* New York 1958.

GARTHOFF, R. L. *Soviet Military Doctrine: How Russia makes War.* Glencoe, Ill. 1953; London 1954.

—— *Soviet Strategy in the Nuclear Age.* New York and London 1958.

—— *The Soviet Image of a Future War.* Washington 1959.

GATLAND, K. W. *Development of the Guided Missile.* New York 1958.

GAVIN, J. M. *War and Peace in the Space Age.* New York 1958; London 1959.

GERMANY, FEDERAL REPUBLIC. Bundestag. *Protokolle des deutschen Bundestags über mündliche Verhandlungen zu Fragen der Militär- und Aussenpolitik, insbes. zwischen Adenauer, Strauss, Erler, Kiesinger, Schmidt u.a.* Bonn (n.d.).

GHAIT, E. LE. *Pas de carte blanche au capricorne.* Bruges 1960; Eng. trans. *No Carte Blanche to Capricorn: The folly of nuclear war strategy.* New York 1960.

GINZBER, E., and others. *The Ineffective Soldier; Lessons for Management and the Nation.* New York 1959. VOL. I, *The Lost Divisions*; VOL. II, *Breakdown and Recovery*; VOL. III, *Patterns of Performance.*

GLASSTONE, S. *Sourcebook on Atomic Energy.* 2nd edn. Princeton, Toronto, New York, and London 1958.

GODDARD, V. *The Enigma of Menace.* London 1959.

GOLDBERG, A. (ed.). *A History of the United States Air Force 1907-1957.* New York and London 1957.

GOLLANCZ, V. *The Devil's Repertoire; or, Nuclear Bombing and the Life of Man.* London 1958; New York 1959.

GONARD, S. *La Récherche operationelle et la décision.* Institut Universitaire de Hautes Études Internationales. Geneva 1958.

GOODMAN, E. R. *The Soviet Design for a World State.* New York 1960.

GÖTTINGER ARBEITSKREIS. *Das östliche Deutschland: Handbuch.* Würzburg 1959.

GRABER, D. A. *Crisis Diplomacy: A History of U.S. Intervention Policies and Practices.* Washington 1959.

GREAT BRITAIN. Ministry of Defence. *Defence. Outline of Future Policy.* Cmnd. 124. London 1957.

HAHN, W. F., and J. C. NEFF (eds.). *American Strategy for the Nuclear Age.* New York 1960.

HALLE, L. J. *Choice for Survival.* New York 1958.

—— *Dream and Reality: Aspects of American Foreign Policy.* New York 1959. Under title *American Foreign Policy: Theory and Reality,* London 1960.

—— *Guerre nucléaire et paix nucléaire: Comment survivre.* Geneva and Paris 1958.

HALPERIN, MORTON H. *Nuclear Weapons and Limited War.* Cambridge, Mass. 1960.

HANDKE, W. *Die Wirtschaft Chinas: Dogma und Wirklichkeit.* Frankfurt am Main 1959.

HARRIMAN, A. *Peace with Russia?* New York 1959; London 1960.

HEALEY, D. *A Neutral Belt in Europe.* Fabian Society. Dorking 1958.

HERRICK, J. W., and BURGESS, E. (eds.). *Rocket Encyclopedia,* illustr. Los Angeles 1959.

HERZ, J. H. *International Politics in the Atomic Age.* New York 1959.

HILSMAN, R. *Strategic Intelligence and National Decisions.* Glencoe, Ill. 1956.

HINTERHOFF, E. *Disengagement.* London 1959.

HOAG, M. W. *The Place of Limited War in NATO Strategy.* Princeton 1959.

HÖCKER, K. H., and K. WEIMER. *Lexikon der Kern- und Reaktortechnik.* Stuttgart 1959.

HOWARD, M. *Disengagement in Europe.* Harmondsworth 1958.

HOWE, G. (ed.). *Atomzeitalter, Krieg und Frieden.* Contributors include C. von Weizsäcker. Witten and Berlin 1959.

Humphrey Report: *see* UNITED STATES. Congress: Senate, Committee on Foreign Relations, *Control and Reduction.*

INSTITUTE FOR STRATEGIC STUDIES. *The Communist Bloc and the Free World: The Military Balance.* London 1960.

INSTITUT ROYAL DES RELATIONS INTERNATIONALES. *Le Désarmement; chronique de politique étrangère.* Brussels 1960.

INTERNATIONAL ASSOCIATION OF DEMOCRATIC LAWYERS. *Contribution to the Study of the Problems of Disarmament.* Brussels 1958.

ISMAY, H. L. I. *NATO; the First Five Years.* Utrecht 1955.

JANOWITZ, M. *Sociology and the Military Establishment.* New York 1959.

—— *The Professional Soldier. A Social and Political Portrait.* Glencoe, Ill. 1960.

JESSUP, P. C., and H. J. TAUBENFELD. *Controls for Outer Space and the Antarctic Analogy.* New York and London 1959.

JOOST, W., and H. FÜHRING. *Wie stark ist die Sowjetunion?* Bonn 1958.

JORDAN, G. R. *From Major Jordan's Diaries.* New York 1958.

KAHN, H. *On Thermo-nuclear War.* Princeton 1960.

KAUFMANN, W. W. *The Requirements of Deterrence.* Princeton 1954.

—— (ed.). *Military Policy and National Security.* Princeton and London 1956.

KAWAN, L. *La Nouvelle Orientation du commerce extérieur soviétique.* Brussels 1958.

KECSKEMETI, P. *Strategic Surrender. The Politics of Victory and Defeat.* Stanford, Cal. and London 1958.

KENNAN, G. F. *Russia, the Atom, and the West.* London and New York 1958.

KENNEDY, J. F. *The Strategy of Peace.* New York 1960.

KING-HALL, S. *Defence in the Nuclear Age.* London 1958.

KINGSTON-McCLOUGHRY, E. J. *Global Strategy.* London and New York 1957.

—— *Defence Policy and Strategy.* New York and London 1960.

KINTNER, W. R. *Forging a New Sword: A Study of the Department of Defense.* New York 1958.

KISSINGER, H. A. *Nuclear Weapons and Foreign Policy.* New York, London and Moscow 1957. (*See also under* LARIONOV, V., in Section (ii) Periodicals.)

—— *The Necessity for Choice: Prospects of American Foreign Policy.* New York 1960.

KNORR, K. *The War Potential of Nations.* Princeton 1956.

—— (ed.). *NATO and American Security.* (Authors include Knorr, Hilsman, Hoag, Kaplan, Burns, Schelling, Healey, Nitze.) Princeton and London 1959.

KOCH, H., and others. *Sowjetbuch.* Contains over 400 short bibliographical references to Western publications on the Soviet Union. Cologne 1957.

KRAKOWSKI, E. *Chine et Russie.* Paris 1957.

KRIEGER, F. J. *Behind the Sputniks: A Survey of Soviet Space Science.* Washington 1958.

LAGOVSKIY, A. N. *Strategiya i Ekonomika.* Moscow 1957.

LAPP, R. *Atoms and the People.* New York 1956.

LEE, A. (ed.). *The Soviet Air and Rocket Forces.* New York and London 1959.

LIDDELL HART, B. H. *The Soviet Army.* London and New York 1956.

LIDDELL HART, B. H. *Deterrent or Defence.* London and New York 1960.

LÖWENSTEIN, H., PRINZ ZU, and V. VON ZÜHLSDORFF. *Die Verteidigung des Westens.* Bonn 1960.

LORT-PHILIPPS, P. *The Logic of Defence.* Purley, Surrey 1959.

LONSDALE, K. *Is Peace Possible?* Harmondsworth 1957.

MALLAN, L. *Russia and the Big Red Lie.* Greenwich, Conn. 1959. (Not a serious contribution to scholarship.)

MAO TSE-TUNG. *Selected Works.* New York 1954; London 1956. (*Strategic Problems of the Chinese Revolutionary War*, in VOL. I, pp. 203 ff.)

—— *On the Protracted War.* Peking 1954.

MARTIN, L. J. *International Propaganda: Its Legal and Diplomatic Control.* Minneapolis 1958.

MATAXIS, T. C., and S. L. GOLDBERG. *Nuclear Tactics.* Harrisburg, Pa. 1958.

MAY, E. R. *The Ultimate Decision: The President as Commander-in-Chief.* New York 1960.

McCLOSKY, H., and J. E. TURNER. *The Soviet Dictatorship.* New York 1960.

McINNIS, E. *The Atlantic Triangle and the Cold War.* Toronto 1959.

McKINSEY, J. C. C. *Introduction to the Theory of Games.* New York 1952.

MÉGRET, M. *Armes nucléaires et politique étrangère.* Geneva 1958.

MEISSNER, B., and J. S. RESHETAR, jr. *The Communist Party of the Soviet Union.* New York and London 1957.

—— *Russland unter Chruschtschow.* Munich 1960.

MELMAN, S. (ed.). *Inspection for Disarmament.* New York and London 1958.

—— *The Peace Race.* New York 1961.

MIKSCHE, F. O. *Tactique de la guerre atomique, retour aux tranchées?* Paris 1955.

—— *Atomic Weapons and Armies.* New York and London 1955.

—— *The Failure of Atomic Strategy.* New York and London 1959.

MILLIKAN, M. F., and W. W. ROSTOW. *A Proposal: Key to an Effective Foreign Policy.* New York 1957.

MILLS, C. W. *The Causes of World War Three.* New York 1958; London 1959.

MOCH, J. *Wir sind gewarnt.* Frankfurt am Main 1955.

—— *Le Problème du désarmement devant les Nations Unies.* Paris 1957.

MOORE, B. T. *NATO and the Future of Europe*. New York 1958.

MORGENSTERN, O. *The Question of National Defense*. New York 1959.

MÜLLER, W. D. *Atom ABC*. Düsseldorf 1959.

MURRAY, T. E. *Nuclear Policy for War and Peace*. New York 1960.

NATIONAL PLANNING ASSOCIATION. *An Adequate Military Shield for U.S. Foreign Policy*. Washington 1958.

—— *1970 without Arms Control*. Washington 1958.

—— *The Nth Country Problem and Arms Control*, by W. C. Davidon, M. I. Kalkstein, and C. Hohenemser. Washington 1960.

NORTH ATLANTIC TREATY ORGANISATION. *Facts about NATO*. Paris 1959.

NOEL-BAKER, P. *The Arms Race: A Programme for World Disarmament*. London and New York 1958.

NUTTING, A. *Disarmament. An Outline of the Negotiations*. London 1959.

OGORKIEWICZ, R. M. *Armour. The Development of Mechanised Forces and their Equipment*. London 1960.

OSGOOD, R. E. *Limited War: The Challenge to American Strategy*. Chicago and Cambridge 1957.

—— *NATO: Problems of Strategy and Independence*. Chicago 1959.

PARSON, N. A., jr. *Guided Missiles in War and Peace*. Cambridge, Mass. and London 1956.

PARTEL, G. *Technisches Wörterbuch fur Raketen und Weltraumfahrt*. Rome 1956.

PAYNE, R. *Mao Tse-tung: Ruler of Red China*. New York 1950.

—— *Red Storm over Asia*, New York 1951.

PEARSON, L. B. *Diplomacy in the Nuclear Age*. Cambridge, Mass. and London 1959.

PEETERS, P. *Massive Retaliation: The Policy and its Critics*. Chicago 1959.

PIRIE, A. (ed.). *Fall-out*. London 1957; Philadelphia 1958.

PLATT, W. *Strategic Intelligence Production. Basic Principles*. New York and London 1957.

POKROVSKIY, G. I. (Engineering and Technical Service, Soviet Army). *Science and Technology in Contemporary War*, trans. with a commentary by R. L. Garthoff. New York and London 1959.

POLITICAL AND ECONOMIC PLANNING (P.E.P.). *Prospects for Nuclear Powers*. Planning, VOL. XXV, No. 431. London 1959.

Q

POSSONY, S. T. *A Century of Conflict; Communist Techniques of World Revolution.* Chicago 1953.

PUGWASH CONFERENCES OF INTERNATIONAL SCIENTISTS ON BIOLOGICAL AND CHEMICAL WARFARE. *Proceedings.* Pugwash, Nova Scotia 1957 ff.

RAND CORPORATION. *Report on a Study of Non-Military Defense.* Santa Monica, Cal. 1958. Cf. also periodical bibliographies of the Rand Corporation on this subject.

REINHARDT, G. C. *American Strategy in the Atomic Age.* Norman, Okla. 1955.

RIEZLER, W., and W. WALCHER. *Kerntechnik.* Stuttgart 1958.

RITCHIE, R. S. *NATO: The Economics of an Alliance.* Toronto 1956; London 1957.

ROCKEFELLER BROTHERS FUND. *International Security: The Military Aspect.* Special Studies Project, Report of Panel II. New York 1958.

—— *The Mid-Century Challenge to U.S. Foreign Policy.* Special Studies Project, Report of Panel I. New York 1959.

RUSSELL, B. *Common Sense and Nuclear Warfare.* London and New York 1959.

SÄNGER, E. *Zur Strahlungsphysik der Photonenstrahlantriebe und Waffenstrahlen.* Munich 1957.

—— *Raumfahrt, technische Überwindung des Krieges.* Hamburg 1958.

SARGANT, W. W. *Battle for the Mind.* New York and London 1957.

SAUNDERS, M. G. (ed.). *The Soviet Navy.* New York and London 1958.

SCHELLING, T. C. *The Strategy of Conflict.* Cambridge, Mass. 1960.

SCHELLING, T. C., and M. H. HALPERIN. *Strategy and Arms Control.* Twentieth Century Fund. New York 1961.

SCHRAMM, W. R. VON. *Staatskunst und bewaffnete Macht.* Munich 1957.

SHTERNFELD, A. *Artificial Satellites,* trans. Technical Documents Liaison Office, Wright-Patterson Air Force Base, Ohio. Washington 1958. 2nd. edn., *Soviet Space Science,* New York 1959. Translations of *Iskusstvenniye Sputniki,* Moscow 1958.

SIEGLER, H. *Wiedervereinigung und Sicherheit Deutschlands.* Bonn 1958.

—— *Abrüstung und Sicherheit. Dokumentation 1943-1959.* Bad Godesberg 1960.

SINGH, N. *Nuclear Weapons and International Law.* Indian Council of World Affairs. London 1959.

SLESSOR, SIR J. *Strategy for the West.* London and New York 1954.

—— *The Great Deterrent.* London 1957; New York 1958.

SLICK, T. *Permanent Peace: a check and balance plan.* Englewood Cliffs, N.J. 1958.

SMITH, B. L., and CH. M. SMITH. *International Communication and Political Opinion: A Guide to the Literature.* Princeton 1956; London 1957.

SMITH, D. O. *U.S. Military Doctrine.* New York 1955.

SNYDER, G. H. *Deterrence by Denial and Punishment.* C.I.S. Research Monograph No. 1. Princeton 1959.

Soviet Writings on Earth Satellites and Space Travel. New York 1958; London 1959.

SPAAK, P.-H. *Why NATO?* Harmondsworth 1959.

Space Encyclopedia. A Guide to Astronomy and Space Science, ed. M. T. Bizony. New York and London 1957.

Space Weapons. Handbook of Military Astronautics. New York and London 1959.

SPANIER, J. W. *The Truman-MacArthur Controversy and the Korean War.* Cambridge, Mass. and London 1959.

SPEIER, H. *German Rearmament and Atomic War: The Views of German Military and Political Leaders.* Evanston, Ill. 1957.

—— *The Soviet Threat to Berlin.* Rand Corporation Report P-1912-1. Santa Monica, Cal. 1960.

STARLINGER, W. *Russland und die atlantische Macht.* Würzburg 1957.

—— *Grenzen der Sowjetmacht.* Würzburg 1955.

STERN, F. M. *The Citizen Army.* New York 1959.

STERNBERG, F. *The Military and Industrial Revolution of our Time.* London and New York 1959.

STOCKWELL, R. E. *Soviet Air Power* (with supplement). New York 1956.

STRAUSZ-HUPÉ, R., and others. *Protracted Conflict.* New York 1959.

STRAUSZ-HUPÉ, R., W. R. KINTNER, and S. T. POSSONY. *A Forward Strategy for America.* Foreign Policy Research Institute. New York 1961.

SULZBERGER, C. L. *What's Wrong with U.S. Foreign Policy?* New York 1959.

TASHJEAN, J. E. *Where China Meets Russia* (Analysis of Dr Starlinger's theory). Central Asian Collectanea. Washington 1959.

TAYLOR, M. D. *The Uncertain Trumpet.* New York 1959; London 1960.

TELLER, E., and A. L. LATTER. *Our Nuclear Future: Facts, Dangers, and Opportunities.* New York and London 1958.

THOMAS, N. *The Prerequisites for Peace.* New York 1959.

THORPE, C. *Pure Logistics.* Kansas City 1917. (Out of print.)

TOYNBEE, P. (ed.). *The Fearful Choice.* London 1958; Detroit 1958.

UNITED STATES. AIR FORCE. Air Training Command. *Fundamentals of Guided Missiles.* Los Angeles 1960.

UNITED STATES. ATOMIC ENERGY COMMISSION. *In the Matter of J. R. Oppenheimer. Transcript of the Hearing before the Personnel Security Board.* Washington 1955.

—— *The Effects of Nuclear Weapons.* Prepared by the Department of Defense. Washington 1957.

UNITED STATES. CONGRESS: HOUSE OF REPRESENTATIVES. Committee on Appropriations. *Department of Defense Appropriations.* Hearings for 1960, 1961.

—— Committee on Government Operations. *Reports* (Annual).

—— Committee on Science and Astronautics. *Basic Scientific and Astronautic Research in the Department of Defense.* Hearings. Washington 1959.

—— —— *Missile Development and Space Sciences.* Hearings. Washington 1959.

—— —— *Scientific Manpower and Education.* Hearings. Washington 1959.

—— —— *1961 NASA Authorisation.* Hearings. Washington 1960.

—— —— *Space, Missiles and the Nation.* Washington 1960. Reports on various aspects of outer space 1959, 1960.

—— Select Committee on Astronautics and Space Exploration. *Space Handbook: Astronautics and its Application.* Staff Report. Washington 1959.

UNITED STATES. CONGRESS: JOINT COMMITTEE ON ATOMIC ENERGY. Special Subcommittee on Radiation. *The Nature of Radioactive Fallout and its Effects on Man.* Hearings. Washington 1957-8.

—— —— *Biological and Environmental Effects of Nuclear War.* Hearings. Washington 1959.

—— —— *Fallout from Nuclear Weapons Tests.* Hearings. Washington 1959.

—— Subcommittee on Research and Development. *Aircraft Nuclear Propulsion Program.* Hearings. Washington 1959.

UNITED STATES. CONGRESS: SENATE. Committee on the Armed Services. *Department of Defense Reorganisation Act of 1958.* Hearings. Washington 1958.

—— —— Preparedness Investigating Subcommittee. *Inquiry into Satellite and Missile Programs.* Hearings. Washington 1957-8.

—— —— Preparedness Investigating Subcommittee. *Missiles, Space and other Major Defense Matters.* Hearings. Washington 1960.

—— —— Subcommittee on the Air Force. *Reports.*

UNITED STATES. CONGRESS: SENATE. Committee on Foreign Relations *Statements by Secretary of State John Foster Dulles and Admiral Arthur Radford, Chairman, Joint Chiefs of Staff, on Foreign Policy and its Relationship to Military Programs.* Washington 1954.

—— —— *Control and Reduction of Armaments. Final Report of the Subcommittee on Disarmament.* Washington 1958. (Chairman of the Subcommittee, Senator H. Humphrey: hence popular name "Humphrey Report.")

—— —— *Background Documents on Germany 1944-1959.* Washington 1959.

—— Committee on Government Operations. *Reports* (Annual).

UNITED STATES. President's Committee to Study U.S. Military Assistance Program. *Composite Report and Final Report.* Washington 1959.

VALLUY, GENERAL. *Se défendre: contre qui? pour quoi? et comment?* Paris 1960.

WALKER, R. L. *The Continuing Struggle: Communist China and the Free World.* New York 1958.

WARBURG, J. P. *Disarmament: The Challenge of the Nineteen Sixties.* New York 1961.

WASHINGTON CENTER OF FOREIGN POLICY RESEARCH. *East-West Negotiations.* A collection of studies and minutes of a session of 3 May 1958. Washington 1958.

—— Military Policy Papers. Series includes: R. Hilsman, *On NATO Strategy*; P. H. Nitze, *Brinkmanship and the averting of War*; J. E. King, jr., *Collective Defense, The Military Commitment*; P. H. Nitze, *Symmetry and Intensity of the Great Power Involvement in Limited Wars*; A. Wolfers, *Europe and the NATO Shield.* Washington 1958.

—— *United States Foreign Policy. Developments in Military Technology and their Impact on United States Strategy and Foreign Policy.* Washington 1959.

WEINSTEIN, A. *Keiner kann den Krieg gewinnen.* Bonn 1955.

WEIZSÄCKER, C. F. VON. *Mit der Bombe Leben.* Hamburg 1958.

—— *Ethical and Political Problems of the Atomic Age.* London 1958.

WELTON, H. *The Third World War: Trade and Industry, the New Battleground.* New York and London 1959.

WESTERN EUROPEAN UNION, Assembly. Approved Texts and Explanatory Memoranda. These materials, published after every regular sitting of W.E.U., are of extraordinary value for the information they provide on the current state of European discussion on the problems of NATO. See especially:

WESTERN EUROPEAN UNION, Assembly. *The State of European Security: Nuclear Weapons.* Assembly explanatory memorandum Doc. 169, Apr. 1960 (by F. W. Mulley).

WETTER, G. A., S.J. *Der dialektische Materialismus. Seine Geschichte und sein System in der Sowjetunion.* Vienna and Freiburg 1952.

—— *Die sowjetische Konzeption der Koexistenz.* Cologne and Bonn 1959.

—— *Philosophie und Naturwissenschaft in der Sowjetunion.* Hamburg 1958.

WIENER, N. *The Human Use of Human Beings: Cybernetics and Society.* Boston 1950; London 1951.

WILLIAMS, W. A. *The Tragedy of American Diplomacy.* Cleveland 1959.

WINT, G. *Dragon and Sickle.* London 1959.

WOLFERS, A. (ed.). *Alliance Policy in the Cold War.* Baltimore 1959.

WORLEY, M. L., jr. *New Developments in Army Weapons, Tactics, Organisation and Equipment.* Harrisburg, Pa. 1959.

YOUNG, W. *Strategy for Survival: First Steps in Nuclear Disarmament.* Harmondsworth 1959.

Periodicals and Articles

ACHESON, D. "The Illusion of Disengagement." *F.A.,* Apr. 1958.

AILLERET, CH. "Guerre nucléaire limitée ou 'drôle de guerre'." *R.D.N.,* May 1958.

ALEXINSKY, G. "Genèse de la doctrine soviétique de 'guerre revolutionnaire'." *R.M.d.I.,* Mar., May, Jul. and Oct. 1959.

ALSOP, J. "Die strategische Lage: ein neues Gleichgewicht der Kräfte." *Der Monat,* No. 118, Berlin 1958.

ARALDSEN, O. P. "Globale Strategie der Sowjetunion." *A.P.,* Aug. 1958.

ARON, R. "A New Member of the Nuclear Club: France's Motives for Joining the Club." *Le Figaro,* Paris, 14 Aug. 1959; *Surv.,* May-Jun. 1960.

BÄUMLER, E. "Auf der Suche nach einer Strategie." *Politische Studien,* No. 108, Munich 1959.

BAGDAHN, H. "Die territoriale Verteidigungsorganisation der Bundeswehr." *W.K.,* No. 2, 1958.

BALDWIN, H. "What Kind of Deterrent?" *N.Y.T.,* Feb. 1959; *Surv.,* Mar.-Apr. 1959.

BAUFRE. "Les Armements modernes et la stratégie." *R.M.G.,* Jun. 1960.

BAUMANN, G. "Atomrüstung in sowjetischer Sicht." *W.K.,* Jul. 1959.

BAZ, I. "The Characteristics of modern war." *Military Herald*, Moscow, Jun. 1958; *Surv.*, Nov.-Dec. 1959.

BECHTHOLD, H. "Mao Tse-tung bëhalt die Führung Chinas." *A.P.*, Feb. 1959.

BETHE, H. A. "The Case for Ending Nuclear Tests." *Surv.*, Sept.-Oct. 1960.

BIDLINGMAIER, G. "Das Atom-U-Boot und seine Verwendungsmöglichkeit." *R.M.G.*, Dec. 1958.

BILLOTE. "Considérations stratégiques." *Encyclopédie Française*, Paris, VOL. XI: *La Vie internationale*.

BIÖRKLUND, E. "Lenkwaffen und die Zukunft." *W.W.Rd.* 1957.

―― "The Pros and Cons of partly demilitarised zones in Europe." *R.M.G.*, Jun. 1958.

―― "Grand Strategy and Missile Strategy." *Air Power*, Aldershot, winter 1958-9.

―― "Modern aspects of limited warfare in general and local wars." *R.M.G.*, Apr. 1959.

―― "Soviet Policy in times of crisis." *R.M.G.*, Nov. 1959.

―― "Das Konzept der sowjetischen Atomstrategie." *Intav.*, No. 7 1960.

BLACKETT, P. M. S. "Critique of some contemporary defence thinking." *Enc.*, Apr. 1961; *Surv.*, III, No. 3, May-Jun. 1961.

BLOCH-MORHANGE, J. (Author of *La Stratégie des fusées*). "Frankreichs Aufgaben und Möglichkeiten in der Übergangszeit von der Strategie des kalten Krieges zur Raketen-Strategie." *E.A.*, Jul. 1958.

BÖHMER, G. "Das technische Hilfsprogramm der Vereinten Nationen." *A.P.*, Aug. 1958.

BOGDANOV, V. "Der sowjetische Plan einer allgemeinen Abrustüng und das Völkerrecht." *Sovetskoye Gosudarstvo i Pravo*, Moscow 1960.

BOHLEN, C. E. "Auslandshilfe und Aussenpolitik der U.S.A." *A.P.*, Jun. 1960.

BOHN, H. "Strategische Information: Aufgaben und Probleme des Nachrichtendienstes." *E.A.*, Jun. 1960.

BOWLES, C. "Grosseuropa vom Atlantik bis zum Ural." *A.P.*, Oct. 1960.

BRAUNTAL, G. "Die Aussenpolitik der Vereinigten Staaten." *E.A.*, Jun. 1960.

BRODIE, B. "Strategy as a Science." *W.P.*, Jul. 1949.

―― "Nuclear Weapons: strategic or tactical?" *F.A.*, Jan. 1954.

―― "Unlimited Weapons and Limited War." *The Reporter*, New York, 18 Nov. 1954.

BRODIE, B. "About Limited War." *W.P.*, Oct. 1957.

—— "The Anatomy of Deterrence." *W.P.*, Jan. 1959.

BUCHAN, A. "Strategic Factors and the Summit." *World Today*, London, Apr. 1960.

BURCKHARDT, G. "Die Veränderung der Welt durch die Atomwaffen." *Frankfurter Hefte*, Special issue, Sept. and Oct. 1959.

BURNS, L. "Disarmament or the Balance of Terror." *W.P.*, Oct. 1959; *Surv.*, Jan.-Feb. 1960.

BUZZARD, A. W. "Massive Retaliation and Graduated Deterrence." *W.P.*, Jan. 1956.

CALENDER. "Le Javelot, le bouclier et l'Europe." *R.M.d.I.*, Nov. 1958.

CHARBONNIER, J.-PH. "Objectif sur la Chine." *R.M.d.I.*, May 1958.

CHASSIN, L. M. "Harmagedon oder Fontenoy?" *Intav.*, Apr. 1958.

—— "Ein Vierteljahrhundert Militärluftfahrt. Von der 'Luftherrschaft' Douhets zum 'Deterrent' Konzept der USAF." *Intav.*, Jun. 1958.

—— "Totalitarisme ou liberté." *R.M.G.*, Jun. 1959.

CHRISTIANSEN, H.-CH. "Disarmament. A Critical Investigation." *Les Cahiers de Bruges*, 1959.

CHURCHILL, W. "Defence through Deterrence," in *Vital Speeches of the Day*, New York, XXI, 15 Mar. 1955.

COHEN, C. "The Future of the Submarine." *F.A.*, Oct. 1959; *Surv.*, Nov.-Dec. 1959.

CORNIDES, W. "George Kennan und die Probleme des Friedens in Europa" (critical examination of the Reith Lectures). *E.A.*, Feb. 1958.

Daedalus. Special Issue on Arms Control, with contributions by K. E. Boulding, R. R. Bowie, H. H. Humphrey (author and rapporteur of a U.S. Senate Report of the same name), H. Kahn, H. A. Kissinger, T. Schelling, E. Teller and others. Fall 1960.

DALMA, A. "Die Gipfelgefechte des kalten Krieges." *W.K.*, Nov. 1959.

DAVIDSON-HOUSTON, J. V. "The Place of China in World Strategy." *R.M.G.*, Apr. 1960.

DELMAS, C. "Poignard ou bombe atomique?" *R.M.G.*, May 1959.

DEMANGE. "La Guerilla, I. De Vercingétorix à Mao Tse-tung." *R.M.G.*, Feb. 1960.

"Disarmament Bibliography." *Surv.*, Jan.-Feb. 1960.

DOOLITTLE, J. H. "By the End of the Century." *A.F.*, May 1958.

DUFOURCQ. "Equivoque autour de la guerre totale." *R.M.G.*, May 1959.

EHRHARDT, K. "Aufgaben, Möglichkeiten und Grenzen der operationalen Forschung." *W.K.*, Oct. 1959.

EITNER, H.-J. "Die militärische Führung der Volksrepublik China." *A.P.*, Apr. 1960.

ELIOT, G. F. "Mobile Strategy for the Mobile Age." *M.R.*, Jun. 1958.

ERLACH, H. U. VON. "L'Arme idéologique qu'il nous faut: le réarmament moral." *R.M.G.*, Apr. 1960.

ERLER, F. "Möglichkeiten einer Politik des Disengagement." *Die neue Gesellschaft*, Bielefeld, No. 6, 1958.

—— "Disengagement und die Wiedervereinigung Deutschlands." *E.A.*, Sept. and Oct. 1958.

FERGUSON, A. R. "Air Force Logistics." *Aeronautical Engineering Review*, New York, Jan. 1957.

FRANK, J. D. "The Great Antagonism. The Psychology of the Americans and the Russians as viewed mutually." *Atlantic Monthly*, Boston, Jan. 1957; *Surv.*, Mar.-Apr. 1959.

GAERTNER, F. VON. "Deutschland und die Verteidigung der deutschen Bundesrepublik im Rahmen des NATO-bündnisses." *R.M.G.*, No. 6, 1959.

GALLOIS, P. M. "Weltkrieg ausgeschlossen, lokale Konflikte wahrscheinlich." *Intav.*, No. 4, 1958.

—— "Eventail des menaces et panoplie de la défense." *R.M.G.*, Dec. 1958.

—— "Mobilität im globalen Krieg." *Intav.*, No. 3, 1959.

—— "Au bord d'une guerre impossible." *C.R.*, Mar.-Apr. 1959.

—— "Collective Defence." *C.R.*, Mar.-Apr. 1959; *Surv.*, May-Jun. 1959.

—— "Bordgestützte Fernwaffen werten den Unterschallbomber auf." *Intav.*, No. 7, 1960.

—— "New Teeth for NATO." *F.A.*, Oct. 1960.

GASTEYGER, C. "Der Atlantikpakt und das Problem der europäischen Sicherheit." *E.A.*, Apr. 1958.

GAULLE, CH. DE. "Integration or Co-operation." *Surv.*, May-Jun. 1959. Excerpts from press conference of 25 March 1959. Cf. P. M. Gallois, "Collective Defence," etc.

GENEVEY, P. "Le Désarmament devant les 'experts'." *R.M.G.*, May 1959.

GERARDOT, P. "La Compétition pour la suprematie thermonucleaire." *R.D.N.*, May 1958.

—— "Menaces nouvelles sur l'occident." *R.M.G.*, Feb. 1960.

GERMANY, FEDERAL REPUBLIC. Bundestag. "Aufgaben der Bundeswehr (Soldaten und Waffen)." 110th Session of the 3rd Bundestag, 8 Apr. 1960. Debate on the state of the Bundeswehr and Operational Plan 14. Federal Minister for Defence. *Parlament*, Hamburg, 4 May 1960.

GIBBS, N. "And the Reply" (to Kennan—cf. the latter's "Disengagement and Disarmament"). *List.*, 19 Nov. 1959; *Surv.*, Jan.-Feb. 1960.

GIESSE, J. H. VAN. "L'OTAN, intégration ou coopération?" *R.M.G.*, May 1960.

GLASER, H.-G. "Aktuelle Aspekte der chinesisch-sowjetischen Beziehungen." *E.A.*, No. 1, 1959. Refers to numerous sources.

GOBBI, A. L. "Esperienze ed ammaestramenti tratti dalla futura terza guerra mondiale." *R.M.G.*, Apr. 1958.

GOEDHUIS, D. "The Air Sovereignty concept and the United States' influence on its future development." *Journal of Air Law and Commerce*, Chicago, spring 1955.

GORDON, L. "Nato in the Nuclear Age." *Y.R.*, spring 1959; *Surv.*, May-Jun. 1959.

GREWE, W. " 'Disengagement'—Voraussetzungen und Konsequenzen." *A.P.*, No. 8, 1958.

HALLE, L. J. "Has the Soviet Challenge changed?" *New Republic*, Washington, Jun. 1959.

HARRIS, R. "China and the World." *I.A.*, Apr. 1959; *Surv.*, May-Jun. 1959.

HEALEY, D. "The Atom Bomb and the Alliance." *Confluence*, Cambridge, Mass., Apr. 1956.

HEIMENDAHL, E. "Der Soldat im Atomzeitalter." *Atomzeitalter*, Frankfurt am Main, Nos. 11-12, 1960.

HEINRICH, W., PRINZ VON HANN. "Staatshoheit und Weltenraum." *E.A.*, No. 6, 1959.

HESS, W. "Einführung in die Logistik des Heeres." *W.K.*, Jun. 1959.

HINTERHOFF, E. "Ein Schlüssel zum Disengagement." *A.P.*, No. 5, 1959.

—— "The Problem of Disengagement." *R.M.G.*, Feb. 1960.

HOAG, M. W. "Nato: Deterrent or Shield?" *F.A.*, Jan. 1958.

—— "What Interdependence for NATO?" *W.P.*, Apr. 1960; *Surv.*, May-Jun. 1960.

HÖPKER, W. "Strategische Probleme rund um den Nordpol." *A.P.*, No. 2, 1960.

—— "Neutralisierung und Entmilitarisierung der Antarktis." *A.P.*, No. 4, 1960.

HOOPES, T. "Overseas Bases in American Strategy." *F.A.*, Oct. 1958.

HSIEH, A. LANGLEY, "Communist China and Nuclear Warfare." *China Quarterly*, London, Apr.-Jun. 1960; *Surv.*, Jul.-Aug. 1960.

HUDSON, G. F. "Mao, Marx, and Moscow." *F.A.*, Jul. 1959.

HURE, N. C. "Situation estratégica de los bloques oriental y occidental. Sus posibilidades, en caso de conflicto, para el empleo del arma atómica." *E.S.G.*, Apr.-Jun. 1958.

—— "Estrategia atómica: la aparición del arma nuclear y sus influencias en el orden político, social y especialmente militar." *E.S.G.*, Oct.-Dec. 1958.

HUSTON, J. A. "Korea and Logistics." *M.R.*, Feb. 1957.

ISTEL, W. "Das moralische Element in der amerikanischen Aussenpolitik." *A.P.*, No. 10, 1958.

JACOBS, W. D. "The Limits of Limited War." *R.M.G.*, Dec. 1959.

JOHNSON, E. A. "The Crisis in science and technology and its effect on military development." *Operations Research* (Operations Research Society of America), Baltimore, No. 1, 1958.

JONES, M. "China and the Bomb." *Observer*, London, 24 Apr. 1960; *Surv.*, Jul.-Aug. 1960.

KATZENBACH, E. L. "Zeit, Raum und Wille. Die polit.-milit. Aussichten Mao Tse-tung." *W.K.*, Feb.-Mar. 1960.

KAUFMANN, W. W. "The Crisis in Military Affairs." *W.P.*, Jul. 1958.

KENNAN, G. F. "Disengagement Revisited." *F.A.*, Jan. 1959.

—— "Russland, Deutschland und die Atomwaffen." (German version of a statement made by Kennan to the Subctee. of the U.S. Senate on 4 Feb. 1959.) *A.P.*, No. 4, 1959.

—— "Disengagement and Disarmament." *List.*, 29 Oct. 1959; *Surv.*, Jan.-Feb. 1960. Cf. N. Gibbs, "And the Reply."

—— "Peaceful Co-existence." *F.A.*, Jan. 1960.

KHRUSHCHEV, N. S. "On Peaceful Co-Existence." *F.A.*, Oct. 1959.

KINDERMANN, G.-K. "Peking und Taipeh in der Weltpolitik" (with many bibliographical annotations). *E.A.*, No. 17, 1960.

KING, J. E., jr. "Aggression and Collective Defense." *S.A.I.S. Review*, spring 1959; *Surv.*, Jul.-Aug. 1959.

KISSINGER, H. A. "Der Einfluss der modernen Rüstungstechnik auf die nationale und kollektive Strategie und Diplomatie." *E.A.*, Nos. 20-21, 1957.

—— "Nuclear Testing and the Problem of Peace." *F.A.*, Oct. 1958.

—— "The Search for Stability." *F.A.*, Jul. 1959.

—— "Arms Control, Inspection and Surprise Attack." *F.A.*, Jul. 1960.

KNORR, K. "The Crisis in U.S. Defense." *The Leader*, New York, 30 Dec. 1957.

—— "Probleme der amerikanischen Verteidigungspolitik." *E.A.*, Feb. 1958.

—— "Abschreckung in Nöten." *Atomzeitalter*, Frankfurt am Main, Nos. 11-12, 1960.

KÖLLNER, L. "Die Auslandshilfe der V. Staaten." *E.A.*, No. 11, 1960.

KRUMPELL, I. "Atomare Strategie." *A.S.M.Z.*, No. 12, 1957.

—— "Führungsbegriffe im Atomwaffenzeitalter." *E.A.*, No. 11, 1960.

LABIN, S. "La Défence collective de l'occident sur le plan politique." *R.M.G.*, Dec. 1958.

LARIONOV, LT.-COL. V. "The Doctrine of Graduated Aggression" (Russian review of Kissinger's *Nuclear Weapons and Foreign Policy*). *Red Star*, Moscow, 8 Jul. 1959; *Surv.*, Sept.-Dec. 1959.

LÉCHER, J. R. "Lenkwaffen." *A.S.M.Z.* Annual, 1958.

LEGHORN, R. S. "No need to bomb Cities to win War." *U.S. News and World Report*, 28 Jan. 1955.

LEROY, G. "Être ou ne plus être?" *R.M.G.*, Apr. 1960.

LIDDELL HART, B. H. "Military Strategy versus Common Sense." *The Saturday Review*, London, Mar. 1956.

—— "Überstrategie." *A.P.*, No. 1, 1958.

—— "Is Gas a better Defence than Atomic Weapons?" *Surv.*, Sept.-Oct. 1959.

MACKINTOSH, M. "Soviet Strategy in World War III." *Army Magazine*, San Francisco, May 1960; *Surv.*, Jul.-Aug. 1960.

MANSFIELD, M. "Die kommende Krise in Deutschland." *A.P.*, No. 5, 1959.

MARGERISON, T. "Missiles to Stop Missiles." *New Scientist*, London, 2 Apr. 1959; *Surv.*, May-Jun. 1959.

MARX, W. "Die psychologische Offensive der Sowjets gegen die freie Welt" (report on the technique of revolutionary war). *W.K.*, Sept. 1959.

MAURACH, B. "Die sowjetische Militär-Literatur." *W.W.Rd.* Annual, 1955.

MEDARIS, J. B. "The State of American Defence." *N.Y.T.*, 8 May 1960; *Surv.*, Jul.-Aug. 1960.

MIGIS. "Survie et machination." *R.M.G.*, May 1959.

MIKSCHE, F. O. "Aggressionen und Atomwaffen." *A.P.*, No. 5, 1958.

—— "Ist die NATO noch zu Retten?" *Wehr und Wirtschaft*, Stuttgart, No. 3, 1960.

MIKSCHE, F. O. "Die unvermeidliche Erweiterung des Atomklubs." *A.P.*, No. 5, 1960.

—— "Désarmement et neutralisation de l'Europe centrale." *R.M.G.*, May 1960.

MOCH, J., and P. GALLOIS. "Les Conséquences politiques et stratégiques des nouvelles armes." *Politique Étrangère*, Paris, No. 2, 1958.

MOREAU, R. "La Recherche opérationelle." *R.M.d.I.*, Apr., Jun., Aug.-Sep. 1958.

MORGENSTERN, O. "The Game Theory in U.S. Strategy." *Fortune*, New York, Sep. 1959.

MORGENTHAU, H. J. "The Political and Military Strategy of the United States." *Bu.A.S.*, Oct. 1954.

—— "Has Atomic War really become Impossible?" *Bu.A.S.*, Jan. 1957.

MULLEY, F. W. "Eine europäische strategische Abschreckungsmacht." *E.A.*, No. 6, 1960. Also in *Surv.*, Jan.-Feb. 1960 after W.E.U. Assembly Report, Nov. 1959.

MURRAY, T. E. "Reliance on the H-bomb and its Danger." *Life*, Chicago, May 1957.

NALIN, Y. "Weapon of Aggression" (standard Soviet arguments against NATO). *Red Star*, Moscow, 28 May 1959; *Surv.*, May-Jun. 1959.

"N.A.T.O. Bibliography" (30-40 selected titles, mostly from 1957-8). *Surv.*, May-Jun. 1959.

NEMO. "Suggestions pour l'établissement d'une doctrine." *R.M.G.*, Apr. 1958.

NITZE, P. "Atoms, Strategy and Policy." *F.A.*, Jan. 1956.

NORSTAD, GEN. L. "NATO as the fourth Atomic Power." *Surv.*, May-Jun. 1960.

OSGOOD, C. E. "A Case for Graduated Unilateral Disengagement." *Bu.A.S.*, Apr. 1960; *Surv.*, Jul.-Aug. 1960.

OSGOOD, R. S. "NATO: Problems of Security Collaboration." *American Political Science Review*, Washington, Mar. 1960.

PARET, P. "The French Army and la guerre révolutionnaire." *Journal of the Royal United Service Institution*, London, Feb. 1959; *Surv.*, Mar.-Apr. 1959.

PELTIER. "La Pensée militaire soviétique." *R.M.G.*, No. 10, 1957.

PERGENT. J. "Les Réductions d'effectifs des forces soviétiques." *R.M.G.*, Jul. 1958.

—— "La Réorganisation des forces de l'occident. L'élaboration des formations nouvelles." *A.S.M.Z.* Annual, 1959.

—— "Die Entwicklung der Atomrüstung." *A.S.M.Z.*, Jul. 1960.

POURICHKEVITCH, "Ingérence soviétique et strategie globale." *R.M.d.I.*, Oct. and Nov. 1959.

POWELL, R. L. "Everyone a Soldier" (The Chinese militia—Chinese sources quoted). *F.A.*, Oct. 1960.

QUARONI, P. "Die Entwicklungsländer in der Politik Sowjetrusslands und der Westmächte." *A.P.*, No. 1, 1959.

QUIGG, P. W. "Open Skies and Open Space." *F.A.*, Oct. 1960.

REINHARDT, G., and W. R. KINTNER. "The Tactical Side of Atomic Warfare." *Bu.A.S.*, Feb. 1955.

RENAULD, P. "La Lance et le bouclier." *R.M.G.*, Apr. 1959.

REUSS, H. S. "Konstruktive Politik für Mitteleuropa." *A.P.*, No. 7, 1958.

RIGG, R. B. "Will Warfare be waged in Outer Space?" *R.M.G.*, May 1959.

ROSAS, C. J. "Una Estrategía general atómica." *E.S.G.*, Apr.-Jun. 1958.

ROSTOW, W. W. "Die sowjetische Herausforderung und die V. Staaten von Amerika." Has numerous critical annotations. *E.A.*, No. 11, 1960.

ROUGERON, C. "L'Explosion thermonucléaire haute et la déstruction à distance." *R.M.G.*, Apr. 1958.

—— "Das Atomgetriebene U-Boot, das 'Grosskampfschiff' von heute." *W.K.*, May 1959.

—— "Sous-marins atomiques et engins ballistiques." *R.M.G.*, Jun. 1959.

SÄNGER, E. "Raumfahrt—technische Überholung des Krieges." *A.P.*, No. 4, 1958.

—— "Militärische Bedeuting der Raumfahrt." *A.P.*, No. 7, 1958.

SCHELLING, T. C. "Surprise Attack and Disarmament." *Bu.A.S.*, Dec. 1959; *Surv.*, Jan.-Feb. 1960.

SCHEUER, G. "Materielle Voraussetzungen für eine Wiedervereinigung Deutschlands in der Sicht nichtamtlicher Vorschläge." 130 sources quoted. *E.A.*, No. 6, 1960.

SCHMIDT, H. "Abrüstung in Mitteleuropa-Möglichkeit oder Utopie?" *Die Welt*, Hamburg, 14 Nov. 1959.

SCHNEIDER, F. "Le Rôle du parti communiste dans le processus d'endoctrinement des masses soviétiques." *R.M.G.*, Feb. 1960.

SCHRIEVER, B. A. "Some Hard Facts for a Harder Future." *A.F.*, Feb. 1960.

SCHÜTZE, G. "Französische Vorschläge zur europäischen Sicherheit und zur Lösung der Berlin Frage." *E.A*, No. 11, 1959.

SCHWARZENBERGER, G. "Die Legalität der Atomwaffen." *E.A.*, 20 Apr. 1958.

SCHWELIEN, J. "Atomarer Versuchsverzicht als erste Stufe." Conference of specialists for study of means of discovering possible infringements of a negotiated nuclear test ban. *A.P.*, No. 12, 1958.

SENGER UND ETTERLIN, F. VON. "Wandel der amerikanischen Kriegsdoktrin." *A.P.*, No. 3, 1958.

—— "NATO in umstrittener Entwickelung." *A.P.*, No. 2, 1959.

—— "Militärische Probleme einer verdünnten Zone in Europa." *E.A.*, No. 11, 1959.

SERVAIS, A. "Redoutable javelot mais fragile bouclier." *R.M.G.*, Dec. 1958.

—— "Le Désarmement." *Chronique de politique étrangère*, Brussels, No. 1, 1960.

—— "Le Désarmement—epreuve de patience." *R.M.G.*, Jun. 1960.

SIMON, H. "World-wide Capabilities for Production of Nuclear Weapons." *Dae.*, No. 3, 1959; *Surv.*, Sept.-Oct. 1959.

SLESSOR, SIR J. "The Great Deterrent and its Limitations." *Bu.A.S.*, May 1956.

—— "Deutschland und die Verteidigung des Westens." *A.P.*, No. 12, 1956.

SMALLMAN, W. A. "Mobility and Logistics." *R.M.G.*, May 1960.

SPAAK, P.-H. "New Tests for NATO." *F.A.*, Apr. 1959.

—— "Space Literature Bibliography." *A.F.*, May 1958.

SPEIDEL, H. "Die Rolle der deutschen Streitkräfte in der Verteidigung der freien Welt." *R.M.G.*, Jul. 1958.

—— "Verteidigung Europas so weit wie möglich." *Bu.P.I.*, 19 Aug. 1960.

SPETZLER, E. "Kriegsrechtliche Probleme des Atomwaffeneinsatzes." *W.W.Rd.*, No. 3, 1957.

SPEZIALETTI, B. G. "Evitare un'altra guerra mondiale?" *R.M.G.*, May 1959.

STAEDKE, H. "Les Armes nucléaires—pourront ils garantir notre securité?" *R.M.G.*, Jun. 1958.

STEHLIN, P. "L'Adaptation de la pensée militaire à la révolution technique." *R.M.G.*, Jan. and Feb. 1959.

STEVENSON, A. E. "Hat der Osten der stärkere Morale?" *A.P.*, No. 5, 1959.

STRAUSS, F. J. "Soviet Aims and German Unity." *F.A.*, Apr. 1959.

—— "Fünf Jahre NATO-Partner. Wirksamstes Instrument für die Erhaltung der Freiheit und des Friedens." *Bu.P.I.*, No. 100, 1960.

256   BIBLIOGRAPHY

STUDNITZ, H. G. VON. "Die Irrtümer der sowjetischen Deutschlands-politik." *A.P.*, No. 9, 1958.

SULIAK, H. "Rubel- und Dollar-Diplomatie." *A.P.*, No. 12, 1958.

SUPINO, P. "I Reflessi operativi della concentrazione di potenza." *R.M.G.*, May 1960.

TALENSKIY, MAJOR-GENERAL N. "Military Strategy and Foreign Policy." *I.A.*, No. 3, 1958.

TAM. "De la guerre subversive à 'la guerre'." *R.M.G.*, Jun. 1960.

TELLER, E. "Alternatives for Security." *F.A.*, Jan. 1958.

THILLAUD. "Adaption de l'occident à la guerre psychologique." *R.M.G.*, Dec. 1958.

THOMER, E. "Gemeinsamer Sicherheit und politische Verantwortung. NATO: Integration statt Koordination." *A.P.*, No. 1, 1960.

TROMMSDORF, W. "Raumfahrt und Waffentechnik." *W.K.*, Jul. 1959.

"Twenty-seventh annual inventory of aerospace power." *Aviation Week,* New York 1960.

VARRONE, E. "Stand und Einsatzmöglichkeiten der Raketen, Lenk-und Fernwaffen." *A.S.M.Z.*, Annual, 1958.

VERNANT, J. "Stratégie et politique à l'age atomique." *R.D.N.*, Jun. 1958.

—— "La France et le désarmement." *R.D.N.*, Jun. 1958.

—— "Hauptfaktoren der internationalen politik in der nächsten Dekade." *E.A.*, No. 9, 1960.

VIRPSHA, E. "Constant Factors in Russian Expansion." *R.M.G.*, Jun. 1959.

WEIZSÄCKER, C. F. VON. "Ethische und politische Probleme des Atom-zeitalters." *A.P.*, No. 5, 1958.

WERNER, V. "La Guerre thermonucléaire et le problème de populations civiles." *R.M.G.*, Jun. 1958.

WHITE, T. D. "Leadership in the Conquest of Space." *Air Power Historian*, Montgomery, Ala., Apr. 1958.

WOHLSTETTER, A. "The Delicate Balance of Terror." *F.A.*, Jan. 1959. P. Gallois answered this in *E.A.*, No. 13, 1959.

WOLFERS, A. "Could a War in Europe be Limited?" *Y.R.*, winter 1956.

—— "Europe and the NATO Shield." *International Organisation*, Boston 1958.

—— "Limits of Nuclear Deterrence." *Marine Corps Gazette*, New York, May 1960.

WORSTHORNE, P. "Our Bomb and Theirs: How the Russians see it." *Enc.*, Jul. 1958.

Young, W. "An Abolitionist's Position." *Enc.*, Nov. 1958.

Zimmermann, F. " 'Disengagement' und deutsche Frage: Die polit. und milit. Bedeutung eines Schlagwortes." *W.K.*, No. 4, 1959.

Zitzewitz, H. von. "Wie Steht es um die deutsche zivile Verteidigung?" *W.K.*, Aug. 1959.

R

Index

Acheson, Dean: 150.

Adenauer, Konrad: on Federal German membership of NATO, 5; on Soviet offer of concessions, 12; on nuclear weapons, 102; on *status quo*, 160; on foreign policy, 162, 166.

Africa: 114-5, 119.

airborne alert: 32.

aircraft: bomber, strategic, 10, 13, 15, 21, 49, 55, 76, 78; interceptor, 22, 66; tactical, 30, 31, 49, 65-6, 76, 78, 80, 82, 95, 97, 99, 100, 154, 158, 188, 195, 203.

air defence: 55, 64, 66, 99, 189-91, 212.

Alaska: 10, 89.

Algeria: 20, 39, 81-2, 107-8, 196, 198.

Alsop, Joseph: 56.

analysis, strategic: 6-8, 207; Federal German need of, 174-5, 176-7, 214.

Antarctica: 142.

armour: 64-5, 154, 200, 213-4.

arms control: Chaps. 8 and 9 *passim*; 167, 208, 213-4.

arms limitation: Chaps. 8 and 9 *passim*; 167, 208.

arms race: 121, 124, 168.

assistance, economic and technical: Western, 117-21; Soviet, 118-21.

Aswan Dam: 119.

Atlas (American I.C.B.M.): 24, 30, 218.

Australia: 40.

Austria: nuclear potential, 40; State Treaty, 161.

Azerbaijan: 19.

Bacteriological warfare: 145.

Baldwin, Hanson: 17.

ballistic missiles: *see* MISSILES, BALLISTIC.

Baruch Plan: 130, 146.

Belgium: nuclear potential, 40; tactical targets in, 99.

Berlin: 9, 19, 53, 69, 86, 122-3, 137, 152, 158, 166-8, 227.

Blachstein, Peter: 101.

blackmail, nuclear: 70-1, 72-3, 77 90, 138, 185.

Blue Streak: 82, 219.

Bonin Plan: 148.

Bonn. *See* GERMAN FEDERAL REPUBLIC.

Bowie, Robert: xvi, 88, 134-5, 146, 173.

Bradford, A. H.: 12.

Brandt, Willy: 122, 166, 175.

breakthrough, technological: 128, 146, 196.

Brennan, Donald G.: 42.

brinkmanship: 13, 46.

Brodie, Bernard: 17, 76, 102, 111.

broken-backed (long-drawn-out) war: 47, 74.

Brown, Admiral Charles: 98.

Buchan, Alastair: xvi, 56, 160, 173.

Bug, River: 152, 154.

Bulganin, Nikolai: 71.

Bulgaria: 149.

Bundestag: defence debates, 2-3. *See also* GERMAN FEDERAL REPUBLIC.

Bundeswehr: 65, 68, Chap. 10 *passim*; nuclear weapons for, 2, 104, 169-74; relation to civil departments, 4, 171; weaknesses in equipment, 65, 203; logistic support of, 67; build-up of, 68, 107, 180, 199; role in European zone of control 152-5; integration into NATO, 169-70; status of, 171.

Bush, Vannevar: 17.

Buzzard, Admiral Sir Anthony: xvi, 17.

Canada: 40, 62, 63.

carrier, aircraft: as means of strategic delivery, 10, 30, 77, 158.

"Carte Blanche" (NATO exercise): 101.

Castro, Fidel: 41, 46, 114, 183.

Churchill, Sir Winston: 28.

82-3, 85, 87; prestige issues, 83; effect on French of strategic nuclear forces of, 83; vulnerability in nuclear war, 83-4; unilateral renunciation of nuclear arms, 84, 137; interest in NATO integrated nuclear force, 88; attitude towards Federal Germany, 107; attitude to growth of Bundeswehr, 107, 174; fails to provide conventional forces, 107; as initiator of global war?, 112; attitude towards disarmament negotiations, 133; as base for strategic nuclear forces, 153.

United States: nuclear monopoly of, 9-14; superiority in strategic aviation, 10; overseas bases, 10-11; military pacts of, 10, 19; will to retaliate, 11, 80, 86; forward strategy, 19-20; strategic capabilities, 21-7, 30; strategic aviation, 21-2, 26; stations I.R.B.Ms. in Europe, 27; attitude towards surprise attack, 33; interest in preventing spread of nuclear weapons, 40; overrates Soviet interest in pre-emption, 48; political and strategic difficulties of, 55, 57; inter-service rivalry, 58; ground forces equipment, 65; attitude to independent European nuclear forces, 85-7; interest in NATO integrated nuclear force, 88; economic lead of, 117; attitude towards arms limitation, 129; contradictory attitude towards nuclear tests, 144; withdrawal of troops from Europe?, 149, 180; support

for Berlin, 168; measures for strengthening armed forces, 194.

Vietnam: 19, 108, 122, 198, 208.
Vistula, River: 154.

War: limited, 12, 17, 19, 20, 52, 54, Chaps. 6 and 11 passim; by accident, 15, 26, 41, 152; catalytic, 15, 40, 128; by miscalculation, 15, 41, 52, 72, 105; by proxy, 17; local, 17, 52, 69-72, 73; cold, 17, 113, 185-6; growing danger of 40, 41, 106, 136; Communist theory of, 46-7; limited nuclear, 50, 53, 71, 92-9, 142, 211; all-out nuclear, 52, 55, 71, 80, 185; possible types of, in Europe, 69-73; of liberation, 113.
war games: 34.
warning, early: see RADAR.
Warsaw Pact: 121, 151, 164, 175; military capabilities, 62-7.
Washington Naval Treaty: 126.
Weber, Max: 172.
Wehner, Herbert: 165, 175.
Weinstein, A.: 83.
Weizsäcker, Carl Fr. von: 2, 6, 16, 188.
Weser, River: 68.
Western European Union: 84, 91, 106, 198, 207.
Wetter, Gustav, S. J.: 45.
Wolfers, Arnold: xvi, 5, 101-2.

zone of control, in Central Europe: 146, 148-61, 179-80; as key to Berlin question, 167; Federal German interest in, 214.